VIOLENCE AND SPORT

Violence and Sport

Printed and bound in Canada

The Butterworth Group of Companies

Canada:
Butterworth & Co. (Canada) Ltd., Toronto and Vancouver
United Kingdom:
Butterworth & Co. (Publishers) Ltd., London
Australia:
Butterworths Pty Ltd., Sydney, Melbourne, Brisbane, Adelaide and Perth
New Zealand:
Butterworths of New Zealand Ltd., Wellington and Auckland
Singapore:
Butterworth & Co. (Asia) Pte. Ltd., Singapore
South Africa:
Butterworth Publishers (Pty) Ltd., Durban and Pretoria
United States:
Butterworth Legal Publishers, Boston, Seattle and Austin
Mason Publishing Company, St. Paul
D & S Publishers, Clearwater

Canadian Cataloguing in Publication Data

Smith, Michael D.
  Violence and sport

Includes bibliographical references and index.
ISBN 0-409-86816-7

1. Violence in sports.   I. Title.

GV706.7.S54   796   C83-098461-5

VIOLENCE AND SPORT

by

MICHAEL D. SMITH

York University

Butterworths
Toronto

Preface

Are we presently engulfed in a wave of unprecedented violence? Since the early 1960s, after the fairly tranquil 1950s, this has been a widely held popular belief. It has been revealed directly by public opinion polls (e.g., Hartnagel, 1979) and indirectly by such indicators as the increasing sale of guns to citizens who fear for their safety and a booming private protection industry (Luckenbill and Sanders, 1977). Official concern has grown apace. In the past dozen years, central or local governments in at least eight countries, including Canada, the United States, and Great Britain, and three multinational organizations, including UNESCO, have sponsored commissions of inquiry, symposia, and permanent research organizations focusing on criminal violence, war, terrorism, civil strife of all kinds, violence in the communications industry, in prisons, in schools, in labour relations, in sports, and so on (see Feierabend, 1978). Investigations of violence by private agencies, such as Amnesty International, number in the thousands. Heavy doses of mass media violence, as entertainment and news, have helped convince citizens that violence is rampant (LaMarsh et al., 1977).

That violence is perceived as a serious social problem there is no doubt, but have levels of violence in fact risen in the last two decades? The answer is a qualified yes. The Canadian case seems fairly typical: homicides are up, assaults are up, child battering is up, rape is up, deliquent violence is up, media violence is up (see Beyer Gammon, 1978). This general trend seems true for the United States as well (e.g., Skogan, 1979).

Of course the time span used in computing such trends is important, for short-term fluctuations occur within longer-term periods. Criminal violence in the U.S., for instance, levelled off and even fell slightly between 1975 and 1977, but then rose again in 1978 and 1979. In the longer-term view, however, criminal violence has increased. Some social scientists predict that violence rates will decline in the immediate future as the population between the ages of 15 and 24, the age group committing most of the violent crime, declines (Skogan, 1979). Others predict that rates will increase with accelerating industrialization, urbanization, labour migration, and other social changes related to rising violence throughout the world (Flynn, 1980).

Then there is the uneasy relationship between reported and actual levels of violence. Official statistics, like police records, which provide the basis of most studies of violence rates, are almost always underestimates; most rapes are never reported, for example. Furthermore, official statistics fluctuate not only as actual levels of violence fluctuate but with shifts in police and judicial practices (e.g., crackdowns on crime may produce higher official crime rates) and even with the ways in which governments and social scientists collect and interpret data. Nevertheless, the consistency of the evidence warrants the guarded conclusion that most *real* violence rates have been on an upward trajectory for about two decades.

Sports violence seems to fit this general pattern. Although it is difficult to demonstrate systematically that sports were more violent in 1979, say, than in 1959, the evidence points in this direction. (Changing rules, inconsistent enforcement of existing rules, and the fact that much of what could be considered "violence" does not violate the formal rule of a given sport, and is therefore not officially recorded, renders the official record of violent offences more or less worthless for such comparisons.) To wit: in the 1960s and 1970s mushrooming professional sports provided job opportunities for an unprecedented number of players whose chief occupational skills lay in the use of violence. New teams, new leagues, and new sports were marketed – and delivered – to unsophisticated consumers on the basis of blood and guts. Internationally, expanding competition stimulated the global diffusion of domestic forms of sports violence. The mass media, television particularly, conveyed the "new" violence to huge audiences in a host of direct and subtle ways. Some youth sports became almost indistinguishable from the big leagues. Misbehaviour in the stands seemed to keep pace with misbehaviour on the field.

At the same time, against a backdrop of public concern about violence in general, some elements of the public started to perceive sports violence as a cause for concern. Reacting to what seemed to be an increasing number of ugly incidents, and a reluctance within sports to take meaningful action, individuals and groups began to lobby politicians, legal officials, and the media for attention and support. Shocking reports of injuries and deaths, and a flurry of sensational court cases, further mobilized public opinion. The authorities bowed to the pressure: investigations were conducted, recommendations made, official machinery put in place to monitor and control the "problem."

A modest burst of scholarly activity accompanied the emergence of sports violence as a contemporary social problem. As of November 1982, the Information Retrieval System for the Sociology of Sport and Leisure (SIRLS) at the University of Waterloo listed 325 published and unpublished works on violence and aggression in sport, almost all produced since 1970. The list includes more than a dozen books, but no comprehensive English-language *text*. This is the first.

The material for the book comes from the above sources, from theory and research on violence in general, and from work on violence in other social contexts, such as the family. It also includes a considerable amount of hitherto unpublished data of my own. The primary orientation is sociological, but I have drawn liberally from social psychology, anthropology, law, and, to a lesser degree, history and political science.

Although it deals with a wide range of theories, the book does have a consistent theoretical focus. I argue in Chapter 1 that all violence is essentially *instrumental* behaviour; that is, behaviour designed to achieve some desired end. It follows that violence is best approached theoretically in terms of its short- and long-term benefits and costs or "payoffs" as perceived by parties directly and indirectly involved. Accordingly, theories that explicitly or implicitly treat violence-doers fundamentally as rational decision-makers who wish to maximize the benefits and minimize the costs of violence, given the social and cultural contexts in which they operate, take precedence over theories treating violence as instinctive, compulsive, or impulsive behaviour. This orientation is expounded specifically in places, such as the "game theory" approach to crowd dynamics in Chapter 7, but its logic underlies every chapter. My goals were to organize, criticize, and synthesize theoretical and empirical work relevant to sports violence and to suggest directions for further study from this broad perspective.

The book is intended mainly for undergraduate students in sociology, social psychology, sport sciences, and physical education, but also as a reference work for teachers and scholars within and outside the academic community. It is aimed at an international readership, albeit with a North American slant, a function mainly of the materials on which it is based.

Several friends and colleagues read and commented critically on portions of the manuscript in various stages of completion. My thanks go to David Bell, Eric Dunning, Desmond Ellis, Richard Goranson, Richard Gruneau, Jerry Lewis, David Lumsden, Alice Propper, and Gordon Russell. Because of their advice the book is better than it otherwise would have been. I absolve them from responsibility for its remaining shortcomings. I am also grateful to Barry McPherson for providing me with a count of the sports violence citations in the SIRLS information retrieval system and to York University's LaMarsh Research Programme on Violence and Conflict Resolution for financial assistance. Thanks go as well to Kathleen Hamilton for her meticulous editing and Janet Turner, Managing Editor, for her encouragement and cooperativeness.

Bev Bergman, Debbie Bromley, Denise Gauthier, Sadie Jainudeen, Sue Kirkland, Mary MacFarlane, Jan Maidenberg, Gail Smith, Kathy Wilson, and York University's Secretarial Services typed what must have seemed like innumerable drafts of various chapters. I thank them for their careful work and good humour in the face of my sometimes unreasonable demands.

Portions of the book are revised versions of several of my previously published articles. Acknowledgement of permission to reproduce this material goes to the *Canadian Journal of Sociology* (Smith, 1979c), *Sociological Inquiry* (Smith, 1978c), Human Kinetics Press (Smith, 1983a), and Springer-Verlag Publishers (Smith, 1983b). Permission to quote from the work of other authors has been obtained from a number of additional sources and is acknowledged in the text.

Contents

Tables

Figures

1 What Is Sports Violence?

Scholarly articles on violence and aggression number in the thousands and are found in journals representing the spectrum of academic disciplines literally from anatomy to zoology. There are hundreds of books on the subject, most of them written in the past two decades. Russell (1983) has compiled a bibliography of over 650 books concerned with humans alone. Dozens of theories of violence and aggression vie for attention: genetic theories, neurophysiological theories, biochemical theories, sociobiological theories, frustration theories, learning theories, subcultural theories, ecological theories, structural theories, systems theories, not to mention "unifactor," "multifactor," and "polysystemic" theories. Given this vast range of materials, it is not altogether surprising that conceptions of violence and aggression are varied, to say the least.

Both terms are used to describe a very wide range of phenomena, from insect cannibalism to contact sports to international warfare. Almost any forceful, vigorous, assertive, exploitive, violative, or injurious behaviour may come under either heading. Violence and aggression may both be viewed as adaptive, constructive, and even creative and ennobling, enhancing an individual's, a group's, or an entire species' ability to cope with its environment. More often, however, they are seen as maladaptive, destructive, and dehumanizing.

The concepts have come to have so many meanings that they have lost a good deal of their meaning. One theorist defines violence narrowly as "the threat or exertion of physical force which could cause bodily injury" (Ball-Rokeach, 1972:101). Another defines it broadly as "any violation of the human rights of a person" (Riga, 1969:145). A third defines it mystifyingly as "extensive and radical changes within a short interval of time produced by given forces in the qualities and structures of anything" (Gotesky, 1974:146). Definitions of aggression are just as diverse.

Several interrelated factors account for the definitional and conceptual confusion. First, there are differences in perspective (and terminology) among the disciplines that make violence and aggression part of their domain. These disciplines examine different aspects of the phenomena, or the same aspect from different angles. A psychologist is interested in the personality profiles of violent criminals, a sociologist in the social conditions that generate criminal behaviour.

Second, it is probably a mistake to think of violence or aggression in unitary terms, as if all their forms were merely aspects of the same phenomenon. Research indicates increasingly that different dimensions of these behaviours stem from different sources, not any single source, such as instinct or frustration or culture, as has been claimed in the past. Edward O. Wilson (1978), founder of the new science of sociobiology, describes four completely different categories of aggression in rattlesnakes. Surely homo sapiens is at least as complex. If what are thought of as different forms of violence or aggression are in reality more different than alike, then the search for a single definition satisfactory for all purposes is futile.

Third, the concepts are loaded with moral, social, and political meanings. The assumptions of scholars regarding the goodness or badness of violence and aggression sometimes creep unwittingly into, and sometimes are explicitly stated in, their definitions. Defining violence as "illegitimate and unsanctioned" (Girvetz, 1974:185) does not sit well with viewing it, at least in some circumstances, as justified (Audi, 1974). Popular usages of the terms vary similarly (Blumenthal et al., 1972).

All this is not to suggest that attempting to clarify what violence and aggression are is a waste of time. To the contrary, such an exercise underscores the complexity of the topic and at the same time discourages simplistic explanations and solutions. It helps reveal the range of associated issues. And it forces one to come to terms with how one wishes to employ the concepts.

Thankfully, there is also some agreement on definitions of violence and aggression, especially if the perspective is narrowed to the social sciences, particularly sociology and psychology. Aggression is usually regarded as the more generic concept. More often than not, aggression is defined as any behaviour designed to injure another person, psychologically or physically. Malicious gossip is aggression; so is a punch in the nose. Violence, more often than not, refers to the physical side of aggression, hence the term "violent aggression." Violence is behaviour intended to injure another person *physically*. These definitions are only rough approximations, but I shall adhere to their general sense in what follows.

The focus in this book is on violence, of all the manifestations of aggression, usually the most overt and arguably the most damaging. It is violence that people see as one of the pressing social problems of our time. Research and theory on other forms of aggression — verbal, for instance — are certainly relevant to the study of violence, but in the final analysis, violence is what we will seek to understand.

Violence is Physical

As already noted, some theorists seem to use the word violence more or less interchangeably with aggression; they speak of psychological violence, economic violence, political violence, and the like; any form of injustice is violence (see Audi, 1974:37-38). They argue that these less direct forms of coercive behaviour can be as painful and destructive as physical violence, if not more so. Groups who believe themselves oppressed sometimes justify their own use of physical violence on these grounds. But as Etzioni (1971) observes, physical violence does seem qualitatively different from other forms of violence. Being stabbed, beaten, or shot has a finality the other forms do not. And killing is the ultimate injury. Etzioni states that when it comes to being stabbed, beaten, or shot, the victim's freedom of choice in most circumstances has been eliminated, whereas with other forms of aggression, the victim ultimately has some recourse, some freedom of choice. He argues that most people, in fact, find physical violence more hurtful than psychological or economic pain, preferring a tongue-lashing or having their pay docked to being beaten. If this is so, physical violence represents the end point on a continuum of aggressive behaviour: it is the most extreme form of aggression. The fact that physical violence is usually a means of last resort — a method of attaining some goal when other methods have failed, or seem likely to fail — reinforces Etzioni's contention. Philosopher Ronald Miller (1971:15) puts it forcefully, if perhaps dogmatically: "The phrase 'physical violence' is redundant. Violence is just the *physical* overpowering of a person or object with the intent to injure or destroy. There is no such thing as non-physical violence." For our purposes it would confuse the issue to label all injury-producing behaviours "violence," and I shall use the term only in its physical sense.

Three additional points: first, it goes without saying that psychological injury may accompany bodily injury induced through violence, as when one loses face after a public beating, but loss of face is in itself not violence. Second, although the offence of assault in the Canadian Criminal Code, for example, includes threatened violence, threats are not violence in our definition. Threats are often implicated in violence, but threats are designed to produce psychological, not physical, harm and are not violence per se. Third, in dealing with individual violence, we shall be concerned only with persons as objects of attack, but in the chapters on collective violence we shall widen the focus to include attacks on property as well.

Violence and Intent

Even this rather narrow conception of violence requires considerable elaboration and qualification. To begin with, definitions of violence that hinge on the idea of *intent* to harm or injure — what Toch (1980) terms "process-centered" definitions — run immediately into several difficulties.

What exactly does "intent to injure" mean? Does it include cases in which a so-called aggressor makes no effort to *avoid* injuring a victim, as opposed to deliberately seeking the victim out? Cases in which a so-called aggressor passively *allows* a victim to sustain an injury, by not giving warning of an impending accident, say? In the first instance, the aggressor's intent is unclear (perhaps he or she was just lazy or careless), but in the second the nasty intent is rather more apparent. Yet the first aggressor took an active role in harming another, whereas the second was completely passive; the injury would probably have occurred in the aggressor's absence! Of course, if the second aggressor had *arranged* for the victim to have an accident, this would perhaps be a different story. Baron (1977) writes that one common criterion of intent is: did the harm-doer *voluntarily* injure the victim? But this raises the knotty philosophical question of whether or not any human behaviour, strictly speaking, is a matter of free will. These dilemmas are perhaps best left to legal or philosophical minds for solution, but they do suggest that the degree to which an alleged violence-doer's behaviour was active or passive, and whether the violence-doer used direct or indirect means, should be taken into account in ruling on intent (Buss, 1961).

In any case, intentions are private events, not directly observable, and thus often difficult to ascertain. People lie, they delude themselves, they are occasionally unsure what their intentions were. Rather than dealing with guilt, for instance, aggressors convince themselves that what happened was an accident, or that the victim deserved to be attacked. As Arendt (1970) has pointed out, violence always needs justification. Violence-perpetrators sometimes even become angry *after the fact,* working themselves into a state of moral indignation after an aggressive act in order to justify their conduct to themselves and others. Thus intentions sometimes have to be inferred from the nature of the allegedly violent act, from what happened before and after it, or from the social context in which the act occurred. When one man shoots another following an altercation in a bar, his intent to injure seems clear, compared to that of a football player who knocks an opposing player senseless with a hard tackle. The intensity or magnitude of the assault, the victim's expression of pain or injury, the social characteristics of the assailant and the assailed, are but a few other considerations used in judging intent (Bandura, 1973). In court cases, batteries of lawyers may spend weeks or months determining the extent to which a defendant accused of assault or homicide intended to do what was done. If convicted, punishment is meted out on this basis. This is the principle of *mens rea,* literally, "guilty mind."

Also, emphasis on intent to injure tends to divert attention from what is often called instrumental violence, in which harm-doing is not an end in itself, but only a means of achieving some other end, that is, when inflicting pain is irrelevant or secondary to securing some other goal or incentive; e.g., "cold-blooded" killing for money. One can even conceive of a aggressor wishing to *avoid* inflicting suffering, as when a parent spanks a child as a last resort, only when all else has failed, to dissuade the child from misbehaving in some way. ("This hurts me more than it hurts you.") The emphasis on intent to injure in definitions of violence probably results from the historical dominance of social psychological theories of aggression, like the frustration-aggression hypothesis and its derivatives, most of which seek to explain what is variously called hostile, affective, expressive, impulsive, angry, annoyance-motivated, nonutilitarian, or noninstrumental aggression, behaviour whose main goal *is* to cause suffering.

The distinction between hostile and instrumental violence is a false one, in any case, for all aggressive acts are instrumental, because all are designed to produce some end, whether a victim's expression of pain or the loss of his or her wallet. The difference is in the contrasting nature of the ends sought (Bandura, 1973). Zillman (1978) proposes that the terms "annoyance motivated" and "incentive motivated" aggression replace "hostile" and "instrumental" aggression. Annoyance-motivated acts would be those whose primary intent is the reduction of some noxious internal state, like frustration or anger. Incentive-motivated acts would be those whose primary goal is to obtain some extrinsic reward, like money, power, or status. Zillman's terminology goes some way toward clarifying the semantic muddle, but the word "annoyance" is too weak to be paired with much of what we shall call violence.

It should be added that empirically these types of violence are not so easily partitioned. Because violence almost always produces a variety of outcomes for the aggressor, it is sometimes hard to determine whether the aggressor's act was primarily reinforced by signs of injury, by some non-injurious outcome, like the approval of another, or by both types of consequence. The athlete who, enraged, attacks an opposing player after a deliberate foul, not only vents anger, but may win the approbation of peers. When such approval is indirect and subtle, the aggressor's action is liable to be misjudged as motivated solely by anger, especially by observers not closely familiar with the social context in which the action took place. What Bandura (1973:4) calls "the pull of status rewards rather than the push of aggressive drive" often accounts for what seems on the surface purely hostile behaviour. Of course, a little "aggressive drive" helps get the job done, an insight provided by Georg Simmel (1955:34) in his classic work *Conflict:* "It is *expedient* to hate the adversary with whom one fights, just as it is expedient to love a person whom one is tied to." Thus the football player, motivated by the spoils that accrue to the victors in an important game, generates as much antipathy as he can toward the "enemy"; it facilitates his task. "I never understood the real violence of the game until I played pro ball," says Jean Fugett, a professional player with the Washington Redskins. "I had to work very hard to be aggressive. I had to think stuff like 'This guy raped my mother' to get psyched and mad at the guy opposite" (Underwood, 1979:52). Coaches are aware of this basic psychology; so are military propagandists and the leaders of fighting street gangs.

Furthermore, in the same way that all aggression is instrumental, it can be argued that all aggression is "incentive-motivated," if incentive motivation is taken to mean the wish to obtain desired outcomes apart from hurting the victim, and to avoid undesired ones. But so-called noninstrumental theories of aggression either rule out or play down decision-making on the part of the aggressor, treating aggression as reflex-like instinctive, compulsive, or impulsive behaviour. Sociologist Desmond Ellis, in a forthcoming book on prison violence, challenges this position. He writes that if the anticipation of rewards or punishments for a violent act affects the probability that the act will occur, and how severe it will be, then the act is, to use Zillman's term, incentive-motivated. Ellis argues that most violence falls into this category. Inmates' accounts of violent incidents in which they took part, for instance, almost invariably yield evidence that they were indeed aware of the consequences of their behaviour and modified it on the basis of this awareness. Illustration: a con savagely and apparently impulsively attacks another con with a heavy metal bar after the latter makes a rude sexual advance. Afterward, while admitting that he wanted to kill the offender, the first con concedes that in the back of his mind he knew he would be in jail for a very long time if he did, and this in fact caused him to throw down the lethal bar and finish the job with his boots. He was also aware that a passive response to the sexual advance would have marked him as a target for other prison "wolves." For Ellis, violence "whose probability cannot be influenced by the consequences that attend it" is what Zillman calls annoyance-motivated, and others call noninstrumental, violence, but he finds it difficult to find an example of such violence, in prison or out. Even "going berserk" has strategic overtones. I shall employ the adjectives "hostile," "affective," and "expressive" in this book to refer to particular manifestations of violence having a strong emotional component, but I shall treat violence, both individual and collective, as motivated fundamentally by the desire to gain rewards and avoid punishments.

Hinging definitions of violence on *intent to injure* also renders somewhat ambiguous the status of third parties, those indirectly involved in the violence — the mafia boss who hires a hit man to do in a rival, the professional hockey coach who unleashes his "goon" to take out an opposing player. These third parties are certainly engaged in the production of violence, but they are at least once removed from the ultimate act. Some would insist that they themselves are not violent. The bullfight impresario Don Livinio-Stuyck was in a sense responsible for the death of several matadors and more than 15,000 bulls in Madrid's famous Plaza de Toros from about 1941 to 1946, yet was a gentle humanist who blanched at the sight of blood and who preferred to work in his garden rather than attend the fights he staged (Collins and Lapierre, 1969). Was his behaviour violent? If we insist that third parties implicated in violence are behaving violently, where does responsibility stop? Is the hockey coach's general manager violent? The team owner? The league president? The fans? (These questions are not as academic as they might seem. In 1980 an injured player brought a civil suit against the National Hockey League for creating an "unsafe work environment," a case examined later in this chapter.) We shall indeed be interested in third parties indirectly involved in violence, but we shall not define their behaviour as violence per se. What they do takes place before the violence occurs. Our working definition thus undergoes its first elaboration: violence is *physically assaultive behaviour designed to injure another person physically.* Admittedly this is not altogether satisfactory, for it may seem to exonerate third parties, while placing the entire onus on those who may be merely carrying out orders. However, we are merely trying to define violence as precisely as possible at this point. The assignment of responsibility is another matter. Perhaps, in summary, it can be said that violence is *observable:* it is done actively and directly by an assailant against a victim.

Violence and Outcome

Some of the problems inherent in dealing with the notion of intent can be bypassed by focusing entirely on the outcome of the act for the target-person. Such definitions Toch (1980) describes as "product-centered." Etzioni (1971:713), for instance, along with many others, defines violence as "an act that causes damage, often to a person, sometimes only to property." But this definition raises another set of problems, which then have to be explained away. As it stands, the definition would include purely accidental occurrences resulting in damage. It would also include damage-causing behaviour for almost universally agreed-upon prosocial ends, such as surgery to save a life, and for less widely accepted ends, such as abortion and euthanasia. On the other hand, it would exclude bungled and foiled attempts at violence: the baseball pitcher who throws deliberately at a hitter but misses, the "dusted-off" batter who charges out to attack the pitcher but is intercepted by other players. It seems more in keeping with what most people think of as violence to exclude accidents and helping behaviour and to include thwarted attempts. Yet by making these qualifications, as Etzioni and others do, the notion of *intent*, with its attendant complications, is implicitly reintroduced. My preference is to make clear at the outset that violence is behaviour *intended* to injure others, and then to deal with the problems this may entail. But I also see violence as product-centred; failed attempts, significant as they may be in the genesis of violence, are still not violence. Our basic definition undergoes its second elaboration: violence is *physically assaultive behaviour that is designed to, and does, injure another person or persons physically.*

Violence and Legitimacy

The problem of the social and moral judgements that play a part in determining whether conduct that in objective terms appears violent is labelled as such has been mentioned. This has to do with what could be called the legitimacy of violence: the extent to which violence is perceived as necessary, good, or justified, and hence not "violence." Conversely, that which is regarded as unnecessary, bad, or unjustified *is* "violence." Behaviour that gets labelled as "violence," in legal and scientific terminology, as well as in everyday language, seems to depend in large part (independently of intent to injure) on who is doing what to whom under what circumstances, and on who is doing the labelling (Ball-Rokeach, 1972).

Institutionalized violence — that carried out by individuals and groups, like the police, who are given a mandate by the state to do so — tends to be called "force." But not always. Monica Blumenthal and her colleagues (1972) at the University of Michigan, in a study of attitudes of American men toward violence, found that groups basically sympathetic to black or student protestors were more likely to label police actions against blacks and students "violence" than were groups unsympathetic to protestors; the latter tended to call the protestors' actions "violence." Corporal punishment inflicted by parents on children is another form of institutionalized violence, known widely as "discipline," but in some circles as "violence." Concerned citizens may call hockey fisticuffs "violence," but most professional players scoff at the idea. Nobody gets hurt in a hockey fight, they claim. Definitions of violence also change over time. The brutal, routine flogging of delinquent British soldiers in Wellington's nineteenth-century army was merely "discipline"; today it would be "violence" and as such clearly not tolerated (Stanage, 1974). "Spear" or "butt" tackling in North American football at one time was simply sound technique; now some consider it "violence." Let us examine in detail what sports violence is and is not.

A Typology of Sports Violence

No rules or practice of any game whatever can make that lawful which is unlawful by the law of the land; and the law of the land says you shall not do that which is likely to cause the death of another. For instance, no persons can by agreement go out to fight with deadly weapons, doing by agreement what the law says shall not be done, and thus shelter themselves from the consequences of their acts. Therefore, in one way you need not concern yourself with the rules of football. (Hechter, 1977:444)

These were Lord Justice Bramwell's instructions to the jury in an 1878 British court case, *Regina* v. *Bradshaw*. A soccer player was accused of manslaughter after he charged and collided with an opposing player, who subsequently died, in a game played under Football Association rules. The defendant was acquitted, but the judge's pronouncement has been cited of late in North America by those who wish to make the point that sports should not be exempt from the laws that govern our behaviour elsewhere.

Seventeen years later, in 1895, Robert Fitzsimmons engaged in a public boxing exhibition with his sparring mate, Riordan, in Syracuse, New York. Riordan was knocked unconscious by a punch to the head and died five hours later. Fitzsimmons was indicted for manslaughter. The judge directed the jury as follows:

If the rules of the game and the practices of the game are reasonable, are consented to by all engaged, are not likely to induce serious injury, or to end life, if then, as a result of the game, an accident happens, it is excusable homicide... (Hechter, 1977:443)

Fitzsimmons was acquitted. What is noteworthy about this case is that the rules and practices of the game were taken into account in determining criminal liability, a precedent directly contrary to that established in *Regina* v. *Bradshaw*. It is the Fitzsimmons ruling that has more or less held ever since.

The fact is, sports violence has never been viewed as "real" violence. The courts, except for isolated flurries of activity, have traditionally been reluctant to touch even the most outrageous incidents of sports-related bloodletting; legal experts still flounder in their attempts to determine what constitutes violence in sports. The great majority of violence-doers and their victims, the players, even though rule-violating assaults often bring their careers to a premature close, have always accepted much of what could be called violence as "part of the game." Large segments of the public, despite the recent emergence of sports violence as a full-blown "social problem," continue to give standing ovations to performers for acts that in other contexts would be instantly condemned as criminal. An examination of sports violence that fails to consider these perspectives "does violence," as it were, to what most people, not to mention those involved with criminal justice systems, regard as violence.

Following is an attempt to answer the question: what is sports violence? I shall go about this task by constructing a typology. A typology is a device for categorizing a phenomenon into at least two types on each of one or more dimensions. In the present case, sports violence will be divided into four types, ranging roughly from greater to lesser, on a scale of *legitimacy,* as shown in Table 1.1. I shall take into account the viewpoints of the law, the players, and the public in so doing. This exercise is confined to acts performed by players during the game, or in its immediate context. (A typology of sports crowd riots is presented in Chapter 6.)

Table 1.1   A Sports Violence Typology

Relatively Legitimate

Brutal body contact
Conforms to the official rules of the sport, hence legal in effect under the law of the land; more or less accepted.

Borderline violence
Violates the official rules of the sport and the law of the land, but widely accepted.

Relatively Illegitimate

Quasi-criminal violence
Violates the official rules of the sport, the law of the land, and to a significant degree informal player norms; more or less not accepted.

Criminal violence
Violates the official rules of the sport, the law of the land, and players' informal norms; not accepted.

Brutal body contact

This category of sports violence comprises all significant (i.e., high magnitude) body contact performed within the official rules of a given sport: tackles, blocks, body checks, collisions, legal blows of all kinds. Such contact is inherent in sports such as boxing, wrestling, ice hockey, rugby, lacrosse, football, and to lesser degrees in soccer, basketball, water polo, team handball, and the like. It is taken for granted that when one participates in these activities one automatically accepts the inevitability of contact, also the probability of minor bodily injury, and the possibility of serious injury. In legal terms players are said to "consent" to receive such blows *(volenti non fit injuria* – to one who consents no injury is done). On the other hand, no player consents to be injured *intentionally*. Suppose a blitzing linebacker levels a quarterback with a ferocious but legal tackle; the quarterback is severely injured; a civil court case ensues. Theoretically, the law suggests, if it can be shown that the linebacker foresaw that his blow would severely injure the quarterback, hence *intended* to injure him, the linebacker is culpable. The probability of such a legal outcome, however, is close to zero. In effect, any blow administered within the formal rules of a sport is legal under the law of the land (Lambert, 1978).

Legal body contact is nevertheless of interest as violence when it develops (or as some might prefer, degenerates) into "brutality." A rising toll of injuries and deaths, followed by public expressions of alarm, then demands for reform, typically signal this condition. An "intrinsically brutal" sport like boxing always hovers not far from this point; for this reason, boxing is almost everywhere regulated by the state, albeit often inadequately. When body contact assumes an importance out of proportion to that required to play the game – when inflicting pain and punishing opponents are systematized as strategy, and viciousness and ferocity are publicly glorified – a stage of brutality can be said to have been reached. Such practices may strain the formal rules of sports, but they do not necessarily violate those rules.

Sports brutality is not a new phenomenon. The history of football, to take probably the best example, is in part a chronicle of intermittent waves of brutality, public censure, and reform. In 1893 indignation against alleged viciousness in American college football, smouldering for some time, erupted across the country. A campaign led by the magazines *Saturday Evening Post* and *The Nation* caused several institutions to drop the game, including Harvard, one of the first schools to play it on a regular intercollegiate basis. (Parke Davis [1911:98], then the University of Wisconsin coach and later a historian of the game, wrote that the reports of brutish play were somewhat exaggerated. Among the most hysterical must have been that appearing in a German publication, *Münchener Nachrichten*. This report, quoted by Davis, described the Harvard-Yale game of 1893 as "awful butchery," seven participants reportedly being carried in "dying condition" off the field with broken backs, broken legs, and lost eyes.) A popular vaudeville ditty of the day is revealing (Betts, 1974:244

> *Just bring along the ambulance,*
> *And call the Red Cross nurse,*
> *Then ring the undertaker up,*
> *And make him bring a hearse;*
> *Have all the surgeons ready there,*
> *For they'll have work today,*
> *Oh, can't you see the football teams*
> *Are lining up to play.*

Antifootball sentiment swept the United States again in 1905. In a report somewhat more measured than the one above, a Chicago newspaper published a compilation for the 1905 season showing 18 players dead, 11 from high schools and 3 from colleges, and 159 more or less serious injuries. President Roosevelt called representatives of Yale, Harvard, and Princeton to the White House and threatened to ban the game unless its brutality was eliminated. Stormed Teddy "Rough Rider" Roosevelt, "Brutality and foul play should receive the same summary punishment given to a man who cheats at cards" (Stagg, 1927:253). Rule changes resulted, including the outlawing of the notorious V formation, and the furor abated.

Roughing up and intimidating opponents as a legal tactic, however, seems to have gained new life of late. Football is still in the vanguard. Consider the "hook," a sort of on-field mugging, whereby a defensive back in the course of making a tackle flexes his biceps and tries to catch the receiver's head in the joint between the forearm and upper arm. Professional player Jack Tatum (Tatum and Kushner, 1979:18), who likes to think that his hits "border on felonious assault," fondly recalls a well-executed hook (the tactic was outlawed soon after):

> *I just timed my hit. When I felt I could zero in on Riley's head at the same time the ball arrived in his hands, I moved... Because of the momentum built up by the angles and speed of both Riley and myself, it was the best hit of my career. I heard Riley scream on impact and felt his body go limp.*

The casualty rates, the ultimate result of this type of play, are not insignificant. The rate in the National Football League is said to be 100 per cent — at least one serious injury per player per season (Underwood, 1979). About 318,000 football injuries annually require hospital emergency room treatment in the United States (Philo and Stine, 1977). In the Canadian Football League, according to a survey conducted by the *Toronto Star* (November 25, 1981), 462 man-games were lost in the 1981 season owing to injury (down slightly from the year before). Observers seem to agree that the high injury rates at all levels of the game are attributable in significant measure to the way football is taught and played: brutishly.

Borderline violence

In this category are assaults that, though prohibited by the official rules of a given sport, occur routinely and are more or less accepted by all concerned. To wit: the hockey fist-fight, the late hit in football, the high tackle in soccer, the baseball knock-down pitch, basketball "body language," the sometimes vicious elbowing and bumping that takes place in track and road races. Such practices occasionally produce serious injuries, but these are usually dismissed as unfortunate accidents. Borderline violence is essentially the province of referees, umpires, and other immediate game officials, higher league officials and law enforcement authorities seldom becoming involved. Sanctions never exceed suspension from the game being played, and perhaps a fine.

Borderline violence is nonetheless illegal under civil law, as the U.S. *Restatement of Torts* makes clear (Rains, 1980:800):

> *Taking part in a game manifests a willingness to submit to such bodily contacts or restrictions of liberty as are permitted by its rules or usages. Participating in such a game does not manifest consent to contacts which are prohibited by rules or usages of the game if such rules or usages are designed to protect the participants and not merely to secure the better playing of the game as a test of skill. This is true although the player knows that those with or against whom he is playing are habitual violators of such rules.*

Thus a football lineman who goes offside and injures his opposite number with a legal block has broken a rule designed to "secure the better playing of the game" and is not legally liable under civil law for his action. But a defensive back who hits a ball carrier just after the whistle has blown has broken a safety rule, a rule designed "to protect the participants," and *is* liable on grounds of negligence or recklessness. Playing football does not, in the eyes of the law, include "consenting" to be the recipient of a late hit. Yet the law almost never intervenes in such cases, for reasons that will begin to emerge shortly.

Borderline violence is tolerated and justified on a number of grounds, most of which boil down to some version of the "part of the game" argument. Take hockey fisticuffs. A National Hockey League player, one of sixty interviewed in 1976-77 by the author (see Smith, 1979c), provides this familiar (non) explanation:

> *I don't think that there's anything wrong with guys getting excited in a game and squaring off and throwing a few punches. That's just part of the game. It always has been. And you know if you tried to eliminate it, you wouldn't have hockey any more. You look at hockey from the time it was begun, guys get excited and just fight, and it's always been like that.*

Naturally because fist-fighting is considered legitimate it is not defined by its practitioners as "violence." Also nobody gets hurt in a punch-up, players insist. (This is not precisely true. Of 217 "minor injuries" suffered by players on a Southern Professional Hockey League team over a three-year period in the mid-1970s, most involved the hand or forearm [fractures, sprains, lacerations, etc.] and were usually incurred during fights [Rovere et al., 1978:82].) To the majority of professional players interviewed by the author the periodic public fuss over hockey fighting is simply a product of the rantings of publicity-hungry politicians:

I think it's really blown out of proportion. A lot of these politicians trying to get somewhere are just trying to crack down on fighting to get their name in the paper. Most of the guys that say things like that don't know anything about hockey, and they're trying to talk about violence, and they don't even know what they're talking about. I don't think a punch in the head is going to hurt you, unless it's, you know, a sick thing where a guy pummels a guy into the ice and things like that.

There are, of course, more elaborate folk theories in circulation. Apologists are prone to claim, for example, that hockey fisticuffs are safety valves for aggressive impulses (usually described as "frustration") that inevitably accumulate due to the speed, the contact, the very nature of the game. Because these aggressive urges must be vented, the argument goes, if not one way then another, prohibiting fist-fighting would result in an increase in the more vicious and dangerous illegal use of the stick. In the words of John Ziegler, President of the NHL (*Toronto Star,* December 13, 1977:C2): "I do not find it unacceptable in a game where frustration is constant, for men to drop their sticks and gloves and take swings at each other. I think that kind of outlet is important for players in our games."

The logic is shaky. Would Ziegler argue that the pugnacious Philadelphia Flyers, NHL penalty leaders nine years in a row, get more penalties than other teams because they get more frustrated? Or that the Flyers are somehow compelled to respond to frustration with aggression, whereas other teams are not? Hockey may well have its frustrating moments (what sport does not?), but as researchers have repeatedly shown, human beings may or may not respond to frustration with aggression. Like most human behaviour, responses to frustration are shaped by culture and learning. "Frustration" seems more an excuse for, than a cause of, violence in hockey.

Belief in the inevitability of hockey violence generally is so entrenched, that a judge in the famous Ted Green-Wayne Maki assault trials (stemming from a stick-swinging duel during a 1969 game in Ottawa that nearly ended Green's life) concluded that the game "can't be played without what normally are called assaults." Both players were acquitted, needless to say (*New York Times,* September 4, 1970:31).

As for public opinion, polls have revealed that substantial minorities find the hockey fist-fight more or less acceptable. Just months after the Green-Maki episode, almost 40 per cent of the respondents in a Canada-wide survey sponsored by *Maclean's* magazine said they "liked to see fighting at a hockey game"; among males the figure was 46 per cent (Marshall, 1970). In a 1972 *Canadian Magazine* reader survey (over 30,000 questionnaires were returned), 32 per cent of all respondents and 38 per cent of the male respondents thought NHL players should *not* be given automatic game penalties for fighting (Grescoe, 1972). In the United States a state-wide survey of Minnesota residents conducted by Mid-Continent Surveys of Minneapolis, shortly after the 1975 assault trial in Minnesota of Boston hockey player David Forbes, found that 61 per cent of Minnesotans thought punishment for fighting in professional sports should be left to the leagues. Twenty-six per cent preferred court punishment, and 5 per cent preferred both (Hallowell and Meshbesher, 1977). More recently, 26 per cent of over 31,000 Ontario residents surveyed in 1979 responded "No" to the general question, "Do you feel there is too much violence in professional hockey?" (McPherson and Davidson, 1980).

Quasi-criminal violence

Quasi-criminal violence is that which violates not only the formal rules of a given sport (and the law of the land), but to a significant degree the informal norms of player conduct. It usually results, or could have resulted, in serious injury, which is what brings it to the attention of top league officials and generates public outrage in some quarters. This in turn puts pressure on legal authorities to become involved. League-imposed penalties for quasi-criminal violence usually go beyond the contest in question and range from suspensions from several games to lifetime bans, depending on the sport; each league seems to decide how much and what types of violence it will tolerate. Increasingly, civil legal proceedings follow, though perhaps less often than thought; up to 1978 only about ten civil suits involving personal injury in the National Football League took place; in the National Basketball Association, there were perhaps two (Horrow, 1980). Criminal proceedings, rare in the past, are occurring more frequently, but convictions remain few and far between. In 1976 the Attorney General of Ontario, after several public warnings, ordered a crackdown on violence in amateur and professional sports in the province. According to an internal memorandum provided by the Director of Regional Crown Attorneys, sixty-eight assault charges were laid in less than a year (sixty-seven in hockey, one in lacrosse), but only ten convictions were obtained, although sixteen cases were still pending at the time of the memorandum. Apparently all the convictions, and almost all the charges, were against amateur athletes. (Figure 1.1 lists some of the events that marked the emergence and eventual institutionalization of hockey violence as a contemporary, albeit not a new [Hallowell, 1978], social problem.)

Figure 1.1 **The Emergence of Hockey Violence as a Contemporary "Social Problem"**

- 1969, The Green-Maki Fight: Boston's "Terrible" Ted Green and Wayne Maki of St. Louis engage in a stick duel during an exhibition game in Ottawa. Green is struck on the head by a full-swinging blow. His skull fractured, he almost dies. Both men are charged with assault causing bodily harm; in separate trials both are acquitted on grounds of self-defence. Later, naturally, Green writes a book about his experience.
- 1972, The First Canada-Russia Hockey Series: amid accusations and counter-accusations of dirty play, Canada's truculent Bobby Clarke eliminates the Russian star, Kharmalov, from the remainder of the series with a blatant two-handed stick-swipe across the ankle. Canada has exported hockey violence for years, but never before has it been witnessed by quite so many millions of television viewers. Reaction in the mass media is mixed: some commentators glorify Clarke for his insatiable "desire"; others express embarrassment; a handful, shame.
- 1973, The Paul Smithers Case: Smithers, a seventeen-year-old, black hockey player, engages an opposing player in a scuffle outside a Toronto arena following a raucous Midget hockey game. Kicked in the groin, the other boy collapses, chokes on his own vomit, dies. Smithers is convicted of manslaughter and sentenced to six months in jail, a decision causing bitter and prolonged public controversy.
- 1974, The Hamilton-Bramalea Game: players, officials, and spectators brawl throughout this Ontario Junior B playoff game in which 189 penalty minutes are assessed and five players and one team official are injured. Fourteen policemen finally quell the fighting. The Bramalea team withdraws from the playoffs and is promptly suspended by the Ontario Hockey Association, which finds no justification for the team's refusal to play because, it claims, the game was not as violent as many others in recent years.
- 1974, The Ontario Government Inquiry and Investigation into Violence in Amateur Hockey: Toronto lawyer William McMurtry is commissioned by the province to investigate violence in amateur hockey. In an extensive investigation, culminating in five days of public hearings and producing a 1,256-page transcript, McMurtry concludes that professional hockey is the number one cause of amateur hockey violence. His report is widely circulated and hotly debated.
- 1975, The Forbes-Boucha Case: Boston's Dave Forbes and Minnesota's Henry Boucha engage in a minor altercation for which both are penalized. Forbes threatens Boucha from the penalty box; then, leaving the box at the expiration of the penalties, lunges at Boucha from behind, striking him near the right eye with the butt end of his stick. Boucha falls to his knees, hands over face; Forbes jumps on his back, punching, until pulled off by another player. Boucha is taken to the hospital, where he

receives twenty-five stitches and the first of several eye operations. Forbes is indicted for criminal assault in Minnesota, the first criminal prosecution against a professional athlete in the U.S., but a hung jury results in the case being dismissed.

- 1975, The Maloney-Glennie Fight: Toronto Maple Leaf Brian Glennie body-checks a Detroit player. In retaliation, Detroit's quick-fisted Dan Maloney knocks Glennie down with a forearm blow, punches him repeatedly, and allegedly bounces his head several times on the ice. Glennie goes to the hospital with a concussion and other injuries. Maloney is charged with assault causing bodily harm. Hung jury, charges dropped.

- 1975, Establishment of the Ontario Hockey Council: the functions of this quasi-governmental body are to improve and oversee amateur hockey in the province. Among other steps, it forms a parents' education committee. The committee produces a booklet, *You and Your Child in Hockey,* which contains several antiviolence messages. *You and Your Child* goes through three revisions between 1975 and 1980, as over a quarter million copies are distributed in Ontario arenas.

- 1976, The Jodzio-Tardif Beating: in a World Hockey Association playoff game, Calgary Cowboys' Rick Jodzio administers a devastating beating to top scorer Marc Tardif of the Quebec Nordiques. Both benches empty, and a wild, half-hour melee ensues. Tardif, unconscious, with a severe concussion and other injuries, is out for the season. Quebec threatens to withdraw from the series unless (1) Jodzio is suspended for life, (2) the Calgary coach is suspended for the rest of playoffs, (3) the League president (the official observer at this game) is fired or resigns. The demands are met in part, and the series continues. Jodzio is charged in Quebec with causing bodily harm with intent to wound. He pleads guilty to a lesser charge and is fined $3,000.

- 1976, The Philadelphia-Toronto Playoff: in a brawl-filled playoff contest in Toronto (resulting in a new Philadelphia penalty record) Toronto's Borje Salming, a Swedish nonfighter, is badly beaten by Philadelphia's Mel Bridgman. Further brouhahas involving players, fans, and a policeman result in four Philadelphia players being charged — on orders of Ontario's Attorney General Roy McMurtry — with criminal offences, from possession of a dangerous weapon (a hockey stick) to assaulting a police officer. The hockey establishment, insisting it can look after its own affairs, accuses McMurtry of headline-seeking, but considerable support for his actions is registered in other quarters. Two of the players subsequently plead guilty and are fined; the charges against the two others are dropped.

- 1977, Rapport Néron: the Quebec government conducts an investigation into violence in amateur hockey. The 325-page final report includes recommendations to remove violence from the game, including a "code d'éthique" for players, coaches, managers, parents, spectators, the press, and arena managers.

- 1980, The McPherson-Davidson Report: this Ontario Hockey Council-sponsored report, based on a massive mail survey and thirty-one public forums held throughout the province, contains twenty pages of recommendations designed to improve youth hockey. Some of the recommendations are aimed at reducing violence on the ice and abusive behaviour in the stands.
- 1980, No-Contact Rule for Kids: the Canadian Amateur Hockey Association bans body-checking for players twelve years and under.
- 1983, The Sports Violence Arbitration Act: this legislation, recently introduced in the U.S. Congress, seeks to establish a civil arbitration system "for the settlement of grievances resulting from violent conduct" in major professional team sports, including hockey. A similar bill, the Sports Violence Act, would make "excessive" player violence a criminal offence and is presently being considered by the House Judiciary Subcommittee on Crime (See Horrow, 1982).

Still, a small number of episodes of quasi-criminal violence in professional sports have resulted in litigation, and it is these cases that have generated the greatest publicity. Several civil disputes have received continent-wide attention. One of the first in sport's modern era took place in baseball during a 1965 game between the San Francisco Giants and the Los Angeles Dodgers. Giant batter Juan Marichal felled Dodger catcher John Roseboro with his bat following an acrimonious verbal exchange. Roseboro sustained considerable injury; Marichal was fined $1,750 by the League and suspended for eight games. Roseboro filed a $110,000 civil suit for damages against Marichal and the San Francisco club; it was reportedly settled out of court for $7,500 (Kuhlman, 1975).

A decade and a half later, in 1979, Houston Rocket basketball player Rudy Tomjanovich was awarded the whopping sum of $3.25 million dollars in a civil suit for injuries received as a result of a single, devastating punch thrown by Kermit Washington of the Los Angeles Lakers during a 1977 game, a blow described by a Laker assistant coach as "the hardest punch in the history of mankind." Tomjanovich suffered a fractured jaw, nose, and skull, severe lacerations, a cerebral concussion, and was not surprisingly out for the season. The League Commissioner suspended Washington for sixty days and fined him $10,000. The jury, in making an award of more than half a million dollars above what Tomjanovich's attorneys had demanded, found that Washington had acted "intentionally," "maliciously," and "with reckless disregard for the safety of others." The Lakers as an organization were deemed negligent because they "failed to adequately train and supervise Washington," even though they were aware that "he had a tendency for violence while playing basketball" (nine fights in four years, according to the plaintiff's attorneys). The Lakers paid (Horrow, 1981; Rains, 1980).

case is one that began in 1975, *Hackbart* v. *Cincinnati Bengals* igation arose out of an incident in a National Football League in which the plaintiff, Dale Hackbart of the Denver Broncos, ... an illegal forearm blow on the back of the head by an opposing player, Charles Clark of the Cincinnati Bengals, in a "malicious and wanton" manner five seconds after the play had been whistled dead. The referees did not see the action, and no penalty was called. Hackbart returned to the sidelines, but later discovered he had suffered a career-ending spinal fracture. The district court ruled that Hackbart had taken an implied risk by playing a violent game and that "anything" happening to him "between the sidelines" was part of that risk. The case was dismissed. But an appeals court reversed this decision, stating that although Clark may not have specifically intended to injure, he had engaged in "reckless misconduct"; the accountability of his employer (the Cincinnati Bengals) could therefore now be legally considered (Gulotta, 1980; Rains, 1980). New proceedings have apparently been scheduled. The way now seems clear for a professional sports team, as an employer, to be held accountable under civil law for the actions of the players, its employees. (An alternative approach, the Sports Violence Arbitration Act of 1983, is now before the U.S. Congress. This act would force each major professional sports league to establish an arbitration board with the power to discipline players for using "excessively violent conduct" and to make their teams financially liable for injuries suffered by the victims.)

In none of the above cases were criminal charges laid. Why this near immunity to criminal prosecution and conviction? First, most players seem reluctant to bring charges against another athlete. Based on a mail survey of 1,400 major-league basketball, football, and hockey players (no response rate is given), Horrow (1980) concludes that professional athletes, in particular, tend to believe that player disputes are best settled privately and personally on the field of play; that team management does not appreciate "troublemakers" who go "outside the family" (i.e., the league) for justice, and contract difficulties or worse probably await such individuals; that the sheer disruptiveness of litigation can ruin careers, and so on. Bolstering these beliefs is the apparent willingness of most players to dismiss virtually any during-the-match assault short of using a gun or a knife as part of the game.

From the point of view of the law, says Horrow, based on information obtained from twenty United States county prosecutors, in whose jurisdictions most of the country's major professional teams operate, many officials are reluctant to prosecute sports violence because they believe that they have more important things to do, like prosecuting "real" criminals; that the leagues themselves can more efficiently and effectively control player misbehaviour; that civil law proceedings are better suited than criminal for dealing with an injured player's grievances; that most lawyers do not have the expertise to handle sports violence cases; and that it is almost impossible to get a guilty verdict anyway.

There are two other more subtle, nonlegal reasons for the hands-off policy of criminal justice officials. One is the "community subgroup rationale." As explained by Kuhlman (1975), this is the tacit recognition by law enforcement authorities that certain illegal activities by members of some social groups ought more or less to be tolerated because they are widespread within the group and because group members look upon them as less serious than does society in general. Moreover, it would be unfair to single out and punish an individual member when almost everyone else in the group behaves similarly. In other words, the illegal conduct is rendered less criminal because everybody does it. This rationale sometimes arises in connection with the issue of differential law enforcement for minority groups. In some tough police jurisdictions, for instance, police rarely make an arrest for felonious assault involving family members and neighbours, even though such assaults are frequent. Police in these areas tend to define domestic violence as a mere "disturbance," whereas officers in other jurisdictions are more inclined to define it as genuine violence. It seems that certain assaultive practices in sports are looked upon with the same benevolent tolerance. At the very least, the severity of the penalties for violence provided by the law are widely regarded within the legal community, as well as the sports community, as out of proportion to the seriousness of the illegal acts.

The "continuing relationship rationale" applies in assault cases where offender and victim have a ongoing relationship. Legal authorities may wish to avoid straining the relationship further by prosecuting one or both parties. Husbands and wives may wish to continue living together; neighbours may have to; athletes typically compete against each other at regular intervals (Kuhlman, 1975). Criminal prosecution in sport could exacerbate already-present hostility to the point where league harmony is seriously threatened. The 1976 prosecutions on various assault charges of four Philadelphia Flyers hockey players, arising out of a game in Toronto, caused considerable strain between the Philadelphia and Toronto Maple Leafs hockey clubs, and even a public squabble between the Philadelphia District Attorney and the Ontario Attorney General (*Toronto Star,* April 22, 1976). The assumption underlying this rationale is that society has an interest in maintaining such social relationships, that professional sport in this instance serves some socially useful purpose.

Finally there is the premise of "legal individualism" — the notion that the individual is *wholly* responsible for his or her own criminal acts — which has resulted in a virtual immunity to criminal charges of sports organizations in cases where an individual member of the organization has been indicted for assault. The leading case is *State* v. *Forbes,* apparently the only criminal prosecution ever of a professional athlete in the United States.

On January 4, 1975, during an NHL game in Bloomington, Minnesota, an altercation occurred between David Forbes of the Boston Bruins and

Henry Boucha of the Minnesota North Stars. Both players were sent to the penalty box, where Forbes repeatedly threatened Boucha verbally. As they left the box at the expiration of the penalties — Boucha first and Forbes seconds later — Forbes skated up behind Boucha and struck him with the butt end of his stick just above the right eye. Boucha fell to the ice stunned and bleeding (with a badly damaged eye, it turned out). Forbes jumped on him, punched him on the back of the head, then grabbing him by the hair, proceeded to pound his head into the ice. Eventually another Minnesota player separated the two. The President of the NHL suspended Forbes for ten games, but shortly afterward a Minnesota grand jury charged him with the crime of aggravated assault by use of a dangerous weapon. Forbes pleaded not guilty. The jury, after a week and a half of testimony and eighteen hours of deliberation, was unable to reach a unanimous verdict. The court declared a mistrial, and the case was dismissed (Flakne and Caplan, 1977).

Described in law journals as a "landmark" case because it focused so much legal and public attention on the issue of violence in sports, *State* v. *Forbes* also raised the important and still unanswered question of legal individualism as it applies to the occupational use of violence; namely, who should be held responsible in such cases, the individual or the group? Should not only Forbes, but the Boston Bruins and even the League, have been on trial? Was Forbes merely doing his job, his duty, as a good hockey soldier? The defence counsel tried to ask these questions during the trial, to instruct the jury to consider, for example, the "context" in which the assault took place, but the judge demurred, insisting the indictment applied only to Forbes, the individual (Hallowell and Meshbesher, 1977).

The public, too, is divided on legal individualism, if an opinion poll conducted shortly after Forbes' trial, and regarding accountability in the trial of Lieutenant Calley of My Lai massacre notoriety, is any indicator. As reported by Hallowell and Meshbesher (1977), 58 per cent of the respondents in this survey disapproved of criminal sanctions being applied to an individual acting in a legitimate role and following what that individual believed to be "at least implicit orders." Are orders to perform acts of violence implicit in professional hockey? The question should be: how explicit are such orders?

As for legally raising (let alone demonstrating) criminal liability on the part of an employer in sports violence disputes, Kuhlman (1975) suggests that although problems of proof are substantial (the burden of proof on the prosecution in a criminal trial is heavier than in a civil trial), the most promising route is probably via the statutes on conspiracy; that is, the prosecution should attempt to prove that the organization and the individual conspired to commit an assault. Owners, coaches, and teammates — all members of the "system" — are thus potentially implicated; sociological reality becomes legal fact.

By way of a footnote to *State* v. *Forbes,* the author was engaged in 1980 by the Detroit law firm of Dykema, Gossett, Spencer, Goodnow, and Trigg as a consultant and "expert witness" in a civil suit being brought by Boucha against the Boston Bruins and the NHL. (After several only partly successful eye operations, Boucha's career had ground to a halt.) The charge was, in effect, "creating an unsafe work environment." The case was settled out of court for an undisclosed amount two days before the trial was to begin in Detroit.

Criminal violence

This category consists of violence so serious and obviously outside the boundaries of what could be considered part of the game that it is handled from the outset by the law. Death is often involved, as in the 1973 Paul Smithers case, which received world-wide publicity. Smithers, a seventeen-year-old black hockey player, was convicted of manslaughter after killing an opposing player in a fight in a Toronto arena parking lot following a game (Runfola, 1974). Almost always such incidents, though closely tied to game events, take place prior to or after the contest itself. (One suspects that if Smithers' attack had occurred during the game he would have received a five-minute or match penalty, and the victim's death would have been dismissed as an "unfortunate accident.") On the extreme fringe of this category are assaults and homicides only incidentally taking place in a sports setting.

An extended, first-hand account of another hockey incident provides an illustration of a typical episode of criminal violence in sports, while at the same time conveying something about a social milieu that encourages such misbehaviour. This assault took place in a Toronto arena after the final game of a Midget playoff series that had been marred by bad behaviour in the stands and on the ice, including physical and verbal attacks on opposing players by the assailant in question. The victim was the coach of the winning team. He had been ejected from the game for making a rude gesture at the referee and was standing against the boards some distance from his team's bench when the assault took place. He also happened to be a student at York University. Three days after the incident he came to my office seeking some advice, his face barely recognizable. He left promising to lay an assault charge, which he had not yet done, and to write down in detail his version of what happened. He did both. (The offending player was later convicted of assault.) An excerpt from his six-page account (with fictitious names) is presented in Figure 1.2.

Figure 1.2 Criminal Violence in Hockey

At the final buzzer the parents applauded their sons' victory and the players of our team all left the bench to congratulate the goalie who was down at our end. Out of the corner of my eye I picked up Jones making a wide circle in our end and heading directly over toward me. My only thought was that he would skate over and continue his usual swearing and animal-like antics.

I was wrong. He let his stick drag behind him and with the stick in his left hand he took a full swing with it and made contact across my face. The force of the blow was further increased by the heavy heel-end of the stick, which made contact across my nose, just below my eyes. I went partly down against the seat. Some parents came to my aid, while others, including a couple of impartial fans, went on the ice after the boy, along with my players. Parents from both teams tangled as everyone seemed intent on getting to Jones. I was mostly concerned with the safety of my players and getting them into the dressing room. While I stood bleeding profusely from a widely gashed and multiple-fractured nose, I was approached by an impartial spectator, James Turner, who stated that he had seen the whole incident along with Al Marks and that he was going to call the police. He stated that if charges were laid he would be a witness. stating the whole story as he saw it as an unbiased observer. There is also at least one other impartial witness, along with almost all the parents and some friends of our players. A linesman saw the whole incident also, and the referee supervisor of the league told my assistant coach, who was coaching the team at the time, that it was the "most brutal thing I've ever seen."

After answering the questions of the police who arrived approximately twenty to thirty minutes after the incident, and telling my version of the incident, I was taken to North York General Hospital where I was examined first by a nurse and then by the doctor in emergency at the time. He ordered X rays, which showed a compound fracture of the nose. After stitching the cuts across my nose and under my eye, he showed his disgust and anger at such incidents by informing me that he hoped charges were laid and law suits following. Charges of assault causing bodily harm have now been laid. He really shook me up by telling me that I was actually a very lucky person, because if I had turned my head perhaps a half-inch either way, I might very likely have been killed by such a blow to the temple or forehead. He informed me that the usual procedure for this type of fracture was to wait for three to five days for the swelling to go down and then have it set by a plastic surgeon. Later he suggested I come in that morning at 8:00 a.m. to see the head of plastic surgery. I have an appointment to see him next Tuesday, April 4th. Ever since the incident, I have had little if any sleep, a constant headache, a case of bad nerves, constant shaking, mental strain, and depression has begun to set in due to my thoughts about upcoming exams and activities at school. I have been unable to eat and at this point in time feel like a physical wreck, and the thought of almost being killed in such an incident has loomed on my mind a great deal.

The fact that no apology has been offered by the player, parents, or organization, let alone concern for my health, leaves me also with a bitter feeling for those involved or associated with this assault. I don't feel the boy is as much to blame as the coach who sanctioned and reinforced this type of behaviour, the parents who didn't attempt to discourage him from playing this style of hockey, and the Wallbury organization which seems to condone this type of play throughout their organization. The fact that the boy's father was drunk at this incident only leaves me feeling more sorry for this boy and the environment he has been a product of.

Conclusion

What is called violence and what is not is no trivial matter. The extent to which a behaviour is perceived as violence has a great deal to do with what people are willing to do about it. As philosopher Robert Audi (1974:38) puts it in his essay "Violence, legal sanctions, and the law": "Misnaming the disease can lead to the use of the wrong medicine or none at all." Perhaps we are close to being able to say with some clarity what sports violence is. We may soon know with greater certainty what to do about it.

2 Sports Violence in Time and Space

[The players] all falleth by the eares, eche assaultinge other with their unreasonable cudgells sparinge neyther heade, face, nor anye part of the bodie, the footemen fall soe close to it, beinge once kindled with furie as they wholey forgett the playe, and fall to beatinge, till they be out of breathe, and then some nomber hold theire hands upp over theire heades and crye,... peace, peace, and often times this parteth them, and to theire playe they goe a newe.
(Dunning and Sheard, 1979:28)

Modern versions of football are downright tame compared to the blood baths that passed for football in preindustrial Britain. But behaviour considered barbaric in one historical setting may be civilized in another; the face of violence, like other forms of social behaviour, is contoured by sociocultural forces that vary in time and space.

A sociocultural system can be said to have two principal dimensions: social structure and culture. The nature of the relationship between social structure and culture, and the degree to which and the manner in which each is thought to influence human behaviour, are matters of intense disagreement among sociologists. Some argue that structure, culture, and social behaviour are inseparable. I shall not attempt to address these issues directly. The point in the following pages is simply this: if significant variations in types and rates of violence occur over time, across nations, societies, and cultures, by gender, class, age, and so forth, one is alerted to the probability that sociocultural forces shape the distribution of violence in time and space. This chapter and the following constitute an examination of some of these forces and patterns.

Violence over Time: The "Civilizing Process"

In 1978 the first volume of Norbert Elias's magnum opus *The Civilizing Process,* originally published in German in 1939, appeared in English, thus making available for the first time to a wide English-speaking readership a remarkable synthesis of history, sociology, and psychology, of considerable importance in the study of violence. Elias's theory of civilization, as it applies to violence, provides the framework for the first part of this chapter. In bare-bones form it goes as follows:

A "civilizing" of human "aggressiveness" has been occurring at least since early medieval times in what is now Western urban-industrial society. More specifically, there has been a gradual shift in balance between the *af-*

fective or *expressive* forms of violence and the *rational* or *instrumental* forms of violence as characteristic violence-expressions, the balance tilting in the direction of the latter. Two fundamental changes in the organization of society wrought this transformation. First, the state acquired a monopoly on the use of violence, and violence by individual citizens diminished. Second, the typical pattern of social relationships changed from one based primarily on the ascriptive bonds of family and residence – what Elias's collaborator and protégé Eric Dunning calls "segmental bonding" – to one based primarily on achieved ties governed by a complex division of labour – what Dunning terms "functional bonding." The long-term results of these structural changes have been a decline in people's capacity for obtaining pleasure from ferocity and bloodletting and an advance in their willingness to use violence as a means to an end.

Segmental bonding and expressive violence

When it comes to sheer individual ferocity, modern society pales in comparison to some earlier ones. Next to the battle fury of olden warriors, powerless though they would be against a modern army, the aggressiveness of even the most bellicose "civilized" peoples nearly vanishes. In ancient China, Greece, Rome, Mesopotamia, in Arab societies, in the Europe of the Middle Ages, mutilation, torture, peremptory executions, ritual warhunts, human sacrifices sometimes, were not only endemic, they were gloried in (Elias, 1978a, b; Collins, 1974).

The social structure of these societies fostered a level of ferocious violence almost unknown today. In early medieval Europe, Elias explains, central governments were weak. Countries were typically divided into semi-autonomous provinces, and provinces into independent fiefs, whose lords and warriors, or knights, occupied their time warring against one another. The medieval warrior lived to fight.

Warfare included ruining the enemy's lands, tearing up his trees, cutting down his vines, filling in his wells, storming his castle, killing his people, mutilating whatever prisoners were taken. After all, what could be done with prisoners? Those of rank could perhaps be ransomed, but money was of limited use in this society. Keeping prisoners of lower station meant feeding them. Setting them free allowed the enemy to rebuild his strength. So prisoners were sometimes killed or sent home minus eyes, or an arm, or a foot, thus rendering them unfit for both work and military service.

Ferocious cruelty was not stigmatized as abnormal. To the contrary, because the structure and tensions of society more or less required it, as illustrated above, it seemed perfectly normal. The socially permitted level of ferocious violence was much higher than that of today; individual inhibitions against blood lust were much lower, guilt and shame decidedly weaker. *Not* being ferocious put one at a distinct disadvantage. The literature of the time fairly rings with a love of fighting and killing. From a thirteenth-century French battle hymn (Elias, 1978a:231):

I tell you... that I find no such savor in eating, drinking, or sleeping as in hear-
ing men shout "Get them!" from both sides, hearing the neighing of horses
that have lost their riders, hearing the cries, "Help! Help!," and in seeing men
great and small go down on the grass beyond the fosses, and the dead with
their sides ripped open by the pennoned stumps of lances.

Nor is this mere braggadocio. Battle, and indeed the knightly life in
general, required incredible toughness and stamina, according to historian
Barbara Tuchman (1978:63). A knight fought on foot or horseback wearing
fifty-five pounds of armour. He collided with an enemy at full gallop while
holding horizontal a lance "half the length of an average telephone pole."
He gave and received blows with a sword or battle-ax "that could cleave a
skull or slice off a limb at a stroke." He spent half his life in the saddle in all
weathers and for days at a stretch.

If a knight had the bad luck to live in a time of relative peace, he fought in
tournaments, which in the beginning, except for the spectators, were not
much different from real battle. Tournaments orginated in France, according to Tuchman, and were referred to by others as "French combat."
They started without rules, as mere agreed-upon skirmishes between opposing groups, but in time they became more regulated and stylized, taking two
forms: jousts between individuals and melees between groups of up to forty
on a side, either *à plaisance* (with blunted weapons) or *à outrance* (with no
holds barred). In the latter, combatants were often severely wounded and
not infrequently killed. About a hundred knights usually took part, each accompanied by two mounted squires, an armourer, and several servants in
livery.

Tournaments were the great sporting events of the time. One might last as
long as a week and on great occasions two weeks. On opening day the
players were matched and seeded. This was followed by several days of
jousts and melees and a day of rest before the final tourney, all interspersed
with feasting and revelry. These occasions attracted crowds of spectators
ranging from rich merchants to common artisans, from food sellers and
street entertainers to pickpockets and prostitutes.

Not only the warrior class was imbued with a taste for violence. Official
violence at the hands of secular and religious authorities was the order of
the day. The civil authorities hacked off hands and ears, racked, burned,
flayed, and dismembered. Criminals were publicly flogged and hung in
chains. Corpses were left hanging on the gibbet. Decapitated heads and
quartered bodies remained impaled on stakes in public places for months
and years. The church also sanctioned execution and torture. In the
churches themselves hung pictures of saints undergoing every imaginable
variety of bloody martyrdom (Tuchman, 1978).

As for the common town and country folk, lethal feuds between towns,
between villages, between valleys, between guilds, between families and
cliques were common. Murderous robbers roamed the streets and highways.
In 1250, for example, according to contemporary court records, the

ide rate in England was fifteen times greater than that of today (Gurr,
. "Society from top to bottom was imbued with violence, or the taste
ror it," writes Marc Bloch (1969:83) in his celebrated analysis of feudal life.

If the warrior caste had its war and tournaments, the lower classes had
their feuds and semi-institutionalized fights. In England fights were arranged between local groups on certain days of the year, mainly Holy Days.
These events provided opportunities to dramatize or to vent existing tensions in a fashion sanctioned by tradition if not by law.

Playing with a football was one of the ways in which such fights were arranged and conducted, explain Dunning and Sheard (1979) in their
sociological study of the development of rugby. The authorities usually
tried to suppress "ffotebale" – most references to the game in medieval and
postmedieval English sources are in the form of proclamations by state and
local officials banning it (this happened more than thirty times between
1314 and 1667) or reports of legal proceedings against people who insisted
on playing it – but sometimes local magistrates winked at the goings-on, or
joined them. Such was the case in a 1579 match in which a team of Cambridge students was set upon by stick-wielding Chesterton townsmen, who
"did so beat the sayd schollers that diveres had their heads broken." The
sticks had been secreted on the porch of a nearby church, then produced
partway through the game. Forced to flee, the students later sought out the
local constable to lodge a complaint but gave up when they discovered he
had been a member of the town team. In these wild and riotous games,
bloody faces and broken bones were the order of the day and deaths were
not uncommon. A contemporary account of a traditional Shrove Tuesday
contest between a shoemakers' and a drapers' company reported that " '...
much harme was done, some in the great thronge falling into a trance, some
having their bodies bruised and crushed; some their arms, heades or legges
broken, and some otherwise maimed or in peril of their lives'" (Dunning
and Sheard, 1979:23-24).

Then there was Cornish hurling, one version of which was "hurlinge to
the countrie," a sort of free-for-all ball game ranging over miles of country-
side. This pastime, which was often sponsored by local gentry, typically
pitted the members of one parish against another. The description below
conveys something of the character of the game. It also poses questions
startlingly like those being asked today about some modern versions of
football.

*The ball in this play may be compared to an infernall spirit: for whosoever
catcheth it, fareth straightwayes like a madde man, strugling and fighting with
those that goe about to holde him: and no sooner is the ball gone from him,
but hee resigneth this fury to the next receyver, and himselfe becommeth
peaceable as before. I cannot well resolve, whether I should more commend
this game, for the manhood and exercise, or condemne it for the
boysterousness and harmes which it begetteth: for as on the one side it makes
their bodies strong, hard, and nimble, and puts a courage into their hearts, to*

meete an enemie in the face: so... on the other part, it is accompanied by many dangers, some of which do ever fall to the players share. For proofe whereof, when the hurling is ended you shall see them retyring home, as from a pitched battaile, with bloody pates, bones broken, and out of joynt, and such bruses as serve to shorten their daies; yet al is good play, and never Attourney nor Crowner troubled for the matter. (Dunning and Sheard, 1979:27)

In medieval society most people lived in small, relatively autonomous, isolated communities. Within these communities social relations typically were characterized by kinship, intimacy, moral unity, and emotional intensity. Relationships were limited in number but of long duration. People felt they belonged together because they were of the same kind. Eric Dunning (1981a,b) describes this pattern of social relationships as "segmental bonding": people are socially bonded only – or mainly – to members of their own group, which is a kind of "segment" in the sense that the boundaries between it and other groups are sharp and virtually impermeable. To put it another way, such communities are characterized by "short chains of interdependence"; that is, interdependencies among people do not, or only tenuously, extend beyond the group. In the medieval world of segmentally bonded chiefdoms, war bands, clans, families, cliques, and classes, group boundaries governed in large measure the extent of human cruelty and human sympathy. Moral injunctions against killing, torture, and maiming extended only up to the margins of the group; outsiders, being not quite human, were fair game. A twentieth-century "survival" of a segmentally bonded community might be the Mundurucú headhunters of Brazil who not long ago perceived, and treated, non-Mundurucú literally as game animals, referring to them in words used for their tapir and peccary (Durham, 1976). Such a society stands at a different stage of the "civilizing process" than our own.

In the Middle Ages, as now, an act of violence was repugnant only if it violated the moral order, or what the nineteenth-century French sociologist Emile Durkheim termed the "collective conscience" — the general morality common to all individuals belonging to a community at any given moment of its history — not because shame and revulsion automatically follow an act of violence. If the collective conscience is not disturbed, the violence-doer is not negatively sanctioned and, in turn, does not have to deal with feelings of shame and guilt. No one has put this more clearly than Durkheim himself in his discourse on sanctions, which he thought of as "synthetic links" between violence and the consequences of violence. The relevance of Durkheim's words to the current debate about what constitutes violence in sport is self-evident.

Since sanctions are not revealed by analysis of the act that they govern, it is apparent that I am not punished simply because I did this or that. It is not the intrinsic nature of my action that produces the sanction which follows, but the fact that the act violates the rule that forbids it. In fact, one and the same act,

> *identically performed with the same material consequences, is blamed or not blamed according to whether or not there is a rule forbidding it. The existence of the rule and the relation to it of the act determine the sanction. Thus, homicide, condemned in time of peace, is freed from blame in time of war. An act intrinsically the same, which is blamed today among Europeans, was not blamed in ancient Greece since there it violated no pre-established rule.*
> *(Durkheim 1974:43)* (Reprinted with permission.)

In short, a sanction is the *consequence* of an act that results not from the *content* of that act, but from the violation by that act of some preestablished rule.

To sum up what has been said so far, the social organization of some earlier societies – the lack of strong central authority, the multiplicity of close-knit autonomous groups, the dominance of war and the warrior class, and, it should be added, a primitive technology necessitating that violence be mainly face-to-face – led to a level of socially permitted expressive violence that would be regarded today as unspeakable. British folk football reflected the general social conditions. The authorities tried in vain to suppress it. Games were unregulated, chaotic, and barely distinguishable from "real" fighting. They were intensely personal, and the identity of the entire group was tied up in the struggle, not merely the players. There was little division of labour; not only were player roles relatively undifferentiated, the distinction between participants and spectators was blurred, the latter often directly entering the fray. Compared to modern sport, most versions of folk football were blood baths.

Functional bonding and instrumental violence

Yet, Collins (1974) reminds us, violence has more than one face. Personalized ferocity has been largely replaced in modern times by callousness, violence without passion. The transition began around the sixteenth century as a result of two interrelated developments. First, central government control expanded, initially because of the demands of almost continuous war and the dominance of the military community, for, as Robert Nisbet (1973) points out, it had become clear that the sovereign, territorial, political state was most ideally suited for the waging of war. Subsequently, emerging capitalism, which, with its dependence on regulated production and labour could not tolerate the internal violence of precapitalist society, exerted pressure in this direction. The central authorities increasingly forbade the direct expression of violence by individuals; individual citizens were compelled to live in relative peace. Violence became the monopoly of the state and its agents, the army and police. Second, under internal pacification, the division of labour was allowed to expand. Eventually the industrial revolution, with its urbanism and large-scale work organizations, shattered segmentally bonded society, and a different pattern of social relationship emerged, one based on "functional bonding."

Now social ties were voluntary and based not on a feeling of kinship but on the rational pursuit of self-interest, on achievement rather than ascription. Parties to a division of labour and social relationships in general now exerted a degree of mutual influence over one another, which led to greater restraint in personal relations and more self-control than earlier was the case. Where earlier communities were small, relatively undifferentiated, and characterized by a sense of unity, now communities were large, complex, impersonal, and bureaucratic. In war this trend was manifested in ever larger fighting units (national armies instead of local militias), in the use of mercenaries, in increasingly sophisticated technology that enabled destroying at a distance. All this, Nisbet (1973) shows, combined to take the emotional intensity, the "affect," out of battle. In short, individual aggressiveness on all fronts was "civilized," "humanized," and "impersonalized," first by external agencies and sanctions, and eventually by individual inhibitions, for as social structure changes so does the individual personality.

As "affect control" tightened and violence was confined to specific enclaves in time and space – the state and its agents, the masses in periods of external or revolutionary conflict, rudimentary forms of sport – there was also a general transformation of aggressiveness from direct action to observation, albeit initially with no diminution of blood lust. In sixteenth-century Paris, part of the annual St. John's Day celebrations was the public burning of a basketful of cats (sometimes the king lit the first torch). The mere mention of such a spectacle makes us squirm in horror, but people then took undisguised delight in it (Elias, 1978a). At a public execution in the town of Bruges, where several criminals were being tortured to death, we hear of crowd members protesting because the view was poor (van den Haag, 1976). Such spectacles, Elias claims, were the forerunners of boxing matches and other sports and entertainments in which the majority of citizens took part only indirectly. In time there was also a trend toward moderation and regulation. Nineteenth-century boxing matches appear "civilized" compared to eighteenth-century public executions; most sports in the second half of the twentieth century seem "civilized" next to nineteenth-century boxing.

In England, as industrialization gathered momentum in the eighteenth century, folk football began to wither. As Dunning and Sheard explain it, members of the aristocracy and gentry who had traditionally supported folk football, and in rural areas even played it, began to withdraw their patronage. Threatened by the growing power of the middle classes and the restiveness of the "lower orders," privileged Britons reacted by withdrawing into the exclusive company of their own. From this vantage point they viewed football increasingly as an affront to a modern industrial nation. Sniffed one Old Etonian: "I cannot consider the game of football... gentlemanly. It is a game which the common people of Yorkshire are particularly partial to, the tips of their shoes being heavily shod with iron; and frequently death has been known to ensue from the severity of the blows inflicted..." (Dunning and Sheard, 1979:42).

Gone now was the protective influence of the upper classes, and the central authorities, which had never ceased in their attempts to suppress football, for the first time became successful. The authorities also had at their disposal more effective forces of social control than before, most notably, after 1829, Sir Robert Peel's police: Despite occasional pitched battles between players and police, football was inexorably tamed, beginning with its removal from the streets and placement in enclosed grounds. By the end of the nineteenth century folk football had virtually disappeared. It did survive in modified, and initially still-violent, form in another more isolated context – the public schools – where earlier it had taken hold. But there, Dunning and Sheard show, football was not seen as a threat to property and public order. Eventually the excesses of public school football too were brought under control, though it remained for a long time considerably more violent than any of today's versions of the game.

The typical form of modern-day violence is callousness, Collins states, a reflection of society's organization along impersonal lines. For callousness is impersonal. Callous violence is particularly characteristic of large-scale bureaucracy (the Nazi extermination camps come immediately to mind): rationalized, impersonal, methodical, technologically efficient, the routinized following of orders displaces individual moral responsibility. Outbursts of ferocity still occur (public floggings and limb amputations, stonings and decapitations are still officially sanctioned and carried out in some countries, according to the 1981 *Amnesty International Report*), but they are minor compared to the magnitude of callous destruction. Whereas ferocious cruelty implies a kind of empathy between aggressor and victim (it is *expressive;* the aggressor invests his or her personality and emotions in the act) callous cruelty implies a psychological, even a physical, distancing of aggressor from victim, and of spectators from victim. Callous violence is *instrumental;* the victim's suffering is merely a means to an end, whether to purge the Third Reich of racial impurity or to entertain a sports crowd. It is the end product of a social structure that simultaneously generates strong competitive pressures and the use of rational strategies of goal-attainment.

Given the shift in balance between the expressive and instrumental forms of violence in favour of the latter, it follows that sports violence would be used increasingly as a calculated means of achieving ends, particularly in light of the intense competitive pressures of modern sport. Perhaps nowhere is this better exemplified than in North American football. If you wish to know a society, writes philosophy professor and former Canadian Football League player John McMurtry (1971a,b), look to its games and sport. The Middle Ages had chess with its "all-important monarchs," "disposable pawns," "slanting bishops," and "leaping knights." Capitalist Americanada (McMurtry says "Fascist" — this was the era of Nixon, Vietnam, and countercultural bombast) has football, with its complexity, its acquisitiveness, its corporate obedience, its technological efficiency, its obsession with outcome, its elitism (a tiny few plan in secret and play, the rest watch), its licenced and impersonal violence. In football, claims McMurtry (1971a:83), with the hindsight of five years' professional experience, "the truly professional attitude is not to think of the opponent as a human being at all — he is a 'position,' to be removed as efficiently as possible in order to benefit the team's corporate enterprise of gaining points." For McMurtry life inside and outside the stadium is almost the same, the only important difference being that in football "the antagonism is overt." Hyperbole aside, this depiction of football has the ring of truth. Numerous other first-hand accounts attest to it (e.g., Tatum and Kushner, 1979).

Some of the characteristics of the contrasting types of social bonding and violence-expression, and the broader social configurations within which these forms developed, as set forth by Elias and, later, Dunning, are summarized in Table 2.1. Both authors take pains to emphasize that the second set of forms did not totally replace the first but that a shift in balance between the forms occurred; that the "civilizing process" was not a simple, unilinear one but an uneven, long-term transformation, punctuated by civilizing "spurts" and de-civilizing "counter-spurts" in periods of rapidly changing social conditions; that Elias's theory is not concerned primarily with rates of violence but with the expression of violence; and that the civilizing process did not affect all groups, classes, and societies uniformly. In fact segmental bonding and expressive violence may still typify specific working-class groups, an argument to which we shall return later in the book.

Table 2.1   An Ideal Type Representation of Segmental and Functional Bonding and Their Wider Structural Correlates

SEGMENTAL BONDING	FUNCTIONAL BONDING
Locally self-sufficient communities only loosely tied into a wider, proto-national framework; relative poverty.	Nationally integrated communities, tied together by extensive chains of interdependence; relative affluence.
Intermittent pressure "from above" from a weak central state; relatively autonomous ruling class divided into warrior and priestly sections; balance of power skewed strongly in favour of rulers/authority figures both within and between groups; little pressure generated structurally "from below"; power of rulers simultaneously weakened, e.g., by rudimentary state apparatus and poor means of transport and communication.	Continuous pressure "from above" from a strong central state; relatively dependent ruling class in which the secular and civilian sections are dominant; tendency toward equalization of power chances through the generation of multi-polar controls within and between groups; intense pressure generated structurally "from below"; power of rulers simultaneously strengthened, e.g., by relatively efficient means of transport and communication.

Close identification with narrowly circumscribed groups united principally by means of ascribed kinship and local bonds.	Identification with groups that are united principally by means of achieved bonds of functional interdependence.
Narrow range of occupations; homogeneity of work experience both within and between occupational groups.	Wild range of occupations; heterogeneity of work experience both within and between occupational groups.
Low social and geographical mobility; narrow experiential horizons.	High social and geographical mobility; wide experiential horizons.
Little social pressure to exercise self-control over physical violence or to defer gratification generally; little exercise of foresight or long-term planning.	Great social pressure to exercise self-control over physical violence and to defer gratification generally; great exercise of foresight and long-term planning.
Low emotional control; quest for immediate excitement; tendency toward violent mood swings; high threshold of repugnance regarding violence and pain; pleasure from directly inflicting pain on others and from seeing others suffer; violence openly displayed in everyday life; low guilt feelings after committing violent acts.	High emotional control; quest for excitement in more muted forms; relatively stable temperament; low threshold of repugnance regarding violence and pain; vicarious pleasure from watching "mimetic" violence but not "real" violence; violence pushed "behind the scenes"; high guilt feelings after committing violent acts; rational recourse to instrumental violence in situations where it is perceived as undetectable.
Structurally generated tendency for gangs to form around the lines of social segmentation and for them to fight other local gangs; emphasis on "aggressive masculinity"; ability to fight the key to power and status in the gang and the local community.	Structurally generated tendency for relationships to be formed through choice and not simply on a local basis; "civilized" masculine style expressed in formal sport; chances for more than local power and status; status determined by occupational, educational, artistic and sports ability.
"Folk" forms of sport, basically a ritualized extension of fighting between local gangs; relatively high level of open violence.	"Modern" forms of sport, i.e., of ritualized play-fights based on controlled forms of violence but strong social pressure to use violence in its instrumental forms.

Adapted from Dunning (1981a:15-16). Reprinted with permission.

Violence in Space: The Legitimation of Violence

Just as violence changes over time, it varies across sociocultural boundaries at any given time. This is true for almost any measure of rate or level of violence, the principal concern in this section. Some societies wage war almost continuously; others wage no war (Small and Singer, 1972). Some societies have combative sports; others do not (Sipes, 1973). Some societies exhibit a high degree of attitudinal support for violence; others exhibit a low level of attitudinal support (Gurr, 1970). Parents in some societies punish their children for fighting; parents in others do not (Lambert, 1971). Rape is common in some societies, rare in others (Otterbein, 1979). Rates of criminal and political violence range enormously.

What are one's chances of being criminally assaulted or murdered in the United States, reputedly a violent country, compared to Canada and Great Britain, say? Great. When it comes to these offences, the United States is by far the most dangerous place to live, Great Britain is by far the safest, and Canada occupies a middle position. On the other hand, the United States is as safe as a church next to countries like Mexico, Turkey, Nicaragua, and Columbia. In the latter country, during a period between about 1950 and 1965 known as the *violencia,* an estimated two hundred to three hundred thousand homicides took place. For Columbian males in the age group fifteen to forty-five, homicide was the leading cause of death (Wolfgang and Ferracuti, 1967). Studies of internal political strife similarly show the United States far surpassing Canada and Great Britain, and indeed almost all western democracies, in rates of violent collective protest and deaths incurred during such protests, but well in the bottom half of the world's nations (Gurr, 1979a). A complex combination of structural and cultural factors produce such variations. I shall confine the discussion to the relationships among the cultural legitimation of violence, war, and combative sport.

Entire cultures may turn on a theme of violence or nonviolence. Consider two relatively simple, preliterate peoples, the Tausug and the Semai. Among the Tausug, who live on an island south of Mindanao in the Philippines, interpersonal violence among males is a daily occurrence. A Tausug man must defend his interests and his honour by means of force. Any insult, overt or implied, calls for retaliation. A Tausug fights in any situation in which there is even the slightest chance that *not* fighting could be labelled cowardice, the ultimate disgrace. Obviously trivial conflicts easily escalate into serious, even lethal, ones. The Tausug equivalent of the English word violence is *maisug,* meaning "very masculine" (Kiefer, 1972).

Then there are the nonviolent Semai of Malaya who do not even have an explicit word for "kill." They react to violence, when rarely it occurs, with passivity or flight. Quarrels are typically settled by intermediaries. There is no external social control of violence, no police, no courts. The Semai never strike their children. Children almost never see violence in any form. Beheading a chicken is considered regrettable (Dentan, 1968).

But human behaviour is amazingly malleable. Given the right set of social conditions the most pacifistic people may become belligerent and the most belligerent people pacifistic. Robert Dentan (1968) describes an astonishing about-face of Semai tribesmen trained by the British to fight Communist guerillas in the early 1950s (against the advice of those who insisted that the Semai would be useless as soldiers). Taken out of their nonviolent environment and taught to fight, the tribesmen became ruthless killers, and ultimately were swept up in veritable orgies of blood spilling.

The "legitimation of violence" hypothesis predicts a positive relationship between war and other forms of aggression through the cultural acceptance of violence. In a piece of comparative research impressive for its scope and thoroughness, Archer and Gartner (1976) found that homicide rates after World Wars I and II and several smaller twentieth-century wars rose substantially over prewar rates in most of fifty combatant nations, but not in thirty noncombatant "control" nations. The increases occurred after large and small wars, in victorious and defeated nations, in nations with improved and worsened postwar economies, among men and women, among several age groups, and most consistently among nations suffering large numbers of combat deaths. When Archer and Gartner tested a number of competing theoretical explanations of the war-homicide relationship, the only explanation fully consistent with their data was the legitimation-of-violence model. They concluded that war affects postwar homicide rates through the residual cultural approval of violence. A society's glorification of military violence, it seems, does not abruptly cease with the cessation of hostilities; it lingers for some years afterward in the form of a diffuse violence approval that affects rates of homicide and probably other forms of interpersonal violence.

Employing a research design similar to Archer and Gartner's, anthropologist Richard Sipes (1973) discovered that war and combative sport are associated cross-culturally; that is, warlike cultures tend to have warlike sports, and peaceful cultures do not. The patterns of behaviour and value systems of combative sports, on the one hand, and war, on the other, appear to overlap and support one another, together forming part of a culture pattern based, as we have suggested in the case of very bellicose peoples, on a theme of violence.

From fifty of the world cultural areas listed in Murdock's *Ethnographic Atlas* (ethnography is the branch of cultural anthropology concerned with the descriptive study of individual cultures, especially preliterate ones), for which sufficient ethnographic information was available, Sipes selected ten warlike and ten peaceful societies. A warlike society was defined as one that attacked others frequently or continually. A peaceful society was one that attacked others infrequently or never. A combative sport was defined as one played by two opponents (individuals or teams) and having one or both of the following features: (1) actual or potential body contact, directly or through real or simulated weapons, the object of which is to inflict real or symbolic harm, or to acquire territory; (2) no body contact, but patently warlike activity in which actual or simulated weapons are used against actual or simulated human beings. If a combative sport was described in the ethnographic literature of one of these societies, and if there was no contradictory description, that society was coded "yes" for combative sport. Societies receiving no mention of a combative sport were coded "no."

When Sipes correlated the war and combative sport variables, a strong positive relationship emerged, as shown in Table 2.2. There are only three contrary cases in Table 2.2: two peaceful societies that had combative sports and one warlike society that had no combative sport. In the case of the two peaceful societies, both were *formerly* warlike, a reversal of the Semai experience. Their combative sports were anachronisms, relics of an earlier time. In the case of the one warlike society, a unique social structure precluded any sort of competition among its members, sportlike or otherwise, because of the conflict that competition almost inevitably engenders. Kinship in this society was based on the father's family, but residence was based on the mother's. If men and women came into serious conflict on the basis of kinship, villages and households would be torn apart; if they came into conflict on the basis of residence, the entire kinship structure would be threatened. These people never overtly sought to better one another, even in play. War against outsiders was another story. Sipes' findings are even more unequivocal than depicted in Table 2.2.

Table 2.2 The Relationship between War and Combative Sport

| Societies | Combative Sports | | |
	Yes	No	Totals
Warlike	9	1	10
Nonwarlike	2	8	10
Totals	11	9	20

Adapted from Sipes (1973:71).

Sipes then tested the relationship between war and combative sport in a single society over a relatively short period of time – the United States between 1920 and 1970. (The U.S. averaged one military action every 2.6 years during these decades.) Two indicators of military activity were used: annual percentage of adult males in the armed forces, corrected for population increases; and periods of major conflict, namely World War II, the Korean War, and the Vietnam War.

Popular American sports were divided into participant versus spectator and combative versus noncombative categories. Sipes then selected for extended analysis sports in each category for which appropriate and complete data on participation were available. These were the combative sports of hunting and football and the noncombative sports of horse race betting and baseball. When the military and sports variables were correlated, the results generally supported the cross-cultural results. Of eight correlations between war and sport, six were positive. More specifically, the combative sports of hunting and football rose sharply in popularity during the periods of major conflict (so unexplainedly did horse race betting), while the noncombative sport, baseball, declined. Sipes concluded that war and combative sports are probably components of a broad culture pattern and that his findings are evidence of a general strain toward cultural consistency in human groups.

Research conducted by Kalevi Heinilä (1974) demonstrates that the approval of sports violence varies considerably across modern industrial nations. Heinilä, a Finn, conducted a mail questionnaire survey of association football players aged fifteen to eighteen in Finland, Sweden, and England. The Swedes and Finns were all amateurs; the English sample included professionals and amateurs. The questionnaire sought information about players' acceptance or nonacceptance of violence and other technically illegal tactics during critically important games. Over 900 players representing 109 soccer clubs responded, for a player return rate ranging from 57 per cent (Sweden) to 80 per cent (Finland). Percentages of players accepting the use of certain violent tactics are shown in Table 2.3. Rather large national differences are apparent: either the English junior professionals or the Swedes were most accepting of each statement, and the Finns were least accepting of three of the four statements. (See Figure 2.1 for another cross-cultural example.) We turn next to the relationship between such attitudes and actual behaviour.

Table 2.3   Cross-National Differences in Attitudes Regarding Violence in Association Football

Statements	Percentage of Players Agreeing			
	English pro. (N = 125)	English am. (N = 111)	Swedes (N = 283)	Finns (N = 406)
A fast opponent must be stopped by any means, lawful or otherwise.	55	37	60	37
A player who is in an obvious position to score must be brought down unmercifully.	70	54	40	45
In major games all means are permissible to win the game.	54	38	31	25
The coach urges a player to knock out of the game a dangerous player of the opposing team.	56	35	63	27

SOURCE: Heinilä (1974:21). Reprinted with permission.

Figure 2.1   A Swedish NHL Player's Perception of North American Hockey

Hockey is the most demanding sport in the world. It demands speed, stamina, toughness and a lot of other physical and mental qualities. It also demands tolerance of pain. Hurting is a part of professional hockey. You get banged around, you lose your teeth, you twist muscles, break bones.

You get a stick across your shins and an elbow in the mouth. I'm not crying, just stating facts. Some people have said I don't enjoy the North American style of hockey with the smaller ice surface and rougher style of play. Well, I don't mind a hard-hitting game. Before we started this season, I had a talk with the coach, Red Kelly. He told me I'd have to improve my checking. I wasn't following through, taking the man out completely. I was giving up half way. Well, you have no idea how strong some of the guys are in this league, but I've worked hard to increase my strength and improve my checking. I work out on the weights a lot. I feel certain I've increased my strength and durability. That is the way it is with me. I am concerned about my game, I am relatively honest, and if the style of hockey I played in Sweden needs to be changed, then I will try to change.

Certain people have spoken out and criticized my play. They say I should fight a little more, that I should not turn the other cheek. Okay, I have my faults. Maybe I should fight. I am trying to change my game, but it has been hard. In Sweden I was not brought up to fight, just to play hockey.

Of course, there have been misconceptions about the way I play the game. I know how to skate, and in Sweden I was used to opening up opponents with my speed. My job is to skate and score goals. That is my basic style and it probably won't change. If I don't score at least thirty goals in this league I will never be satisfied. I know I can score at least thirty. Yet I am frequently asked: "What kind of person are you? Why don't you fight back?" Some fans in North America seem so devoted to the idea of hockey as a rough sport that it is easy for them to be misled, particularly by the press. Hockey reporters in North America are always concentrating on concepts such as courage, when 99% of the time it is not the moral quality of courage that is at issue but only the physical fact of tolerance to pain. Am I exhibiting any special kind of courage if they knock me unconscious to the ice and carry me off on a stretcher and later I return to the game? No, I am a hockey player. I am like the businessman who goes to work after he has had the heart operation. He goes back because that is his job and that is what he has chosen to do. Courage has nothing to do with it.

I understand that Harold Ballard, the president of the Maple Leafs, has been critical of my play and has been what the other players call "ripping me pretty good." I have heard all the knocks against me and I'm sure the other European players are hearing the same sort of things: "Chicken Swede" or "Cream puffs" or "They skate around with eggs in their pockets and never break them." If the newspaper guys or players on the other teams knock me it doesn't disturb me one bit, but you don't expect it from your own boss. I would be less than honest if I said it didn't bother me a little.

SOURCE: Hammerstrom (1976). Reprinted by permission of International Sports Properties, Inc.

Violent Subcultures

A great deal of sociological research on interpersonal violence bears directly or indirectly on the concept of *violent subculture*. In the subculture approach, a high rate of violence in some socially definable subcategory of persons (e.g., juvenile fighting gangs) is thought to result from adherence to a set of values and norms that encourages violent behaviour. These values and norms vary from, but are not necessarily completely at odds with, those of the wider culture.

As a descriptive term, "violent subculture" seems clear and quickly catches attention. And some sports appear to fit the description. Finding evidence of support for violence in values and norms, however, only makes the violent subculture thesis *plausible*. The fundamental test of the thesis requires a comparison of individual members' values and norms with those of nonmembers; this seems only to have been done twice, and with mixed results (Ball-Rokeach, 1973; Smith, 1979b). In fact the thesis is more widely and uncritically accepted than its present empirical status warrants. Two alternative versions of the thesis are identified below. Let us examine a study that empirically tested each as an explanation of violence in ice hockey.

The violent societal subculture hypothesis

Probably the most representative, frequently cited, contemporary rendition of the violent subculture hypothesis is that of Wolfgang and Ferracuti (1967). They draw upon research on delinquency, crime, lower-class social structure and values, and upon ethnographic studies of traditionally violent cultures to develop the proposition that violence is the product of subcultural *normative standards* (values and norms). In what they call the "subculture of violence," physical assault is the expected response to a perceived challenge or insult – a jostle, a glance, a derogatory remark, the appearance of a weapon. Conformity to this code is essential in acquiring and maintaining honour, especially for young, lower-class males, and especially when such challenges are associated with one's masculinity. Those who fail to conform are subject to peer sanctions ranging from indifference to disdain and ostracism. This type of subculture can be termed "societal" because it is presumed to stem from the social conditions in which people located at the bottom of the socioeconomic order live.

Wolfgang and Ferracuti propose that verification of the subculture-of-violence thesis should not require proving that violence is the predominant subcultural theme, only that it is an important one. No subculture is completely at odds with the parent culture; culture and subculture always interlock to some degree. Also, though violence is an expected response in many different situations, members of the subculture are not violent continuously or everywhere; normal social functioning would be impossible. Most assaults take place in settings where there is easy access to weapons, where others ready for violence are present, and where precipitating situations are likely to arise; in short, where *normative standards* are salient. The subculture-of-violence thesis would predict that violent athletes fight *mainly* on the playing field but also that they fight elsewhere more than nonviolent athletes or nonathletes.

The violent occupational subculture hypothesis

An occupational subculture is one in which people doing the same work have developed a somewhat unique system of values and norms that guides their conduct in the work context and helps them cope with and make sense of the demands of their job. Several sociological investigations of violence in amateur and professional hockey explicitly or implicitly characterize the game as having an occupational culture based on a theme of violence (e.g., Faulkner, 1974; Vaz, 1976; Smith, 1979a); that is to say, players purportedly adhere to a set of proviolence values and norms derived from the occupation of professional hockey.

The social structure of the hockey system, in Canada especially, promotes such an orientation. Boys typically enter hockey around the age of seven. The ablest are quickly funnelled into highly competitive "representative," "allstar" or "competitive" leagues where they begin their occupational socialization. Fighting and other kinds of borderline assaults tend to be discouraged among younger boys, but not hard, legal body contact (although in 1980 the Canadian Amateur Hockey Association banned contact for boys twelve and under). Around thirteen to fourteen years of age, however, the criteria for player evaluation begin to change, for it is then that potential for junior (preprofessional) and professional hockey is thought to begin to reveal itself. By Midget age, fifteen, coaches are looking for players who can mete out, and withstand, illegal physical coercion. Some boys of this age are upwardly mobile primarily because they are good fighters.

The attributes emphasized in these training years are those desired by professional hockey organizations, which depend upon amateur hockey for a steady output of talent and to whose ranks most of the best players aspire. Because motivation to advance to higher-level teams and ultimately to professional is strong, and because the number of top-level teams progressively diminishes as players get older, competition for positions becomes more and more intense. The structure of the system compels aspirants to conform increasingly to prevailing occupational standards, which include the necessity of employing at least a minimum level of what in another context has been labelled "force-threat" (Goode, 1972).

There is a strong masculinity theme in the use of violence as an occupational tool in hockey. Players develop a finely honed sensitivity to slights; they posture and threaten and fight schoolyard-style, and even employ the same schoolyard argot. "I don't think there's nothing worse than being a chicken," says a professional performer (Faulkner, 1974:299-300). This sentiment pervades the hockey culture, from bubblegum card biographies of players who "don't like to be pushed around" to magazine articles on "Hockey's Top Scrappers." It can be found throughout the testimony for the "defence" in the 1,256-page transcript of the 1974 Ontario Government inquiry into amateur hockey violence (McMurtry, 1974).

Research on players' perceptions of the game's social climate reveals that older boys in "competitive" leagues, in particular, view their teammates, coaches, and fathers as approving of a variety of on-ice assaults. (This research is discussed in detail in Chapter 4.) They approve, it seems, to the extent that violence "works" as an occupational tool and to the extent it expresses masculine "character" – a willingness to stand up and be counted in tough situations. These themes seem to be exaggerated versions of broader culture values. How else could the game have become and remained a national institution in Canada?

Research on professional players in the American Hockey League (Faulkner, 1973, 1974) and the National Hockey League (Smith, 1979a,c) depicts the fully socialized end product of the sport. These performers, upon entering professional hockey, and periodically thereafter, are obliged to "show themselves," to lay claim to treatment as persons whom their colleagues can respect. Although not the only way of establishing a positive identity, displays of toughness, courage, and willingness to fight are important means of doing so. Allowing oneself to be intimidated, on the other hand, results not only in coming to be regarded as of doubtful moral worth but in being rendered relatively useless to the team.

In short, much hockey violence arises out of the occupational experience. Violence is at least partly a response to occupational pressures, and players accept and justify it on this basis, once, that is, the standard rhetoric regarding "frustration" and the "nature of the game" as causes of violent play is put aside.

Testing the violent subculture hypothesis

Adequate empirical confirmation of the basic tenet of the violent subculture thesis would require demonstrating that compared to those who do not, individuals who behave violently endorse values and norms that in some way promote violence. After all, people who act violently do not necessarily develop a culture that condones violence, nor do people who profess proviolence values and norms necessarily behave violently. The key to the violent subculture hypothesis is that which links background and behaviour, namely values and norms.

Verification of the *societal* version of the hypothesis would further require showing that proviolence values and norms get strongest support from lower-class persons, and that such values and norms predict violent behaviour in more than one setting. Verification of the *occupational* version would require showing that these values and norms receive strongest support from individuals for whom occupational criteria regarding the use of violence are particularly salient. In the present case these would be older boys in highly competitive hockey leagues.

Data from a 1976 survey of amateur hockey violence conducted by the author bear directly on this issue (Smith, 1979b). In this research three populations of Toronto males aged twelve to twenty-one were sampled: house-league hockey players, "competitive" hockey players, and nonplayers. From the first two populations, eight hockey organizations were chosen – two house-league and six competitive. Using simple random sampling from the lists of registrants in these organizations, 740 selections were made. Following the removal of nonrespondents and players released, traded, injured, or for some other reason not playing at least half a season, 604 players were interviewed. As for the control group of nonplayers, 153 students from six schools representing a wide range of socioeconomic environments were interviewed.

The hockey organizations and performers represented the spectrum of hockey in the city. Of the six competitive organizations (players win positions in tryouts), two drew their players from local areas only, two recruited city-wide, two – Junior B and Junior A (in effect, junior preprofessional) – recruited from even further afield. The two house leagues (no tryouts, everybody plays) were typical of their kind. All told, 98 hockey teams were represented.

To measure values, a modified version of items used by Blumenthal et al. (1972) in their national study of attitudes toward violence among American men was used. These items are shown in Table 2.4. Responses to each value were scored on a five-point scale from Agree Strongly to Disagree Strongly. Two indexes, labelled Hit and Kindness, were constructed by summing respondents' scores on the appropriate items.

Table 2.4   Values Regarding the Use of Violence

Hit Index	Kindness Index
Hitting a person is acceptable if it is the only way to get what you want.	It is important to be kind to people even if they do things you don't believe in.
Hitting a person is acceptable if it is the only way to achieve an important goal.	When a person harms you, you should turn the other cheek and forgive him.
A man has a right to hit another man to defend his property.	Even if you don't like a person, you should still try to help him.
A man has a right to hit another man to defend his reputation.	
Hitting a person is acceptable if it is the only way to get what is rightfully yours.	

Adapted from Smith (1979b).

Table 2.5   Norms Regarding the Use of Violence in Hockey

Are there any situations you can imagine in which you would approve of a minor hockey player punching another player?

(If Yes)

Would you approve if he had been ridiculed and made fun of by the other player?
Would you approve if he had been challenged by the other player to a fight?
Would you approve if he had been shoved by the other player?

Adapted from Smith (1979b).

Slightly revised versions of items employed by the 1969 President's Violence Commission (Baker and Ball, 1969) were used to ascertain verbal expressions of norms regarding violence. These are shown in Table 2.5. Responses were scored on a yes-no basis. An index, Approval of Hockey Fighting, was created by summing the yes's.

Three measures of violent behaviour were used. First, players were asked how many fist-fights they had been in during the 1975-76 hockey season. Second, the season's official game reports were obtained for a representative subsample of 273 players (156 house-league, 117 competitive), and for each, the number of major or five-minute penalties was ascertained. (Almost all major penalties are for physically assaultive acts.) Third, players and nonplayers were asked how many street altercations (fights not associated with sport) they had been in during the past three years. Each of these variables was coded "0" for no fights or penalties, "1" for one or more fights or penalties.

The results of the analysis of these data support the generic form of the violent subculture hypothesis. Fighting and penalty-getting hockey players scored significantly higher on the Hit Index and the Approval of Hockey Fighting Index and significantly lower on the Kindness Index than their nonviolent counterparts. In the broadest sense of the concept, violent hockey players can be said to share a subculture.

But these connections between values, norms, and violent behaviour say nothing about the basis of such a subculture, whether it is societally or occupationally rooted. Two tests of the societal hypothesis were made. First, youths who endorse values and norms supportive of violence should fight not only on the ice, where normative standards are most salient, but off the ice as well. Only very weak statistical associations emerged, however, between the indexes of values and norms and number of off-ice fights for both players and nonplayers. Values and verbally expressed norms are poor predictors of off-ice violence. Second, the societal hypothesis posits that subculture members come from lower-class backgrounds. But although lower-class boys were in more hockey fights and did receive more major penalties than their higher-status counterparts, they were *not* in more street fights than either the higher-status players or the nonplayers (see Table 2.6). In any event lower-class players did not give greater support to proviolence values and norms. The violent hockey subculture is not the societal sub-culture described by Wolfgang and Ferracuti and others.

There remains the possibility of an occupational subculture, composed mainly of older youths in highly competitive leagues, where professional standards of behaviour are in force. The data in Table 2.6 confirm the existence of this subculture. Older players in professionalized leagues fought more and received more major penalties than younger, house-league boys, and they scored significantly higher on the indexes of values and norms. Future research will show if the violent subculture thesis, in either of its forms, is as useful in accounting for violence in other sports.

Table 2.6   Participation in Hockey and Street Violence by Hockey Involvement, Age, and Father's Socioeconomic Status (in Per Cent)

Hockey Involvement	One or More Hockey Fights	One or More Major Penalties	One or More Street Fights
Nonplayers			53
House-league players	12	3	65
Competitive players	60	68	60
Age			
12-13 years	13	4	79
14-15 years	22	0	64
16-17 years	48	35	52
18-21 years	69	61	42
Father's Ses Score*			
20-29	32	22	58
30-39	54	52	62
40-49	50	49	57
50-59	39	32	65
60-69	24	12	65
70+	20	20	57

*Blishen (1967) Index of Socioeconomic Status.

SOURCE: Smith, unpublished data (1976).

Conclusion

What is normal in one historical period may be repugnant in another. The personal ferocity and open joy in blood-spilling characteristic of medieval times would be unthinkable today. Modern violence tends to be efficient and impersonal, more a rationalized means of attaining goals than a discharge of emotion. This is not to say that violence in earlier times was irrational, only that it had a different visage.

According to Elias's theory of the civilizing process, changes in the structure of society wrought this transformation. First, the state acquired a monopoly on the use of violence, and violence by individual citizens diminished. Second, the typical pattern of social relationships changed from one based on bonds only among members of the immediate group – "segmental bonding" – to one based on a complex division of labour – "functional bonding." Whereas the former was characterized by emotional expressiveness, the latter became marked by rationality, restraint, and self-control. A long-term result was that individuals lost the capacity for obtaining pleasure from engaging in, and eventually observing, ferocious violence. In other words, there was a lowering of the level of socially permitted ferocious violence and, in time, an advance in the individual citizen's "threshold of repugnance" with respect to overt aggressiveness. This transformation took place in all spheres of social life, including sport; British folk football games were blood baths compared to modern versions of football.

Levels of violence also vary enormously across societies and cultures at any particular point in history. No single factor accounts for these differences, but a cultural explanation – the legitimation of violence hypothesis – enjoys considerable research support. The diametric opposite of the popular belief that participation in one form of aggression reduces the desire to engage in another, the legitimation hypothesis holds that levels of violence within and across cultures covary with cultural values regarding the use of violence. Levels of warfare and homicide rise and fall together, as do levels of war and combative games and sports. The value systems that sustain these different forms of aggression appear to overlap and support one another. A culture deserves the violence it gets, one might say.

The idea of violent subculture addresses this notion within a narrower context. The violent *societal* subculture hypothesis predicts that proviolence values and norms receive strongest support from lower-class males and that such values and norms are associated with violent behaviour in a variety of settings. The violent *occupational* subculture hypothesis predicts that pro-violence values and norms get most support from persons in a violent occupation and that these values and norms are associated with violent behaviour mainly in the occupational milieu. Research on hockey violence supports the latter hypothesis.

The central argument in this chapter is that social structural and cultural factors shape the characteristic expression and level of violence in society. Variations in violent behaviour *within* these broad contours is the subject matter of the following chapters.

3 Gender, Class, and Age As Determinants of Sports Violence

Just as violence is patterned in time and space, it is patterned within these dimensions by gender, class, and age. Generally speaking, males behave more violently than females, "rough" working-class environments are more dangerous places than middle-class ones, youths fight more than middle-age adults. The objectives of this chapter are to determine the *extent* to which sports violence is a function of gender, class, and age and to examine some social and cultural forces that seem to explain these associations.

Gender

Although there is evidence that female violence is on the rise, violence is essentially 'a male phenomenon. This is true historically and cross-culturally. Males commit most of the violent crimes and most of the violent delinquency. Males predominate in occupations requiring violence – soldier, policeman, prison guard, football player. Boys and men push, punch, scuffle, and fight more than girls and women. It is mainly boys and men who play rough, sometimes violent, games and sports.

Explanations of gender differences in violence usually have to do with some aspect of gender role socialization, the learning process that begins at birth and continues through adulthood, in which individuals learn and internalize the roles considered appropriate for their sex. The details and outcomes of gender role socialization differ from person to person and group to group, but there are consistencies that transcend these differences. One such consistency across cultures is that maleness and violence go together, and femaleness and violence do not. That the reverse is occasionally discovered, as in Mead's (1935) famous study of New Guinea tribes, only underlines the importance of culture and socialization.

Male violence

In a broad sense "masculinity" refers to stereotyped qualities thought appropriate for males. It is frequently asserted that masculinity is a determinant of male violence. But as suggested in the previous chapter, research bearing on masculinity and violence has produced mixed findings. A more extended examination of the relationship is warranted.

In studies of Latin Americans and Mexican Americans, masculinity, or *machismo,* is usually described as a "cultural trait" predisposing men to an exaggerated sense of honour, hypersensitivity, emotional detachment, authoritarianism, drunkenness, sexual promiscuity, callousness toward women, physical courage and aggression (Erlanger, 1979; Lewis, 1961). The stereotypical Latin or Chicano male is depicted as being under constant pressure to prove his *machismo,* to prove that he has, figuratively, *muy co-jones* (abundant testicles), or alternatively that he is not a woman. The bully does not necessarily have *machismo;* the real man is the man who "does what he has to do" when shame must be erased and honour restored. This may involve violence, but violence is not necessarily a macho trait.

In one of the few empirical studies on the relation between *machismo* and violence, Erlanger (1979) reports that among East Los Angeles Chicano males, *machismo* has to do with courage and personal dignity and with the defence of self in its broadest meaning. Erlanger found that when circumstances permitted the demonstration of these male values in a nonviolent way – notably between 1967 and 1972 when there was a popular political movement to gain unity and local control in the Chicano community and a concomitant rise in the self-worth of its residents – the incidence of gang-related violence fell abruptly; when the movement fizzled out, gang violence rose. Levels of gang violence were determined through interviews with law enforcement officials, including members of the Gang Squad, and gang members themselves. A narrow, somewhat twisted interpretation of *machismo* may prescribe physical combat as the only response to a perceived challenge or insult to one's manhood, but a broader, more generally held interpretation prescribes a violent response only when the wider social context in which men function inhibits the expression of courage, honour, and dignity.

In Figure 3.1, Zurcher and Meadow (1967) reveal some of the subtleties of *machismo* in an interpretive account of the symbolic significance of the bullfight in Mexico, the "national sport" of that country. They view this spectacle as an acting out of tensions generated by the typical Mexican family structure, particularly the relationship between father and son. The matador is the son, the bull is the father, the spectators represent the women in the family, the mother especially. Has the matador (son) enough *machismo* to stand up to the awesome power of the bull (father)? The crowd (mother) looks on expectantly, waiting to pass judgment.

Figure 3.1   Machismo in the Mexican Bullfight

The *matador* provides the spectator with an amazingly flexible psychological figure. He can identify with the *matador's* courage, with his expertise, with his skill, and yet he can project upon the *matador,* especially in a bad performance, accusations of cowardice and powerlessness he has experienced himself in the constantly losing battle with his father. It is interesting that many bullfighters take nicknames with diminutive denotations — Jose*lito,* Armillita *Chico,* Amoros *Chico,* Gall*ito,* Machaqu*ito,* etc. Similarly, well over three hundred *matadors* whose names have been

entered in the records have somewhere in their nick
(child) — En Nino de la Palma, etc. Thus is emphasi
helplessness of the child *vis-à-vis* the father. Streng
valued an attribute of the *matador* as is demonstrable
matadors are not remembered for their muscle, but for
sign of fear is acceptable, even desirable, if the *faena*
highlighted the fact that the *matador* has in spite of
dominated, and killed the bull. A too calm, too noncha
matador, without the emotion of fear (and pride in controlling that fear),
who cannot convey to the crowd that his is in fact a struggle in which he has
faced, averred, and administered death to an over-powering force, may be
viewed as a *matador* without *salsa* — without "sauce." The fact of the matter is that the Mexican father *is* threatening, does physically hurt and *does*
strike fear in the heart of his sons. To dominate and destroy him *would* be a
remarkable feat. If the bullfight is to provide symbolically a resolution of
this one-sided affair then it must be representative of its acts, events, and
especially of its emotions.

SOURCE: Zurcher and Meadow (1967:107). Reprinted with permission.

Closely related to the concept of *machismo* is that of "compulsive
masculinity." This refers to the exaggeration of behaviour differentiating
males from females. It is generated by anxiety about maleness. Compulsive
masculinity is thought to be largely a product of family structure common
to urban industrial society, in which, it is argued, boys do not easily grow
up confident of their fundamental masculinity (Toby, 1975). The main tenet
of this hypothesis is that young boys tend to have a problem of masculine
identification owing to the relative unavailability to them of male role
models, fathers especially. Although more and more North American
mothers now work outside the home, mothers are still more available to
children than fathers and still do the lion's share of the child-rearing. The
typical father not only is relatively absent from the home, his children often
have but a hazy idea of what he does at work. Also, in the case of divorced
and separated parents, children tend to live with the mother, not the father.
In fact, the specifics of how gender identity is acquired are somewhat
unclear, but what is clear is that boys and male adolescents tend to have
greater problems than girls establishing their gender identity (Mackie,
1979).

Compulsively masculine behaviour, then, becomes a way of bolstering
the male image, of dealing with the unconscious fear of being feminine, and
if we broaden the notion, the conscious fear of *appearing* feminine. What
specifically is compulsively masculine behaviour? Toby (1975) offers these
illustrations, derived in part from interviews with reformatory inmates: (1)
fascination with body-building; (2) use of profanity, symbolically
associated with masculinity, especially in fear-provoking situations where

...ger that men may respond "like women"; (3) frenetic striving ...sexual conquest; (4) violence as a way of protecting honour, ...g courage, or concealing fear, particularly the fear of revealing ...kness. Toby speculates that males who grow up in female-headed households are more likely to behave violently than males from male-headed households, and that males who come from lower-class or deprived minority backgrounds, where men have little symbolic masculine power (e.g., success in business, authority over others), are more likely to behave violently than males from backgrounds where symbolic masculine power is clearly evident. Toby is not suggesting that the majority of males in urban industrial society have a serious problem of masculine identification, only that a sufficient number of males are insecure enough to influence the cultural image of the "ideal" male.

But sources of anxiety about masculinity do not necessarily relate to the psychodynamics of gender identity. A male may be secure about his gender identity but still anxious regarding his anticipated or perceived ability to fulfill traditional male role expectations; e.g., occupational success. This is "masculine status anxiety" (Greenberg, 1977). Males alleviate it by exaggerating traditional male traits they *can* express, like aggressiveness. The structural sources of masculine status anxiety lie in the long-standing barriers to the achievement of traditional male role expectations experienced by some disadvantaged groups.

What better place to deal with anxiety about masculinity, whatever its source, than rough contact sports? Mere participation conjures up an image of rugged manliness. This is the theme of Sheard and Dunning's (1973) essay on the rise of British rugby in the second half of the nineteenth century. They attempt to show that, as women of the time stepped up their demands for political and economic power, largely through the Suffragette movement, some middle- and upper-class men – their social position and self-image threatened – withdrew into the all-male rugby subculture, for many simply a perpetuation of the all-male community of the boarding school.

Rugby clubs from the beginning were places for testing, expressing, and accentuating masculinity: by mocking and vilifying women in obscene song; by ridiculing homosexuality through songs and male stripteases; by extremes of drunkenness; by initiation ceremonies in which initiates were stripped, often forcibly, and their genitals defiled with noxious substances; by exceedingly rough and violent behaviour on the field of play. These traditions have lasted wherever rugby is played, though usually in diluted form, at least in Britain, where women now are not only visitors at the Saturday night beer-up, but welcome ones. In the past they were told to leave before the rowdiness began. All-female rugby clubs at some American universities now have their own beer-ups (*Time,* June 26, 1978). And some women rugby players now engage in a ritual rejection of female stereotypes by mocking the alleged femininity of their opponents in on-field chanting before games, by wearing T-shirts emblazoned with "Iron Ovaries," and so on (Sherry, 1980). Perhaps what has changed least about the game is its violence, if John Raper, former captain of the Australian National Football League team is right (Dunstan, 1973:243): "Rugby league is for the tough. Outside the side line is the only place for the chicken-hearted or the weak-bodied. It's violent most of the time and, I'd say, a lot harder than professional boxing. The unwritten rule book for this game is based on the word... survive." Rituals somewhat similar to those of the rugby subculture have been documented in popular literature on other male-dominated team sports, e.g., American football (Shaw, 1972; Plimpton, 1973) and baseball (Bouton, 1971).

Paradoxically, while such sports provide opportunities to prove manliness, they also present conditions that systematically generate anxiety about it. In an interesting if highly speculative paper on this theme, Hughes and Coakley (1979) compare the experiences of participants in "heavy contact" team sports with those of prison inmates. In both circumstances, men undergo a set of deprivations and repressions that call into question their masculinity. In both circumstances violence becomes a means, one of very few, of shoring up that masculinity. To be sure, there are fundamental differences between a prison and a sports team. A prison is a total institution, whereas a team is only one of many social settings in which an athlete functions. A prison term is coerced, whereas team membership is voluntary. A prison inmate is stigmatized, whereas an athlete is usually admired. On the other hand, Hughes and Coakley cite college and professional athletes who refer to their sports, especially the preseason training camp phase, as "going to jail," "penal institutions," "Devil's Island," and the like. Their argument, in any case, is not that the physical or social environments of prisons and sports teams are exactly the same, only that the subjective meanings of the deprivations individuals experience in each setting are similar.

First, they argue, prison inmates have greatly reduced opportunities to make the decisions that are an integral part of normal adult life. Their dependence on their captors reduces them, as Sykes (1971) has put it, to the "weak, helpless, dependent status of childhood." Similarly the popular literature on sport is full of references to tyrannical managers and coaches treating men like boys: dictating when to go to bed, what to eat, what clothes to wear, length of hair, when and where team members may drink alcoholic beverages; demanding unquestioning obedience. Most professional soccer teams in South America require something called "concentration," in which players are restricted to club grounds for four or five days before games so that the director can monitor their eating and sleeping and make sure they abstain from sex (Otero, 1982). When men are kept in doubt about their status as male adults, aggressive behaviour offers a long-accepted way of asserting that status, one usually not discouraged by sports coaches, who see fights and other forms of borderline violence, even among teammates, as signs of "desire," "character," and "intensity."

Second, the physical well-being of prison inmates often depends on their willingness and ability to hand out and absorb physical abuse. New arrivals are usually subjected to some sort of character test. Those who can be intimidated are victimized thereafter; those who put up a fight achieve a measure of physical security, plus the respect of their peers. On heavy contact sports teams, players, rookies especially, are similarly tested. Unnerving the opposition, whether a teammate vying for a position or a player on another team, is clearly to any would-be aggressor's benefit. Teammates want to know, too, on whom they can rely not to "chicken out" in a brawl or other rough going. When physical survival, in a sense, hinges upon gameness, a two-fisted colleague naturally comes to be held in some esteem.

Third, the masculine identities of prison inmates are severely threatened by lack of heterosexual relations. Prisoners are not only deprived of heterosexual sex but of the sexual complementarity important in giving meaning to one's identity. Sykes (1971) notes that an inmate's self-image often comes to consist only of that part of his self that is recognized or appreciated by men. A violent streak is so recognized and appreciated – or at least feared. When male athletes are deprived of female contact, as in some training camp situations, violence similarly offers a method of asserting manhood.

Fourth, prisons tend to engender in inmates a sense of failure and inadequacy. For one thing, convicts have no, or few, material goods and services. This lack symbolizes failure and inadequacy in a world where, for men, material possessions are a symbol of success. Violence becomes a way to bolster one's sense of personal adequacy. Professional and other top-level athletes usually do not suffer for lack of material possessions, but they do have to cope constantly with threatened or actual failure and the loss of identity that accompanies it (e.g., Smith and Diamond, 1976). Like convicts, they may employ violence in an effort to keep these spectres at bay. Naturally too much, or otherwise inappropriate, violence can also lead to failure.

It would be misleading to suggest that male violence stems solely from some form of masculine insecurity or anxiety. Male aggressiveness is also a cultural norm found to some degree in almost all cultural groups and at all levels of the social hierarchy. It is particularly salient, however, in some lower-working-class environments; we shall examine male violence as a cultural norm in this context later in the chapter.

Female violence

Is female violence on the rise? How violent are females compared to males? Sensationalistic stories in the mass media, alarmist pronouncements by law enforcement authorities, impressionistic evidence presented by a few scholars, and misreadings of official statistics on crime have produced a public impression of female violence run rampant. What are the facts?

Gender differences in violence rates   Statistics Canada's annual *Crime Statistics* and the FBI's *Uniform Crime Reports* provide the best official statistics on female crime in Canada and the United States, though as we shall see, these data also have their shortcomings. The latest research employing these materials has uncovered the following general pattern of female crime applicable to both countries: from about 1960 to the mid-to-late 1970s, the *total* crime rate (usually arrests per 100,000 population) for females rose significantly and at a faster pace than the rate for males, but nonviolent offences against property accounted for most of this increase. The arrest rate for crimes of *violence* by females rose slightly but no faster than the male rate, and in the United States the female rate even declined between 1974 and 1977 (Adams, 1978; Steffensmeier et al., 1979). Males account for approximately nine of every ten arrests for criminal violence in North America, and this has not changed in almost two decades. Nor have levels of violent female crime risen in Israel and Japan, to cite just two other countries for which data are available (Simon and Sharma, 1979).

It should be noted that percentage changes in levels of female violence are usually based on relatively small *absolute* numbers, especially in the baseline year. A small increase in an absolute figure can appear huge when translated into percentage form. Smart (1979) observes that there was a staggering 500 per cent increase in female murder in Great Britain between 1965 and 1975 – based on absolute figures of one for 1965 and five for 1975! In terms of absolute numbers, as opposed to proportions, the criminal violence statistics are overwhelmingly male.

It can be argued, of course, that the official statistics tell more about the responses of the criminal justice system to female crime than about female crime itself. The flaws in these materials have been described at length elsewhere (e.g., Bowker, 1978), but one purportedly biasing factor deserves comment here because it is so frequently cited as obscuring the true level of female crime. This is the chivalry hypothesis — the notion that the predominantly male members of the criminal justice system, reacting to the alleged weakness and dependency of women, treat women more leniently than men at every stage of the criminal justice process, from arrest to trial to punishment. If chivalry does operate then obviously the actual level of female crime is higher than the officially reported level. Suffice it to say, evidence can be mustered for and against the hypothesis, but recent reviews of this evidence conclude that on the whole the chivalry hypothesis does not have much support; indeed, a few studies indicate that females are treated *more* harshly than males by the law, especially when it comes to "unfeminine" crimes of violence. Here, the female has committed two offences: one against the law and one against her traditional role (Bowker, 1978; Feinman, 1980).

The second major source of information on female violence is self-report studies, most of which have to do with youths and with relatively minor delinquent and deviant behaviour, including minor acts of violence. Self-reports, says Bowker, are more valid indicators of violence than official statistics because they do not undergo as many "filtering" or biasing processes between the actual commission of an act of violence and its appearance or nonappearance in some official report. To be sure, self-report research on violence has its own weaknesses, ranging from typically unrepresentative samples to response biases; e.g., female respondents may be inclined to underreport their involvement in violence because they define it as masculine behaviour. But, as Bowker notes, there are methodological safeguards against such biases, and sophisticated self-report studies that employ such safeguards probably yield the most accurate data on female violence.

Bowker has reviewed the most important self-report research up to 1976 on gender differences in violent behaviour among juveniles in the U.S. In general, he concludes, these studies reveal that male-female differences in rates of involvement in fist-fights, gang fights, property destruction, and other relatively low-magnitude violence are smaller than male-female differences in violent crime rates as shown by official statistics. Several self-report studies reveal male-female ratios of about three to one for delinquent violence compared to nine to one for criminal violence (the approximate official statistics figure). Subgroup differences are present, of course. In two mid-1970s studies reviewed by Bowker, lower-class black girls *outstripped* lower-class black boys on a variety of violence measures. Two more recent self-report surveys disclose a male-female ratio of only about two to one on several measures of violence (Shover et al., 1979; D. Smith, 1979).

An impressive piece of research by Smith and Visher (1980) more or less settles the matter. They reduced to a single data base forty-four studies published between 1940 and 1975 reporting data on the relationship between sex and deviance/criminality – the extant literature on the subject. They did this by rearranging the data in each study into ordinal contingency tables and then computing a measure of statistical association (gamma) for each table. This produced 1,118 separate associations between sex and deviance/criminality, some of which had to do with violence. After analyzing the patterns in these associations, Smith and Visher confirm that the deviance/criminality gap between the sexes is smaller for self-report versus official data sources and that a general narrowing of the gap has occurred over time in all categories of deviant and criminal offences, including violence, though least so for violence.

The discrepancy between official statistics and self-reports can be plausibly explained in at least two ways, neither of which discredits the claim that when *all* violence is considered, not just the criminal variety, the level of female violence is rising faster than the level of male violence. First, because the criminal violence statistics incorporate both adult and juvenile offences, whereas almost all the self-report studies pertain to juveniles only, the higher levels of violence noted in the latter may be a function of age; that is to say, younger females may be more violent than older ones. Some concrete support for this conjecture can be gleaned from the crime statistics, which, broken down by age, show that the violent crime rate has risen faster of late among females under eighteen years than among those over eighteen in the U.S. (Bowker, 1978; Feinman, 1980). Smith and Visher's data also indicate a similar trend for deviance and criminality in general.

Second, acts of violence by females may be of lower magnitude on the average than acts of violence by males. If so, female violence naturally shows up more frequently in self-reports than in official statistics because the former are primarily concerned with relatively minor delinquent acts while the latter have to do with more severe criminal ones. Supporting evidence again comes from the official crime statistics, which indicate that in the U.S. between 1960-77 the gap between the sexes decreased for robbery and simple assault but widened for the more serious crimes of homicide and aggravated assault (Steffensmeier et al., 1979). Additional evidence comes from Straus et al.'s (1980) nation-wide survey of American couples. This research reveals that although wives "beat" their husbands almost as frequently as husbands "beat" their wives, it is the husbands who inflict the most damage.

Crime statistics and the self-reports aside, other strands of research point to upswings in female violence, albeit usually marginal ones. The rather sparse literature on female involvement in juvenile gang violence indicates that violence by independent female gangs, female gangs auxilliary to male gangs, and individual females in mixed-gender gangs increased somewhat in the U.S. during the 1960s and 1970s. Gang violence was and still is predominantly male, however. Miller's (1975) study of gangs in six U.S. cities having serious gang problems found that boys made up approximately 90 per cent of gang membership overall.

Several laboratory experiments on aggression in the 1970s demonstrated that women administer just as strong and long-lasting electric shocks to victims as do men. Earlier experiments almost invariably produced findings depicting men as markedly more aggressive than women. The subjects in these experiments were usually college students (Baron, 1977). Parenthetically, critiques of the experimental literature on sex differences in aggression underline the importance of gender role socialization as the major source of these differences. In a review of the experimental literature on male-female differences in aggression among children, Caplan (1975) concludes that sex differences have been most pronounced in studies in which an adult observer-experimenter was conspicuously present. This suggests an "experimenter effect," whereby boys and girls perceive in sex-stereotyped ways what they think are the expectations of the adult observer-experimenter, and behave accordingly. In a review of the experimental literature on male-female differences in aggression among adults, Frodi et al. (1977) conclude that differences were not significant in studies in which an observer-experimenter gave verbal provocation or justification for aggression. This suggests that women's reluctance to aggress can be lowered by such justifications. Taken together, Caplan's and Frodi's conclusions imply that females' inhibitions against aggression can be overcome, thus reinforcing the claim that socialization produces these inhibitions in the first place.

Theories of female violence   Assuming female violence is increasing, how can this increase be accounted for? The crime and delinquency literature offers several theoretical explanations, one of which is the *equal opportunity* hypothesis. Women's increasing freedom and access to positions long occupied by men, so this argument goes, expose women to new opportunities for violence, both legitimate and illegitimate, and women are availing themselves of these opportunities as men have always done, presumably for the same reasons (Figueira-McDonough and Selo, 1980). Naturally this hypothesis only makes sense if it can be demonstrated, not merely asserted, that females have indeed made inroads into the occupational and social positions traditionally dominated by males. There are some who claim that this has not occurred to any signficant degree, particularly in the occupational sector. To the contrary, they argue, a *lack* of opportunity is the continuing lot of most women. Such deprivation produces frustration and anger, and frustration and anger produce violence. The fact that female violence, even more than male, is a lower-class and disadvantaged ethnic group phenomenon — these groups have the fewest opportunities of all — bolsters this argument (Bowker, 1979; Feinman, 1980).

It is true, nonetheless, that women's opportunities to engage in violence have grown on *some* fronts. Consider their increased participation in the armed services and police work. By the late 1970s women were serving in the armed forces of at least thirty-six countries, sometimes in combat roles, usually in Third World wars of liberation; one front-line North Vietnamese unit in the Vietnam War was forty per cent female (Boulding, 1978). Several Western nations are now considering the question of arming women. A sizeable portion of the public is for it, if a recent Canadian Gallup Poll is any indication. Asked if Canadian military women should fight alongside men, a slight majority of the respondents in this poll said yes (Grescoe, 1980).

In 1977, 2.7 per cent of all law enforcement officers in the U.S. were women, 1,644 of whom, representing 375 police departments, actually went on patrol, where they occasionally encountered violence. Women officers on patrol were pretty much nonexistent before the late 1960s. This advance, however, should not obscure the fact that most policewomen continue to do "women's" police work, like matron duty (Feinman, 1980).

Violent sport? The influx of females into this once exclusively male domain was remarkable in the 1970s. According to *Time* (June 26, 1978), 294,000 U.S. high-school girls took part in interscholastic sports in 1970; by

1977, 1.6 million were playing, some of them in body contact sports. This is a sixfold increase. In 1980, 33 per cent of all high-school athletes and 30 per cent of all college athletes in the U.S. were females. The latter figure represents a 250 per cent jump since 1970 (Wood, 1980).

Virtually no girls played organized soccer in the U.S. in 1970; in 1980 the National Soccer Association reported a membership of 1,000,000 girls under the age of nineteen (Wood, 1980). About 5,000 girls and women played organized soccer in England and Wales in 1979, almost a sixfold increase dating from the formation of the Women's Football Association in 1969 (Bale, 1980). In the Federal Republic of Germany about 400,000 females were participating in soccer by the early 1980s (Pilz, 1982b).

Other contact sports? There were few if any women's rugby clubs in America in 1973, and in 1979 there were at least 140 (Rennert, 1979). In Canada an estimated 30,000 girls and women play in ice hockey leagues for females. Toronto's Dominion Ladies Hockey Tournament, billed as the world's largest, and featuring full body contact, annually attracts about 2,500 players and coaches from 137 Canadian and U.S. teams (*Toronto Star,* April 11, 1982). In Michigan, based on a 5 per cent random sample of the state's population, an estimated 28,000 girls played tackle football in pickup games or community leagues in 1975-76. At least 10,000 boxed and the same number wrestled (Seefeldt et al., 1978). A few female high-school athletes are members of boys' interscholastic football, basketball, and baseball teams (Parkhouse and Lapin, 1980). Women's professional football and basketball flourished briefly in the U.S. during the 1970s (Gilbert and Williamson, 1973; Papanek, 1980), and women currently box professionally in some states. (*Toronto Star,* December 17, 1977). One hundred and thirty-five women from twenty-seven countries competed recently in the first women's world free-style judo tournament in New York City (Levin, 1980). Women play water polo. They fight bulls. They drive race cars. They ride racehorses. "Male" sports remaining uninfiltrated by females are rarities, even at the professional level.

All this is not to say that members of both sexes have not resisted these changes, males more than females, if a study by Nixon and colleagues (1979) is at all representative. They asked 268 college women and 219 college men to respond to this statement: "Contact sports, as well as more physical noncontact sports like basketball and baseball, are too dangerous for females." Fifty-three per cent of the women but only 28 per cent of the men disagreed with the statement. (One wonders what proportions would have said these activities are too dangerous for men.)

Clearly females have made significant gains in terms of participation in sports having considerable latitude for violence, like soccer, and sports requiring violence, like boxing, though it should not be forgotten that violent sport, like violent crime, is still predominantly male. The question now is, given the opportunity for violence, are females in fact behaving more violently? More specifically, are female sports increasingly resembling male sports in terms of brutal body contact, borderline violence, and beyond? And are female athletes increasingly harassing, intimidating, and assaulting opponents as male athletes have always done? The evidence suggests yes, but the evidence is almost entirely journalistic and anecdotal.

- On the Verdun Dodgers, a softball team in Montreal's *Ligue féminine de balle molle:* "We don't play dirty. But some teams do. There are some players who won't let you by a base without doing something. We might step on a foot now and then. But that's it" (Lanken, 1972:16).

- On the Vancouver Chimos, Canadian women's volleyball champions: during a match against the boys' provincial champion high-school team, an indignant boy protests to the referee after being victimized by a devastating spike: "She was *aiming* at me" (Grescoe, 1973:14).

- On the Point Edwards Supremes, the most penalized team in the Michigan-Ontario Ladies Hockey League: says the League president: "They *are* ladies. But they're also hockey players and they lose their tempers just as quickly as men. There's no polite tea party manners when there's trouble – just the five old knuckles in the chops" (Edmonds, 1975:25).

- On girls' ice hockey in Buffalo, New York: in a television programme on violence in hockey, Channel Seven's "Eyewitness News" (February 7, 1980) shows a videotape of several 14-year-old girls fighting during a game. One goes to the hospital with a separated shoulder. Interviewed, another player states matter-of-factly that the other team is well known for its tactics of intimidation.

- On Ontario women's interuniversity basketball: prior to a game between York and Brock Universities, the York coach happens by chance into the dressing room just vacated by Brock. On the blackboard is written the name of York's best player and the statement: "I want this player hurt." A minor furor ensues (personal communication with the York University basketball coach, February 4, 1981).

- On U.S. college basketball star Nancy Lieberman who brings a "new rough-and-tumble style" to the women's game: "Quick, very smart on the court, a good shooter, excellent jumper, very very strong rebounder, *aggressive, hard-nosed,* very strong on defense" (Kirkpatrick, 1979:108; emphasis added).

- On intramural basketball at the University of Toronto: the women's championship game is "marred" by an incident in which a player throws the ball, and her coach a punch, at the referee (Money, 1980).

Some of these incidents smack of a sort of "female masculinity," which suggests another explanation for the general upturn in female violence. If it is argued that masculinity, the attributes traditionally associated with being male, encourages violence, it follows that if females are becoming more violent, it is because they are becoming more masculine.

Female masculinity has been frequently cited as a cause of apparently rising female violence ever since Freda Adler (1975) claimed in *Sisters in Crime*

that a dramatic rise in crimes of violence by women was the resul\
"imitative male machismo," itself a product of women's liberation.\
was wrong about violent crime, of course (she failed to perceive that th\
crease in the total crime rate, based on official statistics, was caused entirely
by an increase in nonviolent offences). What is more, her "data" on female
machismo were mainly impressions gleaned unsystematically from workers
in the criminal justice system. Further, she made inferences about individual behaviour from aggregate data – the ecological fallacy: it is simply
not warranted to "discover" on the basis of aggregate data that the female
violent crime rate is up, and to discover independently that females are
becoming more "masculine," then to infer that females who act violently
are "masculine." Not inconceivably, less "masculine" females perpetrate
more violence than more "masculine" females, perhaps out of frustration;
after all, "masculinity" is not the sole cause of violence. An adequate test
of the female masculinity thesis requires that some measure of violence and
some measure of masculinity be obtained from the *same* individual females
and the association between these two variables then examined.

Two more recent studies *have* tested the female masculinity hypothesis
using individual-level data. Shover et al. (1979) and Cullen et al. (1979) both
report statistically significant relationships between female high-school and
college students' self-reports of various aggressive acts, including fist-
fighting, and their scores on a scale of masculinity (or in the case of Shover,
a scale of "weakened femininity"). Finding a positive correlation between
female masculinity and violence does not prove that the former *caused* the
latter (conceivably some third variable caused both), but it certainly lends
empirical support to the hypothesis.

There seem to be only two scientific studies published in English directly
relevant to female masculinity and sports violence. Their findings are
somewhat contradictory. Brown and Davies (1978) administered a twenty-
three-item Attitude toward Violence Scale (the items had to do with a willingness to accept violence as a way of solving problems) to male and female
varsity athletes and nonathletes in a U.S. college. The mean score on this
scale for the 53 female athletes in contact sports (hockey, basketball,
lacrosse) was much lower (i.e., these women were less accepting of violence)
than the mean scores for (1) 131 male athletes in contact sports (football,
soccer, basketball, lacrosse, wrestling), (2) 89 male athletes in
"noncontact" sports (track, swimming, golf, tennis, fencing, baseball), and
(3) 156 nonathletes. There were no statistically significant differences in the
mean scores of the three female samples (the contact sports participants, 25
females in noncontact sports, and 75 female nonathletes). These results held
regardless of socioeconomic status. Brown and Davies provide no data on
the relationship between attitudes toward violence and violent behaviour.
Their attitudinal data, however, as far as it goes, does not support the
female machismo hypothesis.

Gunter Pilz (1979), a researcher at Hannover University in the Federal

Republic of Germany, goes somewhat further. Pilz compared the attitudes of male and female soccer and team handball performers toward certain "aggressive actions" in sport. The male soccer players were much more approving than the female players of items like "cutting down an opponent from behind"; but there were only 12 female soccer-playing respondents so this finding is of dubious value. The 52 women team handball players, on the other hand, were significantly more approving on the average of elbowing and body-checking in given situations than males participating at relatively low levels of handball competition, though less approving than males in top-calibre leagues (145 male players in all). Pilz does not indicate the competitive level of the women players. Furthermore, on semantic differential scales, the average female handball player emerged as significantly more "aggressive" and just as "pugnacious" as the average male player.

Do the actions of female handball players match their attitudes and self-images? Pilz provides no individual-level data on this question, but he does describe women's team handball in West Germany as a rough contact sport in which deliberately fouling opponents is common practice. As evidence, he cites the results of Tittel et al.'s (1974) analysis of handball injuries in German leagues, which concluded that 41 per cent of the injuries to women performers (63 per cent of the injuries to men) were caused by conscious violations of the rules. It appears that although women's team handball is not as rough as men's, the women's game is not without its share of violence. Pilz's study provides some support for the female masculinity hypothesis (See also Pilz, 1982a, 1982c).

In a paper on aggression and the female athlete published more than a decade ago, (Smith, 1972:107) wrote that

> ... it would be premature to state that aggressive violence in athletics for women is a social problem. Present trends, however, indicate that sport may be moving in this direction.... Impelled by the increasing importance of winning and as the value-climate of sport subtly changes in the direction of the legitimation of female violence, together with the appearance of appropriate reference groups for the social learning of violence, female sport may be moving toward the male model. Soon, perhaps, girl's basketball teams will be recruiting "intimidators," specialists with sharp elbows. (Reprinted with permission.)

Pilz picked up this theme seven years later, speculating that handball players will increasingly show "masculine dispositions" toward violence and that their game will grow progressively more violent as performers have less and less difficulty dealing with the notion that violence "works" when it comes to winning games. Unfortunately, neither Smith, Pilz, nor anybody else has confirmed or disconfirmed this prediction in a systematic way. That females are playing sports with scope for violence in greater numbers than ever before and that they sometimes play them violently are facts. But are women playing these sports more violently than in the past?

And are levels of violence in women's sports approaching men's? It *seems* that this is so, but in the absence of research, these questions, unlike those pertaining to female violence in the home, on the street, and elsewhere, remain basically unanswered.

Class

Research conducted in many countries indicates that persons of low socioeconomic status, compared to the more privileged, commit more homicides, criminal assaults, and violent delinquency (Flynn, 1980; Dinitz and Conrad, 1980), make up the bulk of the membership of fighting gangs (Miller, 1975; Patrick, 1973), get into more fights (Erlanger, 1974), more frequently hit their spouses (Gelles, 1974; Dobash and Dobash, 1978) and their children (Gelles and Straus, 1979). The ferocious Hell's Angels outlaw motorcycle gang was a lower-class phenomenon (Thompson, 1967), so is British soccer hooliganism (see Chapter 7).

When research on violence is based on data collected by official agencies, it can be argued that social class differences result wholly or partly from a greater probability of the poor being caught and processed by the authorities. Yet even studies that have avoided this bias by employing different kinds of data have found an inverse relationship between class and violence (e.g., Straus et al., 1980).

Combative sports

The relationship between social class and violence in sport can be approached by asking questions similar to those asked about women. The first question: to what extent are working- and lower-class persons, relative to those of higher status, found in combative and contact sports? Again the evidence comes in small, isolated fragments, but is fairly consistent.

- In a Polish study, 70 per cent of 86 "elite" boxers came from "working-class" homes, as opposed to "peasant" or "intellectual" (Nowak, 1969).
- Of 1,879 male and female members of clubs representing fifteen sports in the Federal Republic of Germany, wrestlers, team handball players and soccer players were lowest on an index of social stratification (Lüschen, 1969).
- Among 3,806 Belgian adult male sports participants, those in team handball, martial sports, and soccer ranked lowest on an index of occupational status (Renson, 1978).
- In an early study of 68 professional boxers in the United States, all but two had a "low socioeconomic background" (Weinberg and Arond, 1952).
- Among 845 University of California varsity athletes in twenty sports, boxers, wrestlers, and football players ranked lowest on the Duncan Socioeconomic Status Index (Loy, 1969).

- In a sample of 412 male and female U.S. college students, the lowest positions on the Hollingshead Two-Factor Index of Social Position were occupied by those who gave as their most preferred participant sports, football, rugby, wrestling, karate, and basketball (Yiannakis, 1975).
- At the 1971 Canada Games, boxers, wrestlers, judo performers, weight lifters, and hockey players came from families whose fathers scored lower on the Blishen Index of Socioeconomic Status than the fathers of participants in twelve other noncontact sports (Gruneau, 1976).
- "Prole" sports, like motocross racing, roller games, and commercial wrestling appear to have a predominantly working-class membership (Martin and Berry, 1974; Hinrichs, 1979).
- Rugby League, an exceedingly rough, professionalized version of rugby played mainly in Northern England (see Table 3.1), was and is almost exclusively a working man's game (Dunning and Sheard, 1979).

Table 3.1   Rugby League Deaths and Injuries, Yorkshire County, 1890-93

	Deaths	Broken Legs, Etc.	Arms	Collar Bones	Other Injuries
1890-1	23	30	9	11	27
1891-2	22	52	12	18	56
1892-3	26	39	12	25	75
Totals	71	121	33	54	158

SOURCE: Dunning and Sheard (1979:220). Reprinted with permission.

Is it reasonable to label such combative and contact sports "working" or "lower" class? If indeed they recruit the majority of their participants from the lower half of the socioeconomic order, this is a fairly accurate designation. Note, however, that this socioeconomic stratum may still be under-represented in contact sports in terms of its proportion in the general population, in which case the designation is misleading. Most of the above studies do not present such comparisons, but Gruneau's (1976) Canada Games research is an exception. It reveals that the percentage of fathers of combative and contact sports participants in the bottom three Blishen socioeconomic categories was somewhat less than the percentage of the Canadian male work force in these categories. In contrast the percentages of fathers of noncontact athletes in the top three Blishen groups ranged from somewhat greater than to triple the percentage of the labour force in these groups. Similarly, Canadian hockey can hardly be called a working- or lower-class activity; only 33 per cent of Smith's (1979b) representative sample of players came from working- or lower-class backgrounds, compared to 75 per cent of the male labour force (Table 3.2). If this is true for any of the other sports cited above, they may be working- or lower-class only in the sense that working- and lower-class participants play them in greater proportions than they play noncontact sports. The terms "working-" and "lower-class sports" should be used guardedly.

The above are mainly between-sport comparisons. What of within-sport comparisons in sports that can be played at greatly varying levels of seriousness? Some brands of most contact sports are notoriously violent, whereas others are pacifistic.

Take Canadian hockey. It was shown in the last chapter that professionalized, "competitive" leagues are much rougher than house leagues. The most professionalized and roughest of all are the junior (preprofessional) leagues. Table 3.2 compares the socioeconomic status of all players in Smith's survey with the Junior A and B sample alone, the comparison group of nonplayers, and Canadian males in the work force. (A detailed description of these samples is provided in Chapter 2.) It can be seen that taken as a whole, hockey is not a working- or lower-class sport. Precisely the opposite is true. On the other hand, 56 percent of the 120 Junior A and B performers, compared to only 33 percent of all players, came from the lowest three Blishen socioeconomic categories. The most violent brand of hockey indeed recruits the greatest proportion – in this case a majority – of working- and lower-class players.

Table 3.2 All Hockey Players, Junior B and A Players, Nonplayers,* and Canadian Male Labour Force† in Blishen Socioeconomic Categories (in Per Cent)

	All Players (N = 604)	Jr. B. and A (N = 120)	Nonplayers (N = 152)	Male Labour Force (1971)
Upper three categories	67	44	40	25
Lower three categories	33	56	60	75

*SOURCE: Smith, unpublished data (1976).

†SOURCE: Himelfarb and Richardson (1979:187).

A structural explanation of the working/lower-class affinity for contact, as opposed to noncontact, sports might focus on *accessibility:* the degree to which contact sports are (1) inexpensive, either because they require little in the way of equipment, facilities, and coaching or because the community at large foots the bill; or (2) physically available, e.g., the traditional working-class neighbourhood boxing gym. Counter examples of relatively inaccessible contact sports and accessible noncontact sports are not hard to find, but the foregoing arguments would appear to have some substance.

A cultural explanation might focus on *preference:* the degree to which working- and lower-class youths are found in contact sports because they (1) exemplify working- and lower-class values and traditions concerning physical strength, toughness, manhood, and the like, or (2) appear to offer professional opportunities. The Yiannakis (1975) research, mentioned above, provides a bit of support for the preference argument in general; the lower-class respondents in this study said they preferred contact activities. There is also a considerable amount of evidence that standing on your own two feet, being able "to take it," being able to look after yourself, being a man – values that can easily support the use of violence – are most highly regarded in lower-class environments (e.g., Dietz, 1978). As for contact sports offering, or appearing to offer, more professional opportunities, this may be generally true, though again contrary examples are available. In any case, conventional wisdom has it that professional sport exerts more drawing power on lower-class youth than middle-class. In fact, this is true for Canadian hockey. When Smith's 604 players were asked: "Would you like to play professional hockey if you had the ability?" a straight-line negative relationship between class and aspirations emerged. At one extreme, 82 per cent of the boys in the lowest, or sixth, socioeconomic group said yes; at the other extreme, only 46 per cent of those in the highest group said yes. To the extent that contact sports are indeed viewed as offering more professional opportunities than noncontact sports, the former may attract, or as is more likely the case, *hold* lower-class youth for this reason.

One final comment on structural versus cultural explanations: it is somewhat misleading to speak of one without the other because it creates the impression they are unrelated. The truth is, structure not only determines *objective opportunity* for participation, it contours *subjective attitudes* as well (Gruneau, 1976). Marxist theory probably makes this connection most explicitly (see Gruneau, 1982), but one need not be a Marxist to perceive it. Recall the examination in Chapter 2 of the manner in which the structure of professionalized minor hockey progressively narrows and limits the perspective of players as they advance through the system.

Class differences in violence

It is one thing to show that certain contact sports, or levels within a contact sport, recruit members principally from the lower social strata, but is it quite another to show that lower-class individuals perpetrate more violence than middle-class ones. For the sake of argument, the Junior players in the top three Blishen levels in Table 3 *could* have accounted for more violence than players in the bottom three, though one would be hard pressed to explain why.

It appears that three studies, all having to do with hockey, have in some way examined the question: are working- and lower-class athletes more violent than their middle-class counterparts? Vaz (1976; 1982; Clark et al., 1978) administered a questionnaire to 1,915 minor hockey players, aged seven to eighteen, residing in the Canadian city of Kitchener, and found no significant relationship between players' social class and their responses on a multi-item scale of approval of illegal hockey aggression. Smith (1974) also found no relationship between class and assaultive penalties, or between a school's socioeconomic environment and penalties, in a study of 83 Toronto high-school hockey players. In Smith's later research (1979b), however, although no significant associations between class, on the one hand, and attitudes and values regarding violence, on the other, materialized, class *was* significantly related to fights and major penalties, as indicated in Table 2.6 in the last chapter. Table 3.3 presents an even clearer picture, this time using father's educational attainment as an indicator of class: the less the father's educational attainment, the more assaultive the son.

Table 3.3   Violent Behaviour of Hockey Players by Father's Educational Attainment (in Per Cent)

Father's Educational Attainment	One or More Hockey Fights	One or More Major Penalties
Completed elementary school or less	59	50
Some secondary school to completed secondary school	44	39
Some higher education to completed higher education	22	16

SOURCE: Smith, unpublished data (1976).

Because these behavioural measures of violence (self-reported fights and official records of major penalties) are probably more valid measures of violent behaviour than Vaz's attitude scale, and because this sample of players was much more representative than the one in Smith's earlier study, it may be concluded that an individual's social class does affect the probability of that individual behaving violently in sport.

Why? In Chapter 2 we dealt at length with, and found somewhat wanting, the subculture-of-violence thesis, probably the most widely cited explanation of the lower-class-violence linkage and the only such theory that has been applied systematically to sports violence. Several other theoretical points of view deserve attention.

Anomie   Briefly, anomie theory, a general theory of deviant behaviour, holds that the class structure exerts pressure on those disadvantageously located in it to engage in nonconforming behaviour. More specifically, the lower-class experience of being systematically denied equal opportunities, often over several generations, leads to a lowered commitment to society's rules, an absence of stake in conformity, a feeling of more to gain than lose by pursuing deviant, as opposed to legitimate, routes to success. There is some debate about whether the lower-class deviant is consciously aware of the unfairness of his or her position in the class structure, which raises the issue of whether he or she is *pushed* into deviance (a "vengeful victim of injustice") or simply *pulled* by its promised rewards. Whatever the case, not having a stake in conformity supposedly frees the deviant from its constraints (Hagan, 1977). In his classic essay on cultural goals and institutionalized means, Robert Merton (1957:189) uses sport to illustrate how an emphasis on ends can subvert the acceptable means of attaining those ends:

> ... *in competitive athletics, when the aim of victory is shorn of its institutional trappings and success becomes construed as "winning the game" rather than "winning under the rules of the game," a premium is implicitly set upon the use of illegitimate but technically efficient means. The star of the opposing football team is surreptitiously slugged; the wrestler incapacitates his opponent through ingenious but illicit techniques; university alumni covertly subsidize "students" whose talents are confined to the athletic field. The emphasis on the goal has so attenuated the satisfactions deriving from sheer participation in the competitive activity that only a successful outcome provides gratification.* (Reprinted with permission.)

Anomie theory would predict that whereas notions of fair play and sportsmanship tend to inhibit the middle-class athlete from engaging in these sorts of tactics, the lower-class athlete cleaves to a more pragmatic code, of the sort shown in Table 3.4. This of course gives the latter a distinct edge over a middle-class adversary in some types of violent encounter. "Redblooded American boys do not normally intend to inflict serious injury in a fight," writes Hunter Thompson (1967:184) in his exposé of the Hell's Angels motorcycle club. "It is one thing to get punched in the nose, and quite another to have your eye sprung or your teeth shattered with a wrench."

Table 3.4   Rules for the Successful Use of Violence

Be first:	Get your opponent before he gets you. Let him know your intentions.
Be fast:	Hit as quickly, as hard and as often (sic) before he knows what's happening. This will not only discourage him but is likely to hurt him so that he won't be so effective.
Be final:	Get him off his feet and make sure he hasn't the ability or the inclination to attempt to come back at you. Kick him when he's down. If you haven't hit him hard enough and you don't at least temporarily put him out of commission, he is likely to get up mad and really be dangerous.
Be careful:	Keep the *odds* in your favour. Stay in your own territory. Don't get caught off guard. Keep your back to the wall. In strange places locate the exits. Don't "run your mouth" when you're in somebody else's neighbourhood.

Adapted from Dietz (1978:36). Reprinted with permission.

Physical punishment in child-rearing   This perspective on lower-class violence has to do with the effects of parents' physical punishment of their children. The literature on the subject is marked by debate on the extent to which corporal punishment is indeed a lower-class phenomenon. A reexamination of early research on social class differences in child-rearing by Erlanger (1974) concluded that though the tendency for parents to punish their children physically does increase as one goes down the socioeconomic ladder, class differences are not pronounced enough to conclude that lower-class persons *typically* control their children by means of physical punishment, or that middle-class persons *typically* use other means. But this conclusion seems truer for spanking than for more extreme types of abuse. National surveys conducted in the United States by Gil (1973) and Straus et al. (1980) reveal that child battering is rather heavily skewed toward the very bottom of the social class structure — the so-called underclass. The Straus et al. survey also indicates that milder forms of physical punishment are more strongly related to class than Erlanger states. The Straus study is particularly significant because, unlike research based on officially reported data, which tends to inflate the amount of lower- as opposed to middle-class violence, it used parents' own testimony. Although one should certainly be wary of perpetuating erroneous stereotypes about the lower class, as Erlanger warns, it is also wrong, as Gelles and Straus (1979) point out, to purvey a myth of "classlessness" with respect to parents' violence against children.

The significance of the Gil and Straus et al. findings for the present discussion is this: children who are spanked, beaten, or otherwise physically abused by their parents tend themselves to become spankers, beaters, and abusers. "Violence in the family is a major predictor of violence by the child," Bybee (1979:10) concludes in a review of research on the subject. We shall wait until the next chapter to deal at length with the specific ways in which violence is transmitted from parent to child, for these apply to all social strata. Suffice it to say at this point that because lower-class parents are more likely than middle-class parents to hit their children, and to hit them hard, lower-class children tend to make their way in disproportionate numbers into the violence-doer statistics for youths and adults. There is no sound reason why this logic should not encompass sports violence.

Experience theory   No matter how lower-class violence is initially explained, once it is a reality it can acquire a momentum of its own. Experience or education in violence, Dietz (1978) explains, particularly if successful, tends to produce more violence. A violent background heightens one's sensitivity to cues for violence provided by others – insults and challenges, for instance, a look, word, or gesture that may be missed by the uninitiated. Successful experience in violence also serves to reduce the tendency to look for nonviolent alternatives to problems. Further, it helps develop one's self-concept as a winner, a successful fighter, and this leads to a search for similar success experiences. Also, a tough reputation attracts others who are prepared for violence and who want to enhance their reputation. In sports the tough guys take on the other tough guys more often than not; there is no glory in beating up a weak, small pacifist. Thus violence begets violence. The point is that lower-class youth are more likely to get early experience in violence than middle-class youth, and this tends to lead to more violence for all the reasons suggested.

Violent masculine style   In a perspective not dissimilar to the subculture-of-violence thesis, but more explicit as to the subculture's sources, Dunning et al. (1982) have developed the hypothesis that norms of aggressive masculinity – they use the term "violent masculine style" – flourish in "rough" working-class environments whose social structure resembles that of the segmentally bonded community characteristic of early medieval times (Chapter 2). Such communities are characterized by a resistance to control by the state and its agencies, territorial unity, ethnic insularity and solidarity, segregation of the sexes, dominance by an age-graded all-male fighting stratum, feuding between families, neighbourhoods, and street-corner gangs. Children and adolescents are relatively free of adult control and tend to interact violently with one another and to develop *dominance hierarchies* based on age, physical strength, and toughness. Great prestige is conferred on males who are willing and able to fight. They develop a love of fighting, coming to see it, in Dunning et al.'s words, as a "central source of meaning and gratification in life." Whereas in the "respectable" working and middle classes, violence is normatively condemned, pushed behind the scenes, guilt-producing, and instrumental, in the "rough" working class, violence is normatively rewarded, highly visible, pleasure-producing, and affective. This is not an either-or conception but a matter of balance; violent masculine style is simply more salient in the lower working class. In Britain, Dunning et al. argue, football crowds traditionally have provided an arena for the expression of violent masculine style, a claim we shall investigate in Chapter 7.

Age

Compared to gender and class, scant attention has been paid to age as a determinant of violent behaviour, and our treatment of this variable will perforce be brief. The scarcity of material, however, should not be construed as indicating that age is only tenuously connected to violence. The contrary is true. Persons between the ages of approximately fifteen and thirty account for the lion's share of most types of violence. (An exception may be conjugal violence, which Gelles [1974] found to peak between forty-one and fifty years.) The largest percentage of homicide suspects in Canada falls into the twenty- to twenty-nine-years age range; the sixteen to nineteen years category is next (Reed et al., 1978). In the U.S., arrest rates for all crimes of violence are at their height between the ages of about nineteen to twenty-one

(Greenberg, 1977). Most members of fighting gangs range in age from thirteen to early twenties (Keiser, 1972; Patrick, 1973); the most active fighters in Chicago's Vice Lord Nation, studied by Keiser, were the sixteen- and seventeen-year-olds (see Table 3.5). The typical British football hooligan is nineteen (Trivizas, 1980). California's dread motorcyclists, Hell's Angels, seem to be mainly in their twenties, or were, in the mid-1960s when Hunter Thompson (1967) rode and drank with them. Prison violence is inversely related to age, and youth prisons are generally much rougher places than adult ones (Ellis et al., 1974). As for sport, the only research available once again has to do with hockey. The reader is referred to Chapter 2, Table 2.6, which shows that on-ice fighting and major penalty-getting are rare among twelve- to thirteen-year-olds but increase steadily with age until over 60 per cent of eighteen- to twenty-one-year-olds are involved in such behaviour.

Table 3.5　Age Hierarchy of Fighting Gangs and Hockey Leagues

Age	Vice Lord City (Chicago)*	Calton Tongs (Glasgow)†	Minor Hockey (Canada)‡
12-13 years		Toddler Tongs	Peewees
14-15 years	Midgets	Tiny Tongs	Bantams
16-17 years	Juniors	Young Tongs	Midgets
18-21 years	Seniors	Big Calton Tongs	Juveniles

* SOURCE: Keiser (1972).

† SOURCE: Patrick (1973).

‡ Excludes Junior hockey, for which there is no formal minimum age.

Biologically, human capacity for most forms of violence is at its peak from adolescence through early adulthood. This explains the age-violence association partly, but not wholly. Greenberg (1977) offers a sociological explanation of the age-violence association, with particular reference to teenagers. The teenage years in industrial society seem to be a holding period between childhood and adulthood. The teenage male, especially, is censured for acting "like a child" but prevented from becoming an "adult" by barriers not unlike those discussed in the earlier comparison of prisons and sports teams. He is exluded from the world of *serious* adult work. He endures a long, mandatory, sometimes repressive stint in school, where he may be treated with considerable disrespect. He typically has difficulty obtaining enough money to support his leisure-time social activities or to acquire other trappings of male adulthood. These factors exacerbate his already devalued position and push him into exaggerated dependence upon peers for validation of his self. Risk-taking activities, including violence, become a way of establishing a positive social identity.

In support of this argument, Greenberg points out that in both the U.S.

and England the peak year for delinquency is the school-leaving year. In peasant and tribal societies, in contrast, which cannot afford to exclude teenagers from serious work, juvenile crime rates are low. When poverty, racial minority status, school failure, and the like intersect with the status of teenager, the symbols of adulthood are even farther out of reach, and it is among these youngsters that the greatest amounts and worst kinds of violence occur. Among the slum boys in Patrick's Glasgow gang and in Ellis et al.'s youth prisons, to take two extreme cases, having the respect of one's peers was of *consuming* concern, and the *only* way of getting this respect was through violence.

Why do violence rates begin to fall off in early adulthood? First, adults presumably have established, or are well on the way to establishing, the adult identity that teenagers are struggling to acquire. Second, full-time employment and marriage reduce time spent with and dependence upon peers. Third, the costs of violence, including its physical toll, start to outweigh the gains: violence disrupts job and marriage; adults are held more accountable for transgressions of the law than teenagers and are punished proportionately. All else being equal, the older one gets the greater one's stake in conforming to the rules against violence – the greater the potential costs, that is, of behaving violently. Fourth, one simply grows up. In Horowitz and Schwartz's (1974) study of fighting gangs, most members lost interest in street warfare as they grew older. In the prisons studied by Ellis et al. (1974) older inmates tended to regard the constantly threatening and fighting con as "stupid" and violence as an activity for "kids" (even though they continued to appreciate the things violence could get).

Adults who *do* cling to violence presumably do so in part because they continue to face barriers to adult status attainment. Occupations that call for and reward violence, of course, are a somewhat different story. Professional athletes continue to scuffle and brawl long after their age peers have abandoned such antics along with other adolescent trappings.

A participant observation phase of Smith's (1979a,c) hockey research reveals something of the age norms governing violence in sports. Six field workers attached themselves to six different hockey teams for a season of play, four in the role of "complete participant" (two coaches, two trainers), two in the role of "participant as observer" (Gold, 1958). The teams ranged from house-league Minor Atom (age nine) through Provincial Junior A. A wide range of participant observation operations was employed in an attempt to understand violence as it is understood by those in whose world it routinely occurs: direct participation and observation, document analysis, use of informants, interviews with players, coaches, league officials, referees, parents, and spectators.

For hockey participants up to about age ten or eleven, violence is not a concern, though the occasional prospective hooligan is in evidence. Most boys look askance even upon rough play. In dressing room talk, the subject of violence arises infrequently. Once, boys of nine were overheard discussing what to do about an overly boisterous player on another team; all suggestions had to do with methods of avoiding him. The few other times violence was mentioned were in reference to professional hockey: "Did you see the fight last night?" "Yeah, did you see Schultz? Fighting is his hobby." What boys this age sometimes do is to parody big-league fights: the slow-motion stick duel, feigned punches, wrestling on the ice. Hockey fighting is rare at this age because expectations that these youngsters act like men are minimal, and their own concern about male status is only in the nascent stage. Besides they are not usually steady enough on their skates to engage in much violence.

Hockey violence begins around age thirteen, when some professionalized minor leagues become rough indeed. Size and toughness now begin to weigh heavily in the player selection process. Players start to evaluate one another's gameness. Reputations are forged. By fourteen most boys are schooled in the informal norms that regulate the use of violence. Deviants, "chickens," suffer varying degrees of disapprobation, depending on how well they compensate for lack of courage with other attributes. At sixteen some boys are veteran brawlers and have developed an extensive repertoire of "dirty tricks." Tough talk, the argot of hockey violence, is standard, coolness *de rigueur*. Notes taken by the author while observing a university team tryout convey something of the character of all this:

> *"Hawk," no. 14, playing for the Red side, slammed hard into no. 10 (unusual helmet) of the Yellow side. The Yellow bench shouts to no. 10, "Get his number," but the shouts are clearly for the "Hawk's" benefit (whom the Yellow bench clearly favours even though he is playing on the other side). Further shouts are to the "Hawk" and are good-natured: "Hawk the backslammer." The "Hawk" looks back. He smiles. The bench laughs. No. 10, though the object of this interaction, is clearly left out of it and is deserted by his teammates. Soon after he seeks reprisal with a spear to "Hawk's" solar plexus. No harm is done. Shouts from the Yellow team: "Hawk, ya got him worried. He's not playing hockey anymore." Laughter from the bench.*

Quantitative data from the same research buttress these observations. On an index of violence approval (described in detail in the next chapter), players' approval rose sharply between the ages of twelve and twenty-one; so did their perceptions of the approval of their parents, coach, teammates, and spectators. Granted, some overt support of violence turns out to be mere talk. Individuals' approval of violence is not as great as that which they attribute to their teammates collectively. Players' private attitudes are one thing; what they express in the presence of their peers is another. As Matza (1964) has shown in his research on delinquents, boys' anxiety about *appearing* tough produces a "shared misunderstanding," whereby each thinks the others value violence more than is actually the case. Also, some of the association between age and hockey violence can be attributed to socialization into the occupational subculture; that is, as players get older, they also get closer to the profession of hockey and conform increasingly to professional criteria of what constitutes a good player. Nevertheless, when age and level of competition are separated statistically, it can be seen that age does exert an independent effect on violence approval and on violent behaviour (Smith, 1979c).

Hockey violence declines slowly in adult amateur leagues as players advance into their twenties, for the same reasons, one suspects, that violence declines in general: male status is more firmly established, the costs of violence become too great, fighting comes to be regarded as childish. The onset of this fall-off is retarded in professional ranks, but the same inverse relationship between age and violence ultimately takes place. Even "goons" try to semi-retire from fighting as they get older, hoping their reputations will work for them, though this is not always easy, as is indicated in the account in Figure 3.2 of Reggie Fleming, an aging hockey brawler who played and fought in the major professional leagues for eighteen years. At thirty-nine, Fleming now labours in the Continental League. An NHL veteran interviewed by the author explains why it is difficult to vacate the tough-guy role.

> *It's like the fast gun thing. There's always somebody around that's a little bit younger and a little bit stronger, and all of a sudden you're not as much of a threat as you were and you end up on the bad end of fights and beatings and that kind of thing. And so there are very few of those people that last for very long, and I think that's why most of those players make the attempt to become hockey players while they're performing this special function. They realize their career is really going to last only so long as they can make the adjustment into something else, that it's going to be a very short-lived career if you just stay as the fighter, as the brawler. It's a tough life for those kinds of guys because even if you win fights you take some physical abuse in winning, and if you are in fights often that builds up and your hands get sore and your face gets sore; you're more susceptible to bleeding and those kinds of things.*

Figure 3.2 Requiem for an Aging Hockey "Goon"

The Kenosha Flyers, playing before 415 fans in a cold, cheerless Madison arena that can seat 8,000, are trailing the Madison Blues 10-7 in the third period when it happens. A kid on the Blues named John Gill trips the Flyers' Steve Anderson. Anderson gets up, skates over to Gill, says something. Gill says something back. Anderson punches him in the face. The crowd roars. Gill brings his stick down on Anderson's head. Anderson collapses to the ice, and now the crowd is going wild. Across the ice charges Reggie Fleming. He lifts his stick and smashes Gill across the back of the neck, sending him to the ice. The benches empty, the fans scream, rush down from their seats to the boards, throw cups and papers on the ice. "You rotten bastard, Fleming," a voice yells. "Kill him, kill Fleming." A tall, skinny bl ⸜ kid with the Blues, Cal Harris, 23, who weighs 170 pounds, turn⸍   ⸍ng. "C'mon, Fleming, drop your stick, drop it you chicken a⸍   ⸍⸍h you are."

"Screw oh,

"Fight, you co,   .s clenched. "Fight, you fat slob." The crowd how   .ıg skates over to the penalty box. He's shouting at the refer⸍   . c be heard over the noise. A fan leans over the rail and spits on Fleming's head. A half-filled cup of Coke hits Fleming on the shoulder and he turns, curses the fan and waves his stick blade in his face. "Fight, c'mon, fight," Harris is yelling in the background. "Chicken," the fans chant. "Chicken! Chicken! Chicken!"

All the wars of all the nights of the past suddenly rage through Reggie Fleming's mind and, spinning, he attacks Harris, fists up and swinging, the crowd shrieking. Fleming misses with a wild right hook. Harris slams him in the face with a right, a left, drives a right deep into Fleming's belly. Fleming gasps, doubles over and Harris slams his head back with an uppercut. The crowd screams with delight. The other players watch. The officials watch. Fleming swings blindly at Harris but Harris moves in, punches him furiously in the face and head and then hurls him against the boards. Harris pulls Fleming's jersey over his head, tosses him to the ice, jumps on him and flails away. Blood appears on Fleming's jersey, spreading fast like ink on a blotter. Harris doesn't let up and Fleming is helpless. It's brutal and sickening to watch and finally it's broken up. To boos and thrown debris, Fleming leaves the ice, gasping for breath, blood pouring down his battered face. He heads to the dressing room, alone, closes the door softly behind him, and sits on the bench. From far away come the crowd noises. He says nothing, takes off his jersey, throws it in a corner. He turns back, closes his eyes for a few seconds. He opens them and looks at his hands, turning them slowly. They're trembling.

SOURCE: McRae (1977b:13-14). Reprinted with permission.

Conclusion

When it comes to accounting for basic patterns of violence, gender, class, and age are important variables. Males engage in more violence than females, so-called lower-class persons more than middle-class, teenagers and young adults more than older adults. This is true historically and cross-culturally. It is the pattern in sports as it is in most other social contexts.

Theoretical explanations of violence as a male phenomenon tend to turn on a theme of "masculinity," stereotyped notions about how a man ought to behave. Distorted *machismo*, "compulsive masculinity," "masculine status anxiety," "violent masculine style" – these are the concepts typically employed in attempts to understand violence as a male act. Yet, while it is true that males dominate the violence statistics, there is evidence that the level of female violence, especially where relatively minor transgressions are concerned, is rising faster than the male level. That girls and women currently have unprecedented opportunities to play sports having considerable scope for violence is indisputable. That they are increasingly assaulting opponents as boys and men have always done remains conjecture, though a considerable amount of anecdotal and journalistic evidence suggests this is the case. A new "female masculinity" or "imitative female *machismo,*" itself a product of loosened gender roles, may underlie this apparent trend.

If males account for the lion's share of violence in sports and society, lower-class males seem to account for more than their share of male violence. Of initial interest is the question, do contact and combative sports disproportionately attract lower-class participants? Although the lower and working classes appear to be underrepresented in almost all sports in terms of their representation in the total population, these groups reach their highest representation in violent sports, or in violent versions of a particular sport; the roughest brands of Canadian ice hockey have the highest proportion of lower-class players. Social structural explanations of the lower-class affinity for contact sports focus on the relative *accessibility* of these sports. Cultural explanations focus on *preference;* the degree to which lower-class participants gravitate toward such sports because they exemplify lower-class values or are perceived as offering professional opportunities.

A second question is this: do lower-class players within a given sport behave more violently than their higher-status counterparts? Data on hockey violence indicate that they do. Several theories purport to explain the association. *Anomie theory* suggests that lower-class persons have an absence of stake in conforming to society's rules, hence less compunction about using violent means to achieve desired ends. A compendium of work dealing with *physical punishment in child-rearing* suggests that lower-class parents tend to punish their offspring physically, thus teaching them that violence is an appropriate way of dealing with problems. *Experience theory* predicts that lower-class individuals tend to have early experience in violence, setting in motion social forces that tend to generate further violence, a reputation for fighting, for instance. In the *violent masculine style* perspective, the social structure of "rough" working-class communities is thought to foster the perpetuation of an all-male, age-graded, fighting elite whose members adhere to norms of exaggerated masculine aggressiveness.

The association between age and violence is curvilinear. Violence rates tend to increase through adolescence into young adulthood, then tail off. In the teenage years especially – what some describe as a holding period between childhood and adulthood devalued in many ways by adult society – risk-taking behaviour, including violence, is one of a limited number of ways of achieving a positive peer status, particularly for working-class males. Sports offer a forum for such behaviour. Violence rates decrease in adulthood when, for a number of reasons, the costs of violence begin to outweigh the gains. Even professional athletes, who continue to threaten, scuffle, and fight, years after their age peers have given up these remnants of adolescence, become relatively docile in time.

4 Interpersonal Determinants of Violence in Sports: The Influence of Parents, Coaches, Peers, and Spectators

This chapter attempts to bridge the gap between the sociocultural system and individual behaviour. This is the province of social psychology, the level of analysis lying at the intersection of sociology and psychology. I shall draw upon many different theories and concepts, but use one explicitly social psychological perspective – the "reference other" orientation – as an organizing framework for the chapter.

The "reference other" orientation, in the words of its chief exponent, Raymond Schmitt (1972:8), sets out "to explain an individual's behaviour as that behaviour is related to the individual's significant sociocultural worlds." Said differently, social structure and culture influence one's behaviour through one's relationships with "reference others." These, in the most general sense, are persons or groups who provide some sort of orientation for the individual in the development of a course of action or attitude.

From such a vantage point, violence becomes distinctly *interpersonal,* the product of a reference relationship between the individual and his or her "reference others." Theory and research suggest that parents, coaches, peers, and spectators serve as the individual's principal "reference others" when it comes to sports violence. This chapter is an examination of the ways in which, and the extent to which, these others exert their influence.

Parents

An extensive body of scholarly work attests to the general importance of parents as "reference others" for their offspring. The recent spate of research on family violence and child abuse indicates, more specifically, that children learn much about the uses and justification of violence from their parents. Such parent-child interaction may be categorized as indirect or direct training in violence (Steinmetz and Straus, 1975).

Indirect training in violence

This refers to children's learning of violence through parents' violence against children, the extent of which has recently, and shockingly, come to light. In their survey of a nationally representative sample of 2,143

American families (couples who indicated they were married or living together as a couple), Straus et al. (1980) found that 71 per cent of the 1,146 parents who had children three to seventeen years of age living at home had spanked or used some sort of violence against their child at some time. The researchers included spanking as violence because spanking *is* intended to cause physical pain and if administered to someone outside the family *is* an assault in the eyes of the law. Other, smaller-scale studies have reported that up to 90 per cent of parents spank their children (Bybee, 1979). As for the more severe forms of child "discipline," Straus and his colleagues estimate that 8 in every 100 American children were kicked, bitten, or punched, and nearly 3 in every 100 had a gun or knife used on them by a parent at least once in 1975, the year to which their data refer. They suggest that between 1.4 and 1.9 million children in the United States were in danger of being seriously injured at the hands of a parent (also see Gelles and Straus, 1979).

Straus et al.'s extrapolations should be regarded with caution because of the very broad definition of "violence" employed, the absence of data on the actual physical consequences of violence, and the lack of corroborating information from other family members (one parent in each family was interviewed). On the other hand, their figures may underreport the true level of child abuse. They exclude single-parent families, believed to be more abuse-prone than intact families. They are based on a parent's own testimony, which almost certainly minimizes abuse. They pertain only to children aged three to seventeen, thus excluding very young children, a particularly abuse-prone group. In the Straus survey, rates of parental violence against children peaked at two ages: the youngest (three to four years) and the oldest (fifteen to seventeen years). The latter finding is perhaps surprising, but in two earlier studies more than half of two samples of college students reported being hit or threatened by a parent as late as their senior year in high school (Straus, 1975). More limited research conducted in Canada, the United Kingdom, South Africa, India, and in several Arab countries confirms the suspicion that the physical ill-treatment of infants, children, and adolescents is nearly universal (Eekelaar and Katz, 1978).

Parents hit their children out of frustration and anger, but they hit them mostly, Gelles and Straus (1979) write, for purposes of moral training and character development. Many parents apparently think that children *need* to be hit for their own good and *deserve* to be hit when they misbehave. Yablonsky and Brower (1979), in their book about little league baseball, relate an interview with a youngster who told them that if he played a bad game he could look forward to a beating by his father. Such violence is instrumental, contrary to the popular image of the frustration-induced parental explosion. And because it is done in the name of child-rearing, it is widely regarded as legitimate and thus not violence.

Child-rearing of this kind is a form of indirect training in violence because it tends to produce violent children and, ultimately, adults – a "generational pattern" of violence. Beginning with Sears et al.'s (1957) discovery that children whose mothers spanked them severely behaved more aggressively toward their parents than children who were spanked less severely, a considerable number of studies, employing several different research methods, have yielded a positive correlation between parents' use of corporal punishment and their children's aggression in various forms, including physical (see Feshbach, 1979). Straus et al.'s (1980) statistics suggest over and over again that violent families produce violent children. Ironically, parents often employ physical punishment to control their youngster's own aggressiveness, to teach it *not* to be aggressive.

Several investigations of more serious child battering have demonstrated that battered children tend to batter other, younger children and grow up to be battering parents (Lystad, 1979). Palmer's early (1960) study of fifty-one convicted male murderers, perhaps the ultimate aggressors, revealed that as boys the murderers had experienced much more severe beatings by their parents than did their brothers, who did not become murderers. On the basis of findings like these, Steinmetz and Straus (1975) hypothesize that the effects of physical punishment on tendencies toward violence are directly proportional to the severity of the punishment.

Several theories have been advanced to explain the association between physically punitive child-rearing and subsequent violence by children, but the largest amount of evidence, and the most persuasive, supports social learning theory. The abused child *learns* from the abusing parent through direct experience and observation how to hit, in what circumstances to hit, and that hitting is a swift, effective, and in some circumstances acceptable method of dealing with other people, even people you love, especially when other methods do not work. In the language of "reference other" theory, such a parent and child have a "comparative reference relationship"; the child compares itself to the parent with respect to the use of aggression and is influenced by the comparison (Schmitt, 1972).

Of course because the child learns about aggression in this fashion does not necessarily mean it will behave aggressively as a child or as an adult. Social psychologist Albert Bandura (1973), the leading spokesperson for the social learning theory of aggression, has shown that imitative aggression varies with the observer's perceptions of the rewards and punishments given to the aggressive model and likely to attend the observer's own imitative behaviour. An abused child is more likely to abuse an age-mate, say, if the child thinks it will be rewarded in some way for doing so. In short, imitative aggression is a function of the availability of aggressive models *and* the structure of rewards and punishments for aggressive behaviour. It is worth noting that psychological abuse by parents also may produce violent offspring. We shall not examine this proposition, but the interested reader is referred to a review of literature on the subject by Hirsch and Leff (1975).

There appears to be no research on the relationship between indirect violence training in the home and violence in sports. But the occasional biography, like that of former Canadian professional football player

Angelo Mosca, self-admittedly the dirtiest player in the league for more than a decade, suggests that such a relationship may exist (McRae, 1977a).

Direct training in violence

This refers to the structure of rewards for aggression that exists within the family — more specifically, to parents' subtle or open approval, by word or deed, of their children's aggression. When a child is influenced by this approval, the child can be said to have a "normative reference relationship" with the parent; the child is influenced by its perception of the parent's norms and values regarding violence.

A majority of parents seem to approve of their children's violence in at least some circumstances. This approval usually comes under the heading of teaching boys to be men. In a survey of 1,176 American adults, conducted by the National Commission on the Causes and Prevention of Violence, 70 per cent of the respondents agreed with the statement, "When a boy is growing up, it is very important for him to have a few fist-fights" (Stark and McEvoy, 1970:274). Straus et al. (1980) found that male children were more likely than female to be victims of parental abuse, especially severe abuse, possibly because of the belief that experiencing violence "toughens up" boys in what for boys, more than girls, is a tough, violent world. Parental techniques for hardening boys can be found in most societies. In Lebanon in the 1970s, parents brought wooden Kalashnikov rifles to their hospitalized children who had been wounded by sniper fire and shrapnel (Boulding, 1978). Among the primitive Yanomamö – the "fierce people" of Brazil and Venezuela – parents teach their sons almost from infancy to be fierce and cruel, to develop a large capacity for rage, a hair-trigger temper, a willingness to use violence to attain almost any end; four-year-old boys are rewarded for hitting their own parents. Yanomamö male adults are chronically violent (Chagnon, 1968).

Not only fathers are charged with the responsibility of turning boys into men. Mothers, themselves traditionally inhibited when it comes to the overt expression of aggression, help socialize what Boulding (1978) terms the "battle-ready," "fight-happy," "rape-happy" male. Children typically spend much more of their life in the company of their mother than their father, and for this reason alone, the mother's possible influence ought not to be ignored.

To understand parents' feelings about their progeny's participation in sports violence, one must grasp the extent and nature of parents' involvement in their children's sports. To start with, parents' sheer physical presence is overwhelming. Some 60,000 boys under the age of eighteen play "competitive" hockey in Ontario. Eighty per cent of their parents attend at least three-quarters of the boys' games (McPherson and Davidson, 1980). An estimated 20 million children participate in adult-organized, nonschool sport in the United States (Ogilvie, 1979). If American parents watch their youngsters' games in roughly the same proportion as Ontario hockey parents do – and they seem to in little league baseball (Yablonsky and Brower, 1979) – then about 16 million American parents regularly watch their kids playing community-sponsored sports. Once mainly a North American phenomenon, little leaguism can now be found in varying degrees almost everywhere. A recent Peewee soccer tournament in Toronto featured teams from Denmark, Japan, New Zealand, Mexico, United Arab Emirates, Canada, and the United States, to name but a few of the entries (*Toronto Star,* May 31, 1980).

Parents do more than observe, of course. Together with other adults, they run almost every aspect of youth sports. California's Livermore Soccer Club seems fairly typical: one adult for every four kids in the organization, for a total of 420 adults who do everything but actually play (Yeager, 1979). Inevitably, as Underwood (1979:289) acidly puts it, "the virtues of adulthood are brought down hard upon all those little heads." As one Toronto father said, revealingly, to the present author after a soccer game for boys aged ten: "I love these kids. They play their guts out for us."

In no other social setting are mothers and fathers afforded such a direct, public comparison of their child with its age-mates engaged in such an overtly competitive activity. What parents want to see, perhaps more than anything else, is their youngsters displaying the qualities they themselves value – above all, it seems, competitive zeal and all that it entails. For is not life itself a competition? From here it is but a short step to the encouragement of violence.

Smith's qualitative data on youth hockey help convey something of the intensity of parents' involvement in their children's sports. Typically, minor hockey families arrive at the arena anywhere from one hour to a half-hour before a game, and while the players dress, parents stand in the lobby talking, usually about hockey. Some wear team insignia: jackets, scarves, hats, buttons. During the game most sit together, sometimes behind their sons' bench, distinctly apart from opposing parents. As the action unfolds on the ice, in the stands bodies strain, faces contort, parents jump to their feet. Organized cheering and spontaneous bursts of applause are frequent. Immersion in the game is total and attuned principally to the performance of one's own offspring. Booing and catcalls are directed sometimes at opposing players, frequently at the referees. Occasionally groups of rival parents engage in unfriendly verbal exchanges; fights are not unknown. The rougher the game, the greater the likelihood of this sort of misbehaviour. A typical example (most of these field observations were conducted prior to 1980 when minor hockey leagues in Canada began banning body contact for youngsters twelve and under):

> It took me about thirty seconds after entering the arena to realize that the game in progress was "getting out of hand." The play on the ice between the Don Mills and Red Wing Peewee teams was exceptionally rough, with a lot of heavy body checks and a great deal of pushing and shoving. Even more noticeable was the behaviour of the fans. Apparently the Don Mills parents

felt that the referee was "shafting" them, and they were very vocal in their criticisms. There were standard comments such as, "C'mon ref, there's two teams on the ice, why don't you take a look?" and the old standby, "How much did the Red Wings pay you to throw this one?" to mention only a few.

Naturally these attacks did not go unnoticed by the Red Wing parents who were sitting about 50 feet from the Don Mills group. The Red Wing fans felt that every call was justified and that the Don Mills parents were "poor sports." This led to numerous verbal exchanges between the groups, like this one:

Red Wing fan: "Why don't you stop crying, your kids deserve everything they're getting."

Don Mills fan: "Sit down and shut up, you idiot."

Same Red Wing fan: "Do you want to step outside and make me, bigmouth?"

Don Mills fan: "I wouldn't waste my time."

(All the quotes in this chapter are from the author's field notes and interviews, unless indicated otherwise.)

This particular arena is constructed so that the fans sit close to the players' benches. Given the parents' proximity to the players and the volume of their yelling, the players of both teams must have overheard these exchanges.

Little league baseball, though not as violent as minor hockey, does have a problem of violence, some of which, as in hockey, can be traced to over-involved parents. The only research directly addressing violence in youth baseball seems to be Yablonsky and Brower's (1979). Both sociologists, Yablonsky and Brower wrote the *The Little League Game* for a general audience. They based their observations on five years of first-hand involvement in little league baseball and over 500 interviews with parents, coaches, and players. Baseball parents engage in the same kind of verbal attacks as hockey parents but usually, according to Yablonsky and Brower, against an obnoxious parent cheering for the same team. In fact parents usually sit behind their own team's dugout, one of which is behind the first base line and the other behind the third base line, which makes the rival groups somewhat inaccessible to one another.

In the eyes of parents and others, the *sine qua non* of baseball is "hustling." Little league baseball parents want to see their kids "hustle." So do minor hockey parents, but "hustling" in hockey, a body contact sport, includes "hitting." Among minor hockey parents, hitting, or "taking the body," usually elicits shouts of approval; hitting is regarded as a sign of desire and gameness. A conversation between two fathers at a Peewee game went as follows: "Stick checks, never body checks," exclaims the first father, disgustedly. Then, yelling, "Take the body, for Chrissakes!" Father two: "Boy, little Ian isn't afraid to hit." Verbal encouragement of legal hitting often extends to the encouragement of semi-legal acts, and sometimes to fighting and more extreme behaviours.

Field notes taken while observing a tournament of ten-year-olds suggest that some parents convey their attitudes not just by what they say but by what they do. Only a small minority is guilty of such gross misconduct, but an obtrusive one, clearly.

A man (hockey jacket, big, fat – a stereotype) had been yelling in a booming voice throughout several games, though nothing overly negative. But during the Thornhill-Oshawa game (his son played on the Oshawa team) his yelling at the referee became abusive and constant. I noticed several kids imitating him, using the same words. An assistant coach from the Oshawa bench walked around to him and apparently asked him to stop. The man punched the coach and a fight was on. There was a great commotion at the end of the rink. Several men joined the fray, to break it up I think, and there was much milling about. All this was observed by a couple of hundred kids. The rink was packed. Toward the end of the game the fat man moved down near where I was sitting (I was surprised that he was still in the rink), and as people began leaving engaged in a shouting match with the Oshawa head coach, who informed him furiously that he and his son were finished with the team. They screamed abuse at one another, looking as if they were trying to get closer, but the exiting crowd prevented it. The fat man had a gash on one cheek.

Fisticuffs also appear to be character-building in the eyes of some parents who see sports as a training ground for life. One father, an official in a minor hockey organization, put it this way: "It's a violent society, eh? This is a tough society we're in. I put my own kid in hockey so he would learn to take his lumps." He said he saw "nothing wrong with taking off the gloves" and that "the day they turn hockey into a namby-pamby game for sissies is the day I get out." Picture this arena lobby scene after an Atom game featuring a multiplayer "semi-fight" ("real" fighting starts around age twelve, or used to before the no-bodychecking rule): two of the ten-year-old combatants approach a group of parents. Smiling, the father of one says, "Looks like we've got a couple of scrappers." Approving chuckles all around. Or consider this dialogue, tape-recorded during a party for Bantam parents.

Parent one (father): "There's nothing wrong with a good fist fight in hockey as long as everyone drops their gloves and sticks first. Having skates on is the great equalizer anyway. No one is really going to get hurt during a hockey fight. If the referees see that one guy is killing another guy they'll step in and break it up fast enough."
Parent two (mother): "I agree. The fights seem to do some good. The boys get it out of their systems and they usually end up playing better hockey in the long run."
Parent three (father): "I think if the boys had dropped their gloves earlier in the game the other night that number 5 wouldn't have gone after Joey with his stick."
Parent four (father): "That's the sad part now. Kids today don't know how to get the gloves off and get the fists up. Everyone is hitting everyone else with their sticks. I think fighting with the fist is a good way to toughen a boy up. He's got to learn to take his lumps as well as give them out. The problem is that everyone in hockey is too sneaky now. They hit you when you're not expecting it. I haven't seen a good fist fighter in two years in this league."

As youngsters advance through the competitive hockey system, violence as an occupational tool becomes increasingly important. Fourteen-year-olds with marginal playing ability are upwardly mobile in some leagues because they are good fighters. Parents' parts in the making of one such performer are suggested in what follows. This interviewee, now nineteen, had been an Ontario Junior A penalty leader. ("My first year, 256 minutes," said he, not without a touch of pride.)

Q. So your father played?

A. He was a good hockey player. He wasn't a finesse hockey player. He just used to hit people all the time and take all the penalties. He was rough, really rough. It was the only way he knew how to play the game, knock them down and they can't do anything. You know, if they're sitting on their ass, they're not going to be able to make me look like an idiot, so I guess that's where I picked all that up too, I don't know.

Q. Is he big too?

A. Well he's big, but he's not tall. He's about five nine. He's just naturally strong, strong as a bull. He's kind of got a bad temper.

Q. He was quite an influence, was he?

A. Ya, I'd say so.

Q. What about your mother?

A. Well she's a knowledgeable hockey fan because she used to watch my father play all the time. She doesn't like the rough stuff. I used to get into fights and she wouldn't talk to me. One time I got into a fight and had a bleeding nose and she came down – I was about fifteen – and she gave me a kleenex to wipe my nose, and I just turned to her and said, "Why don't you get the hell out of here?" and that didn't go over too well at all. But I hurt a kid really bad when I was sixteen years old, hit him and broke a bone in his neck. And there was big fights around our place between her and my dad for about a week and a half. I was too rough. I did it accidentally, you know, I didn't mean to do it. I hurt him really bad, and I felt really bad about it. I was going to quit playing. You know, you might get mad at somebody and you want to beat him up or something, but you don't want to deliberately maim him or crack bones or anything; you don't want to do that. So I guess she was kind of upset. She told me if I had to be so rough to quit the game, and my dad just kind of talked her out of it after about a week and a half.

Q. Was that the only time you ever really hurt somebody badly?

A. Well, I broke a guy's leg once. My first year when I played Junior A, my dad told me that if I want to make the team, go out there and pick on the guy that's out for your position. So I went out and picked on him and broke his leg, and I made the team – Junior A. I didn't deliberately go out trying to break his leg; I just wanted to hit him and make him look bad.

How widespread is parents' approval of violence? Six hundred and four Toronto players were asked if they thought their father and mother would approve of a minor hockey player punching another player in four situations: (1) if ridiculed, (2) if threatened, (3) if shoved, (4) if punched by the other player. Indexes of Parents' Approval of Hockey Fighting were constructed by summing the "yes" responses to these items. Table 4.1 shows variations in players' scores on these Indexes, by age and level of competition.

Table 4.1 **Hockey Players' Perceptions of Their Parents' Approval of Hockey Fighting by Age and Level of Competition (in Per Cent)**

	Fathers' Approval			Mothers' Approval		
	Low	Med.	High*	Low	Med.	High*
Age						
12-13 (N = 166)	77	20	3	89	8	3
14-15 (N = 196)	66	25	9	85	12	3
16-17 (N = 130)	47	31	22	81	14	5
18-21 (N = 112)	40	19	41	75	18	7
Level of competition						
House League (N = 330)	76	18	6	94	6	0
Competitive (N = 274)	41	31	29	71	21	8
All players (N = 604)	60	24	16	83	13	4

*Low = approve in no situations; Medium = approve in one or two situations; High = approve in three or four situations.

Adapted from Smith (1979c:113).

The majority of fathers (60 per cent) ranks low on the Fathers' Approval Index, which is to say, these fathers would not, in the eyes of their offspring, approve of a player punching another player in any of the situations presented. But approval increases sharply with age and level of competition. In the older age and competitive rows, the majority of fathers fall into the medium (one or two situations) and high (three or four situations) approval categories. Forty-one per cent of the eighteen- to twenty-one-year-olds felt their fathers would approve of fighting in at least three of the situations, compared to only 3 per cent of the twelve- to thirteen-year-olds; 29 per cent of the "competitive" fathers were seen as high approvers compared to 6 per cent of the house-league fathers. Mothers consistently were perceived as less approving than fathers; still, 25 and 29 per cent in the eighteen- to twenty-one-year-old and competitive rows are in the medium and high approval categories combined.

A massive public opinion poll conducted by the Ontario Hockey Council (McPherson and Davidson, 1980) suggests that the above perceptions approximate parents' own expressed attitudes about violence in minor hockey.

In 1979, 78,000 questionnaires were mailed to the parents of all so-called competitive players in the province. Over 31,000 parents responded, a return rate of 40 per cent, remarkably high for a survey of this kind. Table 4.2 shows responses to several of the questionnaire items relevant to violence. The proportion of "No" and "Ok as is" responses corroborate in a rough way the medium and high approval data in the competitive row of Table 4.1.

Table 4.2 Hockey Parents' Attitudes about Violence in "Competitive" Minor Hockey (in Per Cent)

	Yes	No	No response
Would you support a rule preventing body-checking for Pee Wee and under players?	54	30	16
Do you think there is too much violence in your child's league?	42	55	3

	OK as is	Needs improvement	No response
Do you think enforcement of the rules relating to the use of hockey sticks is OK as is or needs improvement?	32	66	2
Do you think enforcement of the rules relating to fighting is OK as is or needs improvement?	36	62	2

Adapted from McPherson and Davidson (1980:69, 71).

Levels of and variations in parents' approval of fighting and other acts of violence are of considerable interest. But to what extent does this approval affect behaviour? Considerably, the case study of the Junior A player just presented suggests. A substantial correlation between players' scores on the Parents' Approval Indexes and number of (self-reported) hockey fights indicates this case study is illustrative of a general pattern of parental influence (Smith, 1979c).

Other sports? Studies of little league baseball in the United States (e.g., Voight, 1974; Yablonsky and Brower, 1979) document the sort of parental intrusiveness characteristic of minor hockey but, save for Yablonsky and Brower's, do not touch directly on the question of violence. One can only present vignettes like the ones below, which suggest that direct training in violence by parents' words and deeds manifests itself in a variety of sports:

-   A Canadian minor lacrosse official: "I have seen young mothers at tyke and novice games (six to ten years old) screaming at their sons to 'kill' the opposing player" (*Toronto Star,* June 17, 1973:7).
-   In Kissimmee, Florida, a group of parents assault four coaches of a kids' football team after a game. One coach ends up in the hospital (Underwood, 1979).

- The father of a little league pitcher repeatedly exhorts his son to "Stick it in his ear!" – baseball's traditional directive to aim at the batter's head (Michener, 1976:133).
- Lake City, Michigan: a high-school basketball coach is assaulted by a father because his son is not getting enough playing time (Underwood, 1981).
- Junior league rugby in Sydney, Australia: screaming parents run up and down the sidelines: "Don't just run beside him, Brian, TACKLE! TACKLE!... Get 'im by the ear and haul 'im down" (Dunstan, 1973:42).
- the father of a young Sidney footballer is fined $60 for attacking a referee in the dressing room after an L grade rugby league match for nine-year-olds (Dunstan, 1973).
- Mrs. Rigby, mother of "The Fighting Rigby's: America's Best," a brood of dirt track auto racers: Roger Rigby, age five, undefeated in eleven races, ruthlessly rides down opponents, forcing them into bales of hay: "Look at him go!" shouts Mrs. Rigby, "Keep hittin' 'em Roger" (Michener, 1976:124).

Coaches

The status of coach, like that of parent, puts the coach in a position to exert a powerful influence over those in his or her charge. Stories surface occasionally of coaches manhandling athletes, thus training them indirectly in violence in the manner of parents. In the 1978 Gator Bowl, Ohio State University football coach Woody Hayes punched a Clemson University player, then one of his own players, as millions of television watchers gaped in disbelief (Tatum and Kushner, 1979). Jack Tatum, a former Hayes player, writes that the coach frequently struck his own players. The coach of a juvenile hockey team in Manitoba, Canada, was convicted of assault after he punched one of his players in the face (*Toronto Star,* July 19, 1980). Fifty-two members of a high-school football team in New Orleans recently demanded that their coach be fired because he allegedly abused them verbally and physically (*Globe and Mail,* August 23, 1980). Deposed Arizona State University football coach Frank Kush won a lawsuit brought against him by a former player who accused him of punching him in the face during a game in 1978, but Kush did admit striking some players with lengths of rope (Kirshenbaum, 1981). By and large, however, hitting children and youth is a prerogative that parents jealously guard for themselves, and there is no evidence that the practice is widespread among coaches.

When coaches train athletes in violence they typically do so directly. Theoretically, when an athlete is influenced by his or her perception of the coach's norms and values regarding the use of violence, athlete and coach have a "normative reference relationship." Research on hockey violence sheds some light on why coaches approve of violence, the ways in which approval is transmitted, its extent, and the degree to which it affects players' attitudes and behaviour.

Field data suggest that hockey coaches, like hockey fathers, encourage physically aggressive play, including fighting and other assaultive acts, both for what it symbolizes (gameness and strong character) and for its utility in winning games and enhancing players' occupational careers. Since coaches' own careers – or at least their self-images – in most professionalized minor hockey leagues depend to some degree on producing winning teams and upwardly mobile individual performers, coaches tend to choose players on the basis of size and toughness, among other attributes. Almost from the start, big kids who can handle the heavy going are selected over smaller, less aggressive, though sometimes more skilled, performers. By age thirteen or fourteen a boy's willingness and ability to hit are highly important in determining his upward mobility, as the following pregame "pep talk" suggests. This Bantam coach did not conceal his irritation at the team's recent poor performances.

> *I hope you guys realize if you don't start playing better hockey you've probably reached the end of the line at this level. From here on things are a lot tougher. I was talking to Metcalfe [the Midget coach] and he said that right now he figures there are only two guys on this club who can make it in Midget. He saw the way you guys were pushed around by Nats the other night and said there was no way that kind of stuff goes in Midget. You realize that there are only four guys from that club moving up next year and probably a couple of guys will get cut. So at most there are only likely to be six openings, and that's not counting anyone he recruits. You can see that if you hope to move on next year, you've got to start showing some hustle. Teams have just been walking by our defence all year without being touched. We've gotta start knocking them on their cans. Guys know they don't have to keep their heads up when they come into our end!*

Legal hitting almost always leads to the penalty-getting kind, for the line between the two is often fine. Coaches do not approve of penalties per se, of course, but accept a certain number as an inevitable consequence of spirited, aggressive play. Then there is the "good penalty." "You should have tripped him," a house-league coach admonished a wide-eyed boy, eight. "*Never* let a guy go around you." Many hockey coaches also expect players to fight in self-defence and to retaliate against flagrant fouls. So do some little league baseball coaches. According to Yablonsky and Brower (1979), retaliation for rough play is as common in the little league game as it is in the big leagues, the coach typically encouraging his pitcher to throw at the batter's head to "even up a score." A Junior A hockey coach, once an NHL professional, put it this way:

> *It's important to be tough. I don't think it's all that important that you have to go out and knock somebody right off, but I believe its important to be tough because if trouble comes you have to stand up. That's what they taught*

us in the old days. Take the man out clean, but if he raises his stick and goes at you be ready for him. Stand up to it and be counted.

Some coaches habitually lose their poise in stressful situations. Incidents like the following, observed by the author, are not uncommon. As the buzzer sounded to end a penalty-filled Peewee game, one boy appeared to spear another in the stomach. The coaches began shouting at one another as the teams left the ice. Coach A: "What the hell's the matter with you guys? You beat us five-nothing and now you want to take one of our players out for the season." Coach B: "Ah, shut up and go home you goddam crybaby." Coaches and players filed together down a corridor toward the dressing rooms. Coach A said to the player who was speared: "You have my permission to go and punch the shit out of that son-of-a-bitch," indicating the other player. The first player threw down his stick and gloves, charged his opponent, and began pummelling him from behind. Surprised, the latter went down, his assailant on top, punching. Coach B attempted to pull him off. Coach A pushed Coach B. A short, shoving match ensued, which was finally broken up by bystanders.

Another illustration, from the referee's laconic official report of a raucous Junior B game:

At this point the coach of the Belleville team, Reggie Sommers, took his gum out of his mouth and threw it towards the penalty box, where I was standing. He then picked up a helmet and threw it at me. It landed in the alleyway. It did not strike me. I immediately gave him a game misconduct. He then attempted to get at me. Steve Curti, the linesman, restrained him and finally the Belleville general manager, Charley Johnstone, moved him away. I had the Belleville General Manager call to the referee's room and ask for the procurement of policemen. This was done by the start of the third period.

Such ugly scenes are not unique to hockey, as this baseball incident indicates (Yablonsky and Brower, 1979:67-68):

A base runner slid hard into third base and knocked down the third baseman. The father of the fallen third baseman came running onto the field from the stands and started yelling at the aggressive runner. Phil, the runner's coach, grabbed the irate father by the arm and told him, in an angry tone, to "get the hell off the field and back to the stands where you belong." The father grabbed Phil and took a hard clenched-fist swing at him. Phil ducked under the punch and came up recoiling for a counterpunch. The opposing team coach, by now at the third base action, grabbed Phil and restrained him from hitting the father. Another coach grabbed the father and held him back, too. While both combatants were being constrained from further physical aggression, they were exchanging highly charged and foul language. Meanwhile, the umpire did not speak to the father, did not tell him to get back to the stands, and did not reprimand Phil. All he did was to tell Phil that his runner was not allowed to knock basemen down with highflying slides. Phil barked at the umpire, "If the kid (the third baseman) wants to suck his thumb, he should stay

*at home with his mother.'' The umpire then showed Phil his scarred arm
caused by such rough play, in a game from his own youth. Phil lambasted the
umpire for his remarks which Phil argued were inflammatory and contrary to
baseball rules, thus helping to fuel the anger of the father and the discontented
parents in the stands.*

(Copyright© 1979 by Lewis Yablonsky and Jonathan Brower. Reprinted by permission of
Times Books, The New York Times Book Co., Inc. from *The Little League Game.)*

Some amateur hockey organizations have reputations for sponsoring excessively rough or "dirty" teams. There is at least one of these teams in
every age division, almost always accompanied by a coach of matching
notoriety. Opposing coaches make special preparations for contests against
such teams. "C'mon now guys," one exhorted, "we need a win tonight. We
played well on Tuesday. Let's keep it up. Now these guys are gonna be hitting, so we've got to stay cool. We can't afford stupid penalties." Indeed,
this particular game was very rough. Penalties were numerous. The other
coach directed a tirade at the referee and at his own players. "If you're going to hit him after the whistle make it a *good* one." After the game, a boy
who had played for this coach the year before explained: "He's mental.
He's always yelling and screaming at guys. He used to try and make me do
fifty pushups after games. No one else, just me. The guys on the team are
just as crazy as he is."

More than a few minor hockey coaches tolerate, even nurture, "goons"
or "enforcers," some of them as young as twelve and thirteen. One such
youngster was known as "the Animal" by players and coaches in a Toronto
Bantam league. When opposing coaches prepared for games against the
Animal's team they always made special plans to handle him. The Flyer's
coach explained his plan to his team in a pregame talk that went as follows:

*Look, if this character starts anything, take him out early. We can't have him
charging around hammering people. Somebody's going to have to straighten
him out. Just remember, get the gloves off and do it in a fair fight. If you
shake him up early he can't keep it up. Besides, it's best to take the penalties
early in the game before we get too tired to kill them effectively.*

The field notes go on:

*The Flyers jumped to a 3-0 lead before the St. Mikes coach decided to play the
Animal. As soon as he came over the boards he ran at Johnson (the Flyers'
captain) and wrestled him to the ice. They fought and each player got five
minutes. When he came back on the Animal ran at another guy, but he was
ready for him and decked him with an elbow. He got two minutes for elbowing, but it was worth it. He said after that the Animal was like a piece of jello.
In fact, he hardly got on the rest of the game.*

In Junior B and A ranks, employing one or more "enforcers" on a team
is standard practice. Excerpt from an interview with a nineteen-year-old

Junior A player:

Q.   So you think Ron [the enforcer] was brought on the team for that purpose?

A   Well definitely. You can even hear him [the coach] you know. Bill [the coach] would say, "Ron go out and get that guy. " He'd tell him, and I didn't like that, you know, "go out and get that guy," because half the time I knew the guy he was going to get. I've played in this league so long, I've got some pretty good friends in there. What are you going to do?

Such coaches appear to have much the same attitude toward violence as their counterparts in professional hockey. But the professional coach must concern himself more with the ultimate business of hockey: winning games and filling seats. To produce a team that can do this, certain player types are required, among them tough, combative "grinders" who can win the physical battles for the puck and fight if necessary, which inevitably it is. Also needed is at least one "tough guy," "bad guy," "policeman," "enforcer," "animal," "goon," "cement head," "hit man," or "designated fighter" (these roles are not exactly the same). An NHL player, one of sixty interviewed by the author, explains further:

Every team picks up their tough guys. In our case we never got a guy who just fought. Nobody on our team has been sent out just to fight. We've always had, like, Jim Schoenfeld, who was, like, our tough guy, but he always played 30, 40 minutes a game, so he had to do his job the way it should be done. He's tough, but he also plays a lot. There are other teams, of course, who have guys just to fight. They send them out to play about 10 minutes a game, and their only job is to stir up trouble, start fights, and get the good guys off the ice.

Most of these professionals saw the coach as trying to do a difficult job and as having to cope with the caprices of owners and managers in the process. Coaches, players point out, do not expect everybody to be a fighter, or even highly physically aggressive, if it is not their "nature," especially if they are small and possess compensatory skills.

Like, we had guys that were expected to be like a policeman, you know. Straighten a guy out once in a while. That's what they were getting paid for. They [coach and manager] knew this guy wasn't a twenty-goal scorer, so they didn't expect it. By the same token if you were a twenty- or twenty-five-goal scorer and you weren't a rough guy, they didn't expect you to run into the corner and jump on somebody and get into a big fight, because they weren't paying you to fight. They were paying you to score goals. So, you know, I think it was more or less the individual.

How widespread is hockey coaches' approval of rough play? Almost all of eighty-three high-school players interviewed by Smith (1975b) stated that their coaches would approve (most of them "strongly") of "hard but legal body-checking." Over half of the approximately 2,000 boys who were surveyed by Vaz and Thomas (1974) reported that their coaches regularly emphasized "playing rough and being aggressive." When asked, "What are the three most important qualities a coach looks for in selecting players for Allstar teams?" 62 per cent of the oldest boys (aged fifteen to sixteen) included, out of nine possible response choices, "being aggressive at all times"; 56 per cent included "physical size and strength"; 25 per cent included "guts and courage." More than half these boys were house-leaguers, and their responses probably pulled these percentages down.

Such findings are not surprising; much of what is called "aggressive" play is sanctioned by the official rules of the game. What of officially illegal "borderline violence"? Table 4.3 reveals that Toronto minor hockey players see coaches as somewhat more approving of fighting than fathers; yet only 21 per cent of all coaches come under the high approval heading. But again this overall figure obscures differences in age and level of competition. Over 50 per cent of the eighteen- to twenty-one-year-olds and 36 per cent of the competitive players saw their coaches as high approvers.

Table 4.3   Hockey Players' Perceptions of Their Coaches' Approval of Hockey Fighting by Age and Level of Competition (in Per Cent)

	Coaches' Approval		
	Low	Med.	High*
Age			
12-13 (N = 166)	74	17	9
14-15 (N = 196)	59	30	11
~ 16-17 (N = 130)	39	36	25
18-21 (N = 112)	25	23	52
Level of competition			
House League (N = 330)	70	22	8
Competitive (N = 274)	32	32	36
All players (N = 604)	53	26	21

*Low = approve in no situations; Medium = approve in one or two situations; High = approve in three or four situations.

Adapted from Smith (1979c:113).

Players' perceptions of coaches' sanctions for assaultive play do seem to have an impact on players' attitudes and conduct at all levels of hockey. Vaz and Thomas (1974) report statistically significant associations in all age divisions between players' perceptions of how much their coaches emphasized "playing rough and being aggressive" and players' approval of "taking out an opposing player any way you can in order to save a goal even though you risk injuring the opposing player" (Table 4.4). Smith (1979c) has demonstrated statistically that the more coaches approve of fighting, the more players fight and the more major penalties they receive.

Table 4.4 Hockey Players' Acceptance of "Taking Out an Opposing Player Any Way You Can" by Coaches' Emphasis on "Playing Rough and Being Aggressive" (in Per Cent)

Coaches' Emphasis on "Playing Rough and Being Aggressive"	Players' Acceptance of "Taking Out an Opposing Player Any Way You Can"			
	Okay	Sometimes Okay	Seldom Okay	Not Okay
Very often and often (N = 1,024)	24	34	19	23
Seldom (N = 534)	19	22	26	33
Never (N = 345)	15	15	18	52

Adapted from Vaz and Thomas (1974:45). Reprinted with permission.

There seems to be no research on coaches' influence on player violence in other sports. Anecdotal and journalistic evidence is in ample supply, however, and paints pictures not dissimilar to those in hockey. The material below is offered as suggestive:

- In 1974 baseball manager Billy Martin is suspended three days by the League for ordering his pitchers to throw knockdown pitches at Milwaukee batters (*Toronto Star,* June 2, 1981).
- A U.S. college football referee: "I've seen coaches in practice hold onto a boy's neck, then shove him into a pileup. 'That's what I mean by being aggressive! That's what I want!'" (Underwood, 1979:132).
- St. Louis Cardinal baseball pitcher Al Hrabosky is fined by the team manager for *not* throwing at a batter as directed (Atyeo, 1979).
- George Plimpton (1973:288) asks a professional football player how coaches react to "cheap shots": "If a guy on your own team gets a cheap shot, the coaches will run the film back and forth in the classroom, no one saying anything, but everybody's filing it away in their mind who the other player is, and his number."
- Keith Eddy, coach of Toronto Blizzard of the North American Soccer League, on "sorting out" foes: "I wanted Drew Busby, who can do that sort of thing, to physically challenge the Rochester goalkeeper as early as possible. He did and from then on, the man was looking for Drew – and our other chaps – every time the ball came into his area.... Soccer is definitely a man's game, if you get my point" (*Toronto Star,* April 22, 1980:C2).
- U.S. tennis expert Art Hoppe: "The proper method of playing mixed doubles is to hit the ball accidently at the woman opponent as hard and as accurately as possible" (Atyeo, 1979:267).

- A little league baseball coach yells instructions from the bench to his second baseman when the latter is fouled by a runner: "If he (the runner) does it again, kick him in the face!" (Yablonsky and Brower, 1979:70).
- Former baseball star Maury Wills, on manager Gene Mauch: "It felt funny playing for a manager I had learned to hate.... When he was with the Phils and I was with the Dodgers, he used to order them to throw at me all the time" (Kram, 1975:37).
- an Australian soccer coach motivates his team before an important match by showing them Nazi atrocity films. He tells his players to imagine their own families had been gassed and shot, then instructs them to go out and avenge their deaths (Atyeo, 1979).
- Mimeographed instruction list for players on a California football team. Average age: eight (Underwood, 1979:68-69):
  Rules for a Successful Packer to Live By:
  Become an all-out tackler: dig for more yards!
  Punish the tackler! Put fear in his eyes! Bruise his body!
  Break his spirit! Bust his butt! Make him pay a price for tackling you! Dig for more yards!
  Become a competitor! A competitor never quits. Be hostile. Be violent! Be mean! Be aggressive! Be physical! Remember always — loosing [*sic*] is nothing! Winning is everything!

Peers

The importance of peers as "reference others" in understanding violence in fighting gangs, prisons, violent subcultures of all sorts, and among boys and men in general has long been recognized. Respect is what counts. You get it by demonstrating physical courage, gameness, recklessness sometimes, disdain for injury, a willingness to fight if necessary. You lose it by revealing a lack of "heart," "guts," "balls," by "chickening out." "A boy can be big, strong, or athletic," wrote Sexton (1969:129) in her book *The Feminized Male,* "but if he always shrinks from a fight, his reputation as a boy suffers."

Quantitative data on hockey players' violence approval – their own and their perceptions of their teammates' – are shown in Table 4.5. These data indicate that amateur hockey players perceive their teammates as considerably more approving of fighting than their coaches and parents. Sixty-four per cent of the respondents viewed other team members as approving of fighting in at least three of the four situations presented. Comparisons with players' own attitudes, however, reveals an anomaly described by Matza (1964) in his research on delinquency. It is apparent in Table 4.5 that individual violence approval is extensive but not as extensive as that which individuals attribute to teammates collectively. It seems that what individuals say and do about violence in the presence of peers is one thing, but their private attitudes are another. This results in a shared misunderstanding in which individuals think others value violence more than they actually do.

To what extent would athletes privately *prefer* less fighting and other sorts of illegal rough play? The above hockey players were asked, "Would you like to see more, about the same, or less fist-fighting in your games?" Forty-five per cent said less. When asked, "Would you like to see more, about the same, or less illegal stick-work in your games?" 82 per cent said less. How many players quit hockey and other sports because of violence? This question has yet to be adequately answered, but more than a few have done so, one suspects.

Table 4.5 **Hockey Players' Approval of Hockey Fighting and Perceptions of Teammates' Approval of Hockey Fighting by Age and Level of Competition (in Per Cent)**

	Players' Approval			Teammates' Approval		
	Low	Med.	High*	Low	Med.	High
Age						
12-13 (N = 166)	54	25	21	23	23	54
14-15 (N = 196)	37	39	24	11	27	61
16-17 (N = 130)	13	49	38	4	26	70
18-21 (N = 112)	17	24	59	9	13	78
Level of competition						
House League (N = 330)	48	28	24	16	25	59
Competitive (N = 274)	15	42	43	8	21	71
All players (N = 604)	33	34	33	13	23	64

*Low = approve in no situations; Medium = approve in one or two situations; High = approve in three or four situations.

Adapted from Smith (1979c:113).

Closer inspection of the data in Table 4.5 shows that the individual-teammates gap in violence approval closes with age, and between house-league and competitive. Probably selection and socialization processes jointly account for this. As the less proviolent get older, they quit hockey at increasingly faster rates than the more proviolent. In fact the general dropout rate is precipitous after age twelve. Further, as the less proviolent who stay in hockey are socialized into the culture of the game with age, and in competitive as opposed to house-league competition, they bring their attitudes increasingly into line with the attitudes they impute to their peers.

Among the less than half of one per cent of organized hockey participants who in any given year reach the game's zenith, there is even more unanimity. Smith's NHL interviewees were asked how their teammates react to someone who does not fight when challenged. About half were unequivocal: "I'd rather see a guy fight and lose than turn his cheek and not fight at all, and I think a lot of the players are like that. You pretty well realize that you have to fight, otherwise the guys look down on you." The nonfighter is seen as untrustworthy and therefore a threat to group solidarity. "You get a couple of guys trying to beat you up, you know he's not going to be there to help you out. That's a big thing. You don't look at these guys with much respect, really." Being able to depend on colleagues, on the other hand, helps in coping with the uncertainty inherent in a dangerous work environment. This kind of trust is the basis of peer respect in high-risk occupations and environments everywhere, from high steel work (Haas, 1978) to soccer stadium terraces. Several observers of British soccer hooliganism have described it as "the new tribalism," in which the prime value is loyalty to the group – meaning the team and your fellow supporters. One cry such as, "They're beating one of us up in the toilets," is a signal for fellow supporters to rush to the rescue, no matter what the odds or the rights and wrongs of the situation. The cost of failing to do so is contempt, ostracism, or worse (Harrison, 1974).

The other half of the NHL interviewees stated, contrary to Faulkner's (1974) findings on minor league hockey professionals, that fighting per se is not required ("some guys are fighters, some aren't"), but a player must at least be willing to grapple with a man in a melee, to prevent ganging-up, and tough enough to withstand opponents' attempts at coercion. As noted these are also coaches' requirements for players.

As for those whose role is to start fights, the professionals talked about two main types: the "policeman" and the "goon." Both are supposed to (1) protect weaker teammates, (2) put heart into their team by drubbing an opponent, (3) intimidate opposing players. But they go about their tasks differently.

The "cement head" or "goon" does not adhere to the informal rules of fighting (he wields his stick indiscriminately, attacks from behind, etc.) and is thus feared and disliked for his unpredictability and potential to injure (albeit more so by opponents than teammates, who stand to benefit by the havoc he wreaks). "There are crazy people in this game," complained one player, "Why should I get my head whacked by some cement head? A guy whose job is to go out and hit people with a stick! It's crazy! I worry about that."

The "policeman" can be divided into two subtypes. Both stick basically to the rules of fighting; both are respected, even admired, by other players. The first looks for fights – with anyone, anytime; he never avoids a potentially faster gun. The second fights infrequently, but his menacing reputation acts as a deterrent to those who might think of challenging him, or one of his teammates.

Like Bob Kelly, he doesn't get into a lot of fights but everybody knows he can so he keeps the teams balanced. He doesn't have to go out and fight all the time. Then another guy like Maloney, when he was with LA, everybody knew he was tough. It's like, you know, you're sitting in a store, and a policeman is watching you. Just because he's there doesn't mean he has to grab you by the neck. But because he's there, you're not going to try stealing that magazine.

In *Mad Ducks and Bears* George Plimpton (1973:213-14), that master participant observer, recounts a storytelling session at a gathering of former professional football players that conveys something of the esteem in which some violence-users are held in football circles, particularly when it comes to matters of retribution and revenge – what Jack Tatum (Tatum and Kushner, 1979) calls "Big Brother Justice." A player was relating how Charley Trippi of the St. Louis Cardinals once had gotten so angry at another player, he tore the latter's helmet off with one hand, "just like lifting the lid off a pot," punched him with the other, and then walked away. As the listeners nodded, Leon Hart cleared his throat: "Well, you all remember who gave Charley Trippi his – John Henry Johnson, that's who. What a head-hunter he was. He hit Trippi with a roundhouse right, his arm extended, and the plastic surgeons had to redo the whole of Trippi's face."

These player types have their approximate counterparts in other milieus: the Hell's Angels "punchout artist," the Glasgow street gang "gemme boay," the soccer hooligan "nutter." Other sports have their "cheap shot artists," "head hunters," and "hatchet men." Peers judge one another partly on the basis of how these roles are enacted. If not always beloved by their co-workers, these player types at least enjoy in varying degrees a certain notoriety.

Athletes approve of violence, it seems, to the extent that it brings respect and works as a game tactic and career booster. Separable analytically, these uses merge empirically, each reinforcing the other. Though the latter becomes increasingly salient in most sports as players learn the occupational culture, in some sports the former remains important. Professional hockey players, for instance — grown men — cling to rituals of fighting (even when counterproductive in terms of winning) that most males leave behind in the schoolyard.

It was argued in Chapter 3 that prescriptions for violence often take on special importance among males for whom conventional paths to success are more or less closed. Consider the bizarre world of the British soccer hooligan. Marsh et al.'s (1978) account of the seemingly senseless carryings-on of young Oxford United supporters, failures in school and failures in most other orthodox senses, indicates that such youths are in fact "playing a very similar game to the rest of us," namely, struggling to establish themselves as persons of worth in the eyes of their mates.

In the "miniculture" of the stadium terraces, these young supporters carve out hooligan careers. They start as Novices, the only requirement for which is a willingness to learn the role of fan. Some move up to the Rowdies, by far the most colourful, active, and obtrusive group. A few highly committed lads ultimately attain Town Boy status, where they mostly rest on laurels won as Rowdies. Among the Rowdies, the roles of "aggro leader" and "nutter" – rough counterparts of the hockey "policeman" and "goon" – are of particular interest to the student of violence.

According to Marsh and colleagues, the aggro leader ("aggro" refers more to aggravation than aggression) is a boy with proven ability to lead charges against rival fans. The six or seven Oxford United youths who were acknowledged aggro leaders were always out in front in battles against rival fans and always the last to retreat in running skirmishes. They usually wore the heaviest footwear (Dr. Marten boots) and sometimes carried other weapons. An aggro leader may acquire his reputation by actually "clobbering" rival supporters, though this happens infrequently. He may bring to the terraces an already established reputation for challenging teachers, police, and other authority figures, which gives him a "leg up." But essentially he is someone whom the others believe will be man enough to stand up in the stickiest situation – a genuine "hard man," not a "bullshitter." He does not so much seek leadership as he has it conferred on him by his peers, who pay him great deference. One seventeen-year-old aggro leader had this to say about his role (Marsh et al., 1978:69):

> *Lots of the smaller kids really look up to you. Me and Rich – we always get all these kids crowding around us – away matches specially. They look up to you and think you're a good fighter.... [Me] and Rich fight from time to time. Not so much now 'cos they get a big scared – but used to quite a bit. If people start some trouble or something like that then I'll be in there – but I don't go around looking for it or anything like that. If you live up on the Leys [a local housing estate] then you have to fight or else people piss you about and think you're a bit soft or something.... At the football I try to keep out of it. If fans from Millwall or Villa or somewhere like that come down – causing trouble and that, then I'll have a go. I mean, you can't let them come here and think they can walk all over you, because then next time they come they'll get a bit cocky and think they can do what they want. So I'm in there – making them run – that's what you're trying to do – and make them feel small. So we're round outside after the game and down the road after them. But I don't go round thumping people all the time. You don't have to. People know who you are.* (Reprinted with permission.)

The "nutter," of whom there were usually five or six in the London Road End at any given Oxford United match, is an individual whose behaviour is outrageous to the point of lunacy. The key to his status is the sheer insanity of his behaviour, a readiness to do battle no matter what the odds, even if defeat and physical punishment are certain. A typical nutter stunt is to challenge singlehandedly a huge mob of rival fans. Considered somewhat "mad" by the other boys and regarded with ambivalence and even fear by them, the nutter nevertheless enjoys considerable respect and takes a certain pride in being thought half-crazy. The nutter is impelled by the same need as males almost everywhere, the need for peer approval.

Spectators

> *I can remember games with twenty thousand and the place going crazy with sound and action and color. The enormous energy the crowd produces... all focusing in on you. It's pretty hard to resist that (a former professional hockey player).* (Terkel, 1972:500)

One suspects there are few public performers of any sort who are not responsive in some degree to what they perceive their audiences want. Do sports crowds want violence? This is certainly the popular image. Consider McCormack's (1982) content analysis of nine Hollywood prize-fight films made between 1939 and 1980. No matter how crummy, how stupid, how savage the fighters are, the fans are invariably worse. "Kill him! Kill him!" is standard dialogue. In the 1949 movie *Set-Up* the camera lingers on a fat man in the crowd shovelling food into his mouth as the action builds in the ring; a blind man sitting in the arena listening to the fight on a radio screams at one of the boxers to "go for the eyes."

The popular stereotype of the bloodthirsty sports spectator has some basis in fact. "Death as a Spectator Sport," as Australian writer Don Atyeo (1979) puts it, has been a fact of human existence since antiquity. Witness the astonishing durability of some of the animal pit sports, notably cockfighting and dogfighting. The basic mechanics of these gory spectacles have remained virtually unchanged for 3,000 years in some parts of the world. Cockfighting and dogfighting are currently booming in the United States, albeit clandestinely. For several hundred thousand Americans Sunday afternoons mean mutilated and dying animls on blood-drenched dirt floors. Many commentators agree that for watchers, part if not most of the appeal of the blood sports – including automobile racing, rodeo, football, and the other human blood sports – is the promise of violence. "We *are* becoming more civilized," said author Roger Caras in an interview with Atyeo (1979:121). "We do a lot less of this stuff than the Romans did, for instance. But if you were to announce tomorrow that you were going to kill a thousand lions in Shea stadium, the goddam line would stretch from here to Albuquerque, New Mexico and back."

That those involved in the business end of sports believe fans want violence, and merchandise their product on this basis, there is no doubt. Consider the following commercial messages, some merely hinting at the possibility of blood, others more or less promising it:

- "Are you Ready for the Roughnecks!": newspaper advertisement for a professional soccer game between the Toronto Blizzard and the Tulsa Roughnecks, who "swagger into Toronto Wednesday night" (*Toronto Star,* May 15, 1979:B3).
- In a television commercial for professional soccer shown on several channels in southern California, actor Jack Klugman urges viewers to come out and enjoy the thrills of soccer and "see the fans attack the players." On the screen behind Klugman, fans are shown rushing onto a field (Beisser, 1979).
- Winnipeg Jets hockey player and designated tough guy Jimmy Mann breaks the jaw of Pittsburgh's Paul Gardner with a single punch. Several days later a Pittsburgh radio commercial exhorts fans to turn out and see Mann in action at an upcoming rematch between the teams in Pittsburgh (*Sports Illustrated,* February 8, 1982).

- A full-page newspaper advertisement for the Minnesota Fighting Saints, a now defunct professional hockey team, shows one player pummelling another who is lying prostrate on the ice. "When you play as hard as you can all the time," it puffs, "and you've got as many as 17,211 people going nuts every time you touch the puck, things are going to get a little wild. That's the way we play hockey" (unknown Minneapolis newspaper, circa 1974).

- A similar newspaper ad for the Richmond (Virginia) Robins, of the Southern Professional Hockey League, depicts three stupid-looking cartoon characters hitting each other with hockey sticks, and this comment: "Crunching NO NOS are slashing, charging, and high-sticking. Don't let these happen to you; buy a season ticket to the Robins' 74-75 season. Watch it happen to others at our first home game this Wednesday night" (unknown Richmond newspaper, circa 1974).

- The Maryland Arrows, a one-time professional box lacrosse team, hires the Earle Palmer Brown Advertising Agency to come up with a catchy logo and slogan. The result: "Crunch Crosscheck," a Neanderthal brute in lacrosse gear, and the slogan, "You Gotta Be Mean to Play Box Lacrosse," which shortly begins to appear on T-shirts and automobile bumper stickers around the state, sometimes shortened to just plain "Mean" (*Washingtonian*, September, 1974).

- Prior to the 1982 World Squash Championships in Toronto, large colour posters appear around town depicting the two top seeds, Sharif Khan and Michael Desaulniers, glaring at each other nose to nose. "It's a confrontational, combative poster – very real," later explains Desaulniers (*Toronto Star,* January 20, 1982).

- John McEnroe and Jimmy Connors almost get into a fist-fight during a tennis tournament in Rosemount, Illinois, when Connors wags his finger within a foot of McEnroe's nose. A month later television advertisements for the 1982 Molson's Tennis Challenge in Toronto feature footage of both McEnroe and Connor throwing temper tantrums during matches.

The presumptions of promoters of commercial sports regarding what fans seem to want have some foundation in reality:

- Roughly one out of every four interviewees in a survey of roller game fans in Baltimore, Hershey, and Philadelphia cite fighting as one of the appeals of the games (Hinrichs, 1979).

- Quebec City: the city's coordinator of ice sports bans spectators from minor hockey games because they "have been encouraging players to attack their opponents." Six games have been brought to a halt by battling fans (*Toronto Star,* January 25, 1979: A1).

- Muhammad Ali on boxing fans and his alleged lack of killer instinct: "I don't care about all them people yelling, 'Kill him!'... How do I know just how hard to hit him to knock him out and not hurt him? I don't care about looking good for the fans..." (*Sports Illustrated,* December

13, 1971:29).

- 8,000 watchers at the doubles final of the Player's international tennis championship in Toronto roar in expectation when John McEnroe challenges opponent Steve Denton to a fight and strides purposefully toward him (*Toronto Star,* August 16, 1982:C1).
- Australian cricket spectators scream "Kill! Kill!" when fast bowlers Dennis Lillee and Jeff Thomson deliver their 100 m.p.h. "bouncers" at the unprotected rib cages of opposing batsmen (Atyeo, 1979:295).
- Chelsea football team supporters urge British soccer hatchet man, Ron "Chopper" Harris, to drop opponents with a well-placed kick: "Chopper! Chopper! Do your Job!" (Atyeo, 1979:276).
- Over 400 matadors have died from injuries received in Spanish bullrings since 1850, many, perhaps most, as a result of taking dangerous chances in an effort to please the crowd (Collins and LaPierre, 1969).
- Ex-Cleveland Browns football player Bernie Parish (1971:74): "He drove his helmet into the right side of my unprotected rib cage and drove me six yards in the air, straight backwards.... My ribs hurt so bad I thought they might be broken. No official dropped a flag. I heard the Pittsburgh crowd let out a cheer as I hit the ground...."
- The team doctor of the Bath Rugby Club, and a former player, on rugby union: "Before, the crowds would exhort their team to better efforts. Now they exhort their team to maim. Now you hear cries like 'Kill him! Sort him out. Fix him!'" (Atyeo, 1979:189).
- Kladno, Czechoslovakia: fans of Kladno's first division hockey team, well lubricated with *slivovitz*, a potent drink, shout, heckle, whistle, and scream: "Get them Kladno!" "Beat them!" "Belt them!" "Kill them!" Officials, concerned about unruly fan behaviour, organize a highly publicized contest to determine the most sportsmanlike rink in the league (Bell, 1977).
- Dave "Hammer" Schultz, in the mid-1970s the most penalized player in the NHL and a North American byword for "goon hockey": Schultz's army of Philadelphia fans wears World War I German helmets with SCHULTZ lettered in red. They howl in anticipation when he skates onto the ice. Schultz records a tune called "Penalty Box," which shoots to the top of the charts in Philadelphia (Schultz and Fischler, 1981).

The popularity of violent sport is indisputable. But what precisely is its appeal? Theories are plentiful, though sound supporting evidence is not. In *Death in the Afternoon,* Hemingway (1932) claimed that the main attraction of the bullfight for spectators is fascination with the ultimate mystery that awaits us all – death – the certain death of the bull and the possible death of the matador. There is a belief in motor racing circles that many fans go to the raceway for a "death watch," secretly hoping for a spectacular, fiery crash (*Toronto Star,* May 14, 1980). Some theorists maintain that people seek out cathartic experiences, bloody spectacles that serve to purge them of their aggressive feelings, a dubious notion that is dealt with in

Chapter 5. Lasch (1977) has argued that only the ignorant sports fan, the one having no genuine appreciation of the game, is diverted and titillated by extraneous violence and other sensationalism. Others claim that the brutal pseudo-sports – professional wrestling, roller games, demolition derbies – attract a blue-collar following, because they emphasize daring and destruction, thrills and excitement, which particularly appeal to fans trapped in dull, repetitive jobs (Eitzen and Sage, 1978). And so forth.

A sounder explanation of the popularity of violent sports, one based more on research on human behaviour, has to do with the tension- and excitement-generating character of violence – not "mindless violence," as the media are wont to put it, but violence involving genuine drama or "action." In his essay "Where the Action Is," Goffman (1967) writes that spectator sports provide one of several kinds of setting where "action" is readily found. By "action," he means risky, consequential, but avoidable chance-taking: putting it on the line. Professional athletes, for example, place money, reputation, and physical well-being in jeopardy all the time. "It is here," Goffman (1967:185) explains, "that the individual releases himself to the passing moment, wagering his future estate on what transpires precariously in the seconds to come." Will he fail? What attributes will he reveal? Honour, respect, and more are at stake. No matter that some kinds of violence are disreputable; better to demonstrate "bad" character than "weak" character. For those watching and evaluating, this would appear to provide the drama. Spectators at bullfights, auto races, football games, wrestling, daredevil exhibitions, from this point of view, are not so much interested simply in violence as what violence stands for. It is the consequentiality, the fatefulness of violence for those directly involved that explains the appeal of violence to those who watch. Unable or unwilling to risk the costs of violence him or herself, the sports fan seeks action by observing others who are.

When fans identify with performers there is an added dimension; the fans' own worth is now symbolically at stake. This is nicely illustrated in pit sports, where the animals sometimes become extensions of their owners' egos, and to a lesser degree those of the owners' friends and supporters. "Gameness, the willingness to keep snapping or slashing right to death's door, is the quality most prized by dog- and cock-fighters as a reflection of themselves" (Atyeo, 1979:105). If a man's animal *quits* in the ring the humiliation is profound.

In his celebrated study of the Balinese cockfight, anthropologist Clifford Geertz (1972) employs the concept of "deep play" to help explain participants' deep absorption in, and foolhardy betting on, some fights. The notion was first used by the eighteenth-century utilitarian philosopher Jeremy Bentham. By "deep play" Bentham meant a venture in which the stakes are so great it is irrational for people to enter into it, for what can be lost far outweighs what can be won. What Bentham failed to understand from his blinkered utilitarian perspective was that some social acts are engaged in not for their utility or opportunity for material gain, but for something of much greater significance: honour, dignity, respect, esteem, status. Geertz (1972:16) explains why the seemingly irrational sums of money wagered in "deep" cockfights are really seen by those involved as measures of the bettors' moral worth:

*This, I must stress immediately, is **not** to say that the money does not matter, or that the Balinese is no more concerned about losing five hundred ringgits than fifteen. Such a conclusion would be absurd. It is because money **does**, in this hardly unmaterialistic society, matter and matter very much that the more of it one risks the more of a lot of other things, such as one's pride, one's poise, one's dispassion, one's masculinity, one also risks, again only momentarily but again very publicly as well. In deep cockfights an owner and his collaborators, and, as we shall see, to a lesser but still quite real extent also their backers on the outside, put their money where their status is.*

*It is in large part **because** the original disutility of loss is so great at the higher levels of betting that to engage in such betting is to lay one's public self, allusively and metaphorically, through the medium of one's cock, on the line. And though to a Benthamite this might seem merely to increase the irrationality of the enterprise that much further, to the Balinese what it mainly increases is the meaningfulness of it all.* (Reprinted by permission of *Daedalus*, Journal of the American Academy of Arts and Sciences.)

The performer who risks his or her physical well-being – life even – is surely engaged in the deepest of deep play; one's physical health is not worth any amount of money in utilitarian terms. Daredevil Evel Knievel must do what he does for more than money. For the fan the deep play involved in some sports violence thus provides great drama. This, one suspects, is what the sports fan wants to see.

The *extent* to which sports spectators seem to want violence is perhaps best determined by asking athletes. Forty-seven per cent of amateur hockey players put spectators in the high violence-approval category, as indicated in Table 4.6 But this figure masks a wide variation between the perceptions of the youngest (36 per cent) and the oldest (72 per cent). As players get older, crowd composition changes; the proportion of parents – and whatever violence-inhibiting effect they have relative to other crowd types – goes down. Many people who pay to watch junior preprofessional and professional hockey seem to want "action." Twisted faces, shouted exhortations, soaring levels of crowd noise leave little doubt that violence fits the bill for some. Most of the professional players interviewed by Smith considered it obvious when asked if they thought their fans wanted fights. Said one: "Everybody has that insecure feeling that if he doesn't act as the roughest guy in the league, then the owner's not going to want him. The owners believe this is the thing that sells the tickets, and they're right. This is what everybody wants to see." An ex-Junior A hockey player said he quit his team halfway through one season because the fans would not stop booing him. The source of their displeasure: his failure to become a "hitter" like his brother who had preceded him on the team and gone on to professional ranks.

Table 4.6   Hockey Players' Perceptions of Their Spectators' Approval of Hockey Fighting by Age and Level of Competition (in Per Cent)

	Spectators' Approval		
	Low	Med.	High*
Age			
12-13 (N = 166)	39	25	36
14-15 (N = 196)	35	28	37
16-17 (N = 130)	21	24	56
18-21 (N = 112)	16	12	72
Level of competition			
House League (N = 330)	41	23	36
Competitive (N = 274)	15	24	61
All players (N = 604)	30	23	47

*Low = approve in no situations; Medium = approve in one or two situations; High = approve in three or four situations.

Adapted from Smith (1979c:113).

Some players claim to be oblivious to the crowd during a game, but most say they are acutely aware of it when the noise level is high, and they sometimes hear specific comments directed at them personally. Excited spectators can get a team "up," several NHLers emphasize. "The big thing in Buffalo is they really put you up. Like when you score, the fans stand up and cheer, so it's like a medicine; you like the sensation, so you want to do it again."

A former "goon" ("I used to be the policeman on the team, but now I'm the meter maid. Ha, Ha.") paints a picture of the crowd in a different mood and leaves little doubt that hockey practitioners of his ilk, at least, orient their conduct to what spectators seem to want, perhaps in part via the expectations of owner or coach (also see Schultz and Fischler, 1981).

In my first game in the NHL, I played Chicago. We're losing the game six-three, third period, I hadn't got out on the ice. I was called up so people started yelling, "We want Jackson [not his real name]. You brought him up. Play him." So I get on the ice, my first shift, I take a penalty, nine seconds. I two-handed Mikita and I go off. I come back and I run at Hull, and I knock Hull out, and people just go crazy. The next day in the paper in New York you pick up the paper, it was hard to tell what the score was of the hockey game. All it was, was "Bob Jackson fights Hull," "Jackson this, Jackson that...." Next game in Madison Square Garden, we played there, the signs are all over: "Bob Jackson, Pier Six...." (Smith, 1979c:120)

Interaction in Violence

Thus far I have sought to explain violence mainly in terms of social forces that predispose some people to act violently, forces operating for the most part prior to the violent act. I have alluded only in passing to violence as the product of a process of interaction, a dynamic interchange involving two or more actors that spirals into violence regardless of antecedent factors. Some violence *can* be accounted for almost entirely in terms of the aggressor – mugging, for example – but often what an aggressor does is shaped to a considerable degree by what the victim does, and vice versa. Each party orients his or her behaviour to that of the other; in this sense each is the other's "reference other." Viewed in this way violence is preeminently *inter*personal, as opposed to intrapersonal.

Such an interchange may be called a "situated transaction," a term invented by Goffman (1963) to describe a chain of interaction between two or more individuals, which lasts for the time they are in one another's immediate physical presence. Such interactions take place in a social setting where there is some mutual understanding as to what kinds of transactions are appropriate and inappropriate. A situated transaction of violence begins with an initial provocation and ends with a final violent eruption. The events within this time frame constitute our unit of analysis.

Luckenbill's (1977) analysis of seventy situated transactions ending in murder (all known cases of criminal homicide in a California county between 1963 and 1972) reveals that such episodes develop in somewhat predictable ways. Luckenbill reconstructed the "chronology of dialogue and action" associated with each case by analysing all pertinent official documents: police, probation, psychiatric, and witness reports, court testimony, offender interviews, victim statements, etc. From these reconstructions a six-stage model resulted, which, somewhat altered, offers a framework for analysing the dynamics of violent confrontations in sports. All the following quotes are from the field notes of one of the author's hockey participant-observers, a graduate student in sociology, and a veteran of the hockey wars, who at the time was playing in an industrial league.

STAGE 1. In the opening "move" of a situated transaction of violence, 'Other' performs an act that 'Self' interprets as an insult or a threat to his identity, the "situated" identity he claims for himself in this type of situation and perhaps his reputation in general. Other's objectionable behaviour may be unintentional; it is Self's *interpretation* of the behaviour that counts. "Self-image defenders" (Toch, 1969), for example, individuals hypersensitive to actions that appear to discredit their self-image as persons with whom others do not trifle, find such disparaging behaviour everywhere. Other's impropriety may take one or more of several possible forms: (1) a verbal utterance, (2) a physical gesture, (3) physical contact with Self, (4) refusal to comply with a request made by Self, which Self takes as a denial of his ability or right to command obedience and respect,

(5) almost any violation of a norm. To wit:

An opposing player took several strides and hit our defenceman, Mike R., with a high stick. A couple of minutes earlier Mike had shot the puck at their goalie after the whistle (a definite norm violation). Mike retaliated by shoving back with a high stick, and a fight started. (I didn't see details as play was still going on.) Mike eventually was pushed into the open door of the penalty box, with the other player on top. There were two players, one of each team already in the box. Don, our player, tried to shove the fighting players out. The opposing player already in the box (probably construing this as interference in a clean fight – another norm violation) suckered Don (punched him in the face while he wasn't looking – a third norm violation) and another fight started in the penalty box. Both fights were broken up by the referees. Don was still upset at being suckered and made threatening gestures and tried to punch this other guy even though one referee was holding him. One of our players said, "Don't worry, we've got all season to get him."

STAGE 2. Self seeks the meaning of Other's act by (1) asking him, (2) examining his facial expression, (3) seeking eye contact, (4) making an inference from the nature of the act, (5) imputing meaning to the act based on prior interaction with other. In almost half the homicides studied by Luckenbill, offender and victim had engaged in a previous hostile confrontation, a rehearsal, as it turned out. In 26 per cent of these cases at least one of the parties entered the murderous transaction *expecting* trouble. Given such a background, Self has a ready-made "interpretive scheme" for making sense of Other's opening move.

STAGE 3. Self reacts to Other's impropriety by making a countermove aimed at demonstrating strong character and saving face. Not to react is to risk confirming the questions about his character he suspects Other has raised. Self therefore (1) issues an ultimatum to Other to apologize, leave the scene, cease the offensive behaviour, or face physical harm; (2) counters with similar insulting or degrading remarks or gestures; (3) challenges Other to fight physically; (4) retaliates physically. The encounter is over, of course, when either party yields to or is physically incapacitated by the other.

I attempted to check one of the opposing defencemen in their corner and get control of the puck by taking the player out, i.e., physically hitting him off the puck. Play was in the corner for several seconds and one player on each team joined the struggle. After the play was whistled for a face-off, the largest defenceman on their team checked me into the boards, knocking me to the ice, then skated away. The referees then intervened. I got up and told him, "I'm going to break your collarbone." He replied with a menacing stare from a distance. When I returned to the bench, a teammate said, "Don't worry, we'll all take a shot at him."

In a paper with a theoretical bent similar to Luckenbill's, Israeli criminologists Giora Shoham et al. (1974) refer to Other's opening move (Luckenbill's Stage 1), Self's response (Luckenbill's Stage 3), and the relation between opening move and response (Luckenbill's Stage 2) as an *interaction cycle*. They hypothesize that the more intense the acts in the first cycle, the shorter the duration of the transaction; in other words, if an encounter begins with a *very* aggressive act by either party the combatants quickly come to blows, or one backs down immediately. Conversely, the more ambiguous the acts in the first cycle, the longer the duration of the transaction, because the exact meaning of an act having a wide range of possible meanings takes several interaction cycles to clarify. Using a variety of data and methods (analysis of court records, content analysis of fictional accounts of violence, role-playing, field observations), Shoham and his co-workers have obtained considerable support for both hypotheses.

STAGE 4. At this juncture, the completion of the first cycle, Other is in the same problematic situation as Self; return the challenge and demonstrate strong character (and risk a fight), or back down and reveal weak character. The adversaries are now almost committed to what Goffman (1967) terms a "character contest," Lyman and Scott (1970) a "face game" – a dynamic exchange in which each party tries to gain or save face at the expense of the other by appearing tough and cool under pressure.

The presence of an audience renders the situation even stickier, for the cost of appearing weak now becomes public humiliation. Needless to say, in sports there is always an audience of other players and often of spectators. Onlookers were present in 70 per cent of Luckenbill's murders. In every case they contributed to the escalation of the character contest by cheering for one or both parties, by blocking others who sought to interfere (some of whom were injured in the process), by providing a weapon, or by assuming a neutral stance, which seems to have been interpreted by the protagonists as favouring violence. In contrast, approximately half of the already mentioned "rehearsals" of these homicides featured a discouraging audience, which prompted a de-escalation of the conflict. Intervention in these cases usually took the form of onlookers assuring Self that Other's impropriety was unintentional or suggesting that an escalation of hostilities was bad form because the social occasion was supposed to be one for fun and pleasure, as in a "pick-up" game.

Caught in a test of character, Other (1) refuses to comply with Self's demand; (2) responds with inflammatory gestures or remarks (name-calling); (3) issues a counterchallenge to fight; (4) retaliates physically. The latter three responses, unlike mere noncompliance, amount to fairly explicit acceptance of violence as the way out of the impasse. Both parties, their reputations on the line, are now committed to battle, or appear to be. The availability of weapons makes a fight almost certain.

We were down 2-1 with a minute left to play. We pulled our goalie for an extra forward. After the face-off, the puck rolled to the goalie who tried to smother it. I tried to pry it out from under him right on the edge of the crease (a territorial violation). An opponent pushed me from behind, over the goalkeeper. As the goalie got up he poked me with the butt-end of his stick, while I was down on the ice. I managed to get to my feet. I had both hands on my stick: "Anytime, you prick."

STAGE 5. Now, or after more jockeying of the above sort, the physical battle erupts. (1) One person drops the other with a single blow or flurry of blows; or (2) the combatants exchange blows until one falls or gives up, or a third party intervenes.

He dropped his mask and gloves and started punching. Since both of us were right-handed, we traded punches with our right and tried to block with the left. After several seconds, I managed to put a headlock on him, at the same time still punching, but then I lost my balance and fell to the ice with him on top. He got in a couple of close-in shots, then the referees jumped in. They had waited until we were wrestling before attempting to separate us.

STAGE 6. The transaction terminates with the victorious party (1) leaving the scene, (2) voluntarily remaining on the scene for the authorities, or (3) being held for the authorities by members of the audience.

This approach to understanding violence falls under the general theoretical heading of *symbolic interaction*. It rests on the premise that violence takes place in a situation and that the violent actor acts on the basis of his definition of the situation, a definition derived in part from his interaction with the victim and, frequently, bystanders. Whereas up to this point we have tended to depict the violence-doer as a organism responding to external or antecedent forces, symbolic interactionism views the violence-doer as an active agent playing a major part in the formation of his or her own behaviour (see also Athens, 1980; Felson, 1982). But human beings both act and are acted upon. Both approaches are important. The first explains why junior preprofessional hockey players, say, are prone to fighting; the second provides a way of explaining why in any given situation a fight may or may not break out.

Conclusion

"Reference other" theory provides a useful vehicle for the study of interpersonal violence. It facilitates linking within a single framework individual and group behaviour and the sociocultural system. For social structure and culture influence behaviour ultimately *through* reference relationships, and reference relationships are in part sociocultural products; parents, for example, are more or less guaranteed as "reference others" for their offspring. Parents, coaches, peers, and spectators are important "reference others" when it comes to sports violence.

Two types of reference relationship explain theoretically how these "reference others" exert their influence. In a *comparative* relationship the individual learns by observing the "reference other" how to perform an act of violence; in a *normative* relationship the individual is influenced by his or her perceptions of the "reference other's" attitudes regarding violence. Virtually all sports violence research has focused on the latter. Quantitative and qualitative data on hockey violence, in particular, indicate that players perceive a pervasive climate of violence approval, though this varies greatly by "reference other" and by age and competitive level. In the eyes of hockey parents, coaches, and others, violence both expresses strong character and helps win hockey games, the former at all levels of competition, the latter increasingly as performers move upward through the system. Anecdotal evidence suggests that such approval is not confined to hockey. Do players' perceptions of their "reference others' " attitudes regarding violence have an impact on players' behaviour? The evidence is that they do.

The "reference other" approach to the study of sports violence is promising because it offers both a means of indexing the sociocultural climate in which violence takes place and a way of accounting, at least in part, for individual violent behaviour, including that which develops out of a process of interaction. Further analysis of sports violence from this standpoint should include "reference others" and relationships not dealt with in this chapter. The next chapter on mass media effects moves in this direction.

5 Mass Media Effects on Violence in Sports

One winter Saturday afternoon several years ago I was at home when I was startled by a din of shrill voices coming from the garage where my ten-year-old son and several friends were playing ball hockey. Investigating, I found a mock fight in progress. The boys were thrashing in a heap on the garage floor, which was littered with sticks and gloves, wrestling and throwing fake punches in an absurd imitation of a real bench-emptying hockey brawl. One noncombatant, the smallest boy, provided a colour commentary, like the ones then in vogue on professional hockey telecasts. After two or three minutes, the boys disentangled themselves, picked up their gloves and sticks, and continued the game. The "fight" broke out several more times in the course of the afternoon.

This homespun tale may elicit a smile, but its real subject matter – the effects of mass media portrayals of violence on violence in society – has for decades generated heated public debate and a huge volume of research and writing. The Ontario Government-sponsored Royal Commission on Violence in the Communications Industry (LaMarsh et al., 1977), one of the latest in a succession of such official inquiries conducted in about ten countries, amassed a library of some 4,000 titles on the subject, and the flow of work has not appreciably slowed. While this outpouring of energy has not resulted in the conclusive establishment of a direct cause-and-effect relationship between media and real-life violence, the bulk of the evidence, especially that pertaining to television, points strongly in this direction. This chapter is an examination of the evidence regarding media influences relevant to sports violence.

Sports Violence in the Media

How pervasive is sports violence in the media? The omnipresence of media violence in general has been amply documented; 80 per cent of prime-time and weekend daytime television programmes in the U.S., for example, and 60 per cent of the programmes' major characters, are involved in violence in some way, figures that have not deviated more than 10 per cent annually since 1967 (Gerbner et al., 1979). Three content analyses done for the Ontario Royal Commission provide the only quantitative data on sports violence in the media. The first, an analysis of televised sports (whose sampling procedures were exceedingly complex), indicates that an average of about fifteen hours of "very aggressive" and "aggressive" sports (based on a classification scheme involving amount of physical contact, probability of injury, etc.) was televised per week during the years 1961-76. Coverage fluctuated considerably from year to year, but increased over time, from a low of approximately ten hours weekly in 1964 to a high of almost twenty-one hours in 1973. Coverage of "nonaggressive" sports increased at about the same rate (Moriarty and McCabe, 1977). The other two studies are of sports *news* presented in representative samples of Ontario newspapers, and Ontario and U.S. television and radio broadcasts, during a six-day period in late May 1976. Low levels of violence were reported in all cases. Only 8 per cent of the newspaper and television items and 10 per cent of the radio items had anything to do with violence, figures much lower than those for general news (Singer and Gordon, 1977; Gordon and Ibson, 1977). Significantly, however, these analyses were conducted at a time of the year when hockey, lacrosse, and football are, as the authors euphemistically put it, "rather quiescent."

Of course television coverage of live action and violence as news does not exhaust the forms of sports violence in the media. Violence appears in numerous other overt and covert forms. Take televised football, which is edited and manipulated in a variety of ways designed to heighten its dramatic appeal: a devastating hit is replayed in slow motion, the cameras zoom in on an injured player grimacing in pain on the bench, colour commentators argue about who is the hardest hitter in the game. A content analysis of six National Football League games telecast in 1976 (two games from each of the three major networks) found that a full quarter of all the sportscasters' comments was dramatic embellishment of the actual play. Some undetermined portion of this commentary had to do with "interpersonal conflict" (Comisky et al., 1977). An experiment in which groups of college students viewed videotapes of especially rough and not-so-rough segments of a professional hockey game, with and without the original broadcast commentary, revealed that the sportscasters made not-so-rough play seem rougher than it actually was, behaving as if they felt they had to compensate for the lack of a bona fide roughness (Zillman et al., 1977). Precisely how much violence of these sorts appears in the media is not known, but sports violence clearly is not unusual media fare.

Assuming that media presentations of "aggressive" sports often contain substantial amounts of violence, to what extent do presumably impressionable young athletes in fact consume such material? Data from Smith's (1978a, b) hockey survey regarding the consumption of professional hockey perhaps illustrate the general case. To begin with, the majority of these youths (65 per cent) *attended* professional hockey games only two or three times a year at most, consuming the professional game instead primarily through the media, chiefly newspapers and television. Fifty-three per cent said they read about professional hockey in the newspaper on a daily basis, 80 per cent at least once a week. About 70 per cent watched professional hockey on television at least once weekly. Reading about it in magazines and books ranked a distant third. Consumption increased with age, and "competitive" players outconsumed house-leaguers. The comparison group of nonplayers consumed significantly smaller but still substantial amounts of professional hockey through each medium. The only other pertinent data come from Moriarty and McCabe (1977), who report that 83 per cent of 152 youth hockey players, 48 per cent of 45 lacrosse players, and 46 per cent of 44 baseball players, named hockey as their favourite televised sport, all other sports ranking far behind. The hockey and lacrosse players also watched more "aggressive" and "violent" television content in general than the baseball participants. It seems reasonable to conclude that most young athletes get substantial infusions of sports violence from the popular media.

A series of experiments conducted by Dolf Zillman and colleagues (1979) at Indiana University's Institute for Communication Research indicates what has long been suspected: that many fans *enjoy* such content. In the first experiment, groups of college students viewed a videotape of a Grand Master tennis match accompanied by one of three versions of audio commentary. In version one the sportscasters described the play only. In version two they described the play and added comments about what close friends the competitors were (the "friendly contest" treatment). In version three they described the play and added comments about what bitter enemies the competitors were and how they would like to destroy and humiliate each other on the court (the "fierce battle" condition). When the subjects were asked to rate the version of the match they were exposed to in terms of enjoyment, the "fierce battle" group submitted the highest mean rating. Perceiving the match as a tense, hostile confrontation seemed to make it more interesting, exciting, and absorbing to the audience.

In the second experiment, a large number of professional football plays were extracted from televised games and arranged in random order on a videotape. Each play was rated in a pretest on its degree of roughness. Student subjects later viewed the videotape and rated each play in terms of enjoyment. The "very rough" plays elicited substantially higher enjoyment marks than the medium and low roughness plays, especially from the male subjects.

A third already mentioned experiment investigated the effects of rough play in professional hockey. Very rough and not-so-rough portions of a televised game between Boston and Detroit were videotaped and shown with and without the original commentary to groups of student subjects. In the no-commentary experimental treatments, the very rough play videotape received the highest enjoyment rating. In the commentary treatments, the not-so-rough play videotape gained the highest rating, but because, the investigators determined, the broadcasters made the play seem rougher than it actually was, altering viewers' perceptions of the action; not-so-rough play, in other words, when described as rough appeared rougher to the viewers than actual rough play!

"Rough play" is a very broad term. Data in Table 5.1 indicate the proportion of young fans who support fighting in professional hockey (as already indicated, most watch it mainly on television). Players and nonplayers were asked: "Regarding the amount of fighting in professional hockey this year, would you like to see more, about the same, or less fighting?" Although very few of the nonplayers were favourably disposed toward fighting, 36 per cent of the players wanted about the same amount (which is to say, a lot), and 3 per cent wanted more. There is substance to the belief apparently prevalent in the communications industry that promoting sports violence is good business, a point made in Chapter 4 with respect to attendance at live events.

Table 5.1   Fans' Preference for More, About the Same, or Less Fighting in Professional Hockey (in Per Cent)

	More	About the Same	Less
Players (N = 604)	3	36	61
Nonplayers (N = 152)	1	12	87
All respondents (N = 756)	2	31	67

Adapted from Smith (1978a:277).

Learning Sports Violence through the Media

Media models exert their influence theoretically in much the same ways as the "reference others" discussed in the last chapter, but they also differ from these "reference others" in several important respects. First, the media model, unlike a parent or a coach, does not directly sanction, nor is typically interested in sanctioning, the behaviour of those being influenced. Second, the model's influence is always mediated, in ways to be examined shortly, by the communications media themselves. Third, the model's influence may extend to literally millions of people, almost instantaneously in the case of the electronic media, rendering whatever influence is exerted significant in terms of scale alone. Following are the two main ways in which violent media models appear to influence others. We shall refer to these mechanisms as *modelling* and *legitimating* violence, for these are the terms commonly used in the literature on media effects.

Modelling violence

Numerous laboratory and field experiments have shown that subjects exposed to a filmed or televised model displaying aggression tend to exhibit similar behaviour when subsequently given the opportunity. The effect is enhanced when, among other conditions, the aggressive act is novel; when it is realistically presented; when it is justified; when the model is prestigious; when the model is rewarded (or merely goes unpunished); when observers perceive that they will be rewarded for the same behaviour; when the physical and social environments portrayed in the media are similar to those later encountered by the observers (Baron, 1977; Goranson, 1977). These conditions are strikingly apparent in some sports.

Most of this work, however, has taken place in the laboratory, raising inevitable questions about generalizing from this artificial environment to the real world. To wit: most of the laboratory experiments have been concerned with *immediate* effects, subjects usually being tested within minutes of viewing the aggressive model. But in real life, opportunities to aggress do not usually present themselves so readily; the young hockey player who views an NHL game on television does not have an opportunity to engage in imitative aggression immediately after. What about the longer-term and cumulative effects of exposure to an aggressive model? A handful of studies of sports violence, employing both correlational and experimental research designs, goes some way toward answering this question.

Short- and intermediate-run effects   York University psychologist Richard Goranson (1982) has investigated the short-term impact of televised sports violence. Goranson hypothesized that the level of violence in televised professional hockey games should be reflected in amateur hockey games the following day, violent televised games being followed by violent amateur games, and nonviolent televised games being followed by nonviolent amateur games. From the NHL summaries published in the Toronto *Globe and Mail,* Goranson obtained penalty data for all forty-five Toronto Maple Leaf games televised in Toronto during the 1975-76 season. All of these games were played on Wednesday and Saturday nights. Amateur penalty data were obtained from the official game reports of 1,202 games played in the city the following Thursdays and Sundays, within twelve to twenty-four hours of the television games. The amateur players represented a wide range of ages, from six to thirty, and competitive levels, from house-league to junior preprofessional.

Analysis of the data yielded no support for the modelling hypothesis. When the total number of penalty minutes from each televised game was paired with the total from the following day's amateur games, no significant statistical correlations emerged. Nor did the type of penalty (minor, major, or misconduct), the period of the game, the time of the week, the time of the hockey season, the winner of the televised game, the closeness of the televised game score, the age or competitive level of the amateur players affect this result.

Goranson does raise the question of the geographical generalizeability of this result. Toronto is saturated with media coverage of professional hockey, and most amateur players are probably fairly sophisticated fans. Less knowledgeable viewers elsewhere, where hockey is relatively new, such as in parts of the United States, might conceivably be more attuned to and affected by televised professional hockey violence. Laboratory findings showing that *novel* acts of aggression are most readily imitated support this conjecture.

Moriarty and McCabe (1977), in a study combining laboratory and field procedures, have examined the short- and intermediate-term impact of televised sports violence. Two hundred and fifty-nine hockey, lacrosse, and baseball players were randomly assigned by team to "antisocial" or "prosocial" experimental treatments, or to a control group. The experimental procedure consisted of exposure on two separate occasions to half-hour videotapes of sports action, mainly featuring professional athletes, edited to highlight, in the antisocial treatment, physical, verbal, and "symbolic" acts of aggression, such as threatening gestures, and in the prosocial treatment, supportive, encouraging, and approving behaviour. The teams in the control group saw no videotapes. One to seven days after this exposure several observers armed with video machines systemically recorded antisocial and prosocial behaviour in the subjects' own playing. The data analysis produced significant positive relationships between the prosocial experimental treatment and prosocial behaviour in the hockey and lacrosse, but not in the baseball, groups, an effect present at most age levels for as long as a week after exposure. No significant relationships between antisocial media exposure and antisocial behaviour emerged.

Do we conclude that prosocial media models influence the behaviour of children and youth in the short and medium runs, whereas antisocial models do not? The problem is, given the several-week time period during which the Moriarty-McCabe experiment was conducted, a factor that the researchers could not account for could have affected the results: although subjects' at-home television programme preferences were determined, rated on aggressive content, and found unrelated to the subjects' sports behaviour, their television-watching regimen specifically during the experimental period was not ascertained. A heavy dose of prosocial programming during this time could conceivably have negated any effects of the anti-social experimental treatment.

Combined with Goranson's results, however, it must be tentatively concluded that viewing aggressive media models in sport seems to have no *systematic* short or intermediate run impact on the behaviour of viewers of various ages. This is not to say that violence-prone *individuals* suffering from some psychopathology may not occasionally imitate acts of sports violence seen on television. Even a single such event, of course, can have disastrous consequences.

Long-run effects   Two studies examining the relationship between hero selection and violence in hockey address the long-term, cumulative impact of exposure to professional sports violence. In the first study (Smith, 1974), interviews with 83 Toronto high-school players aged fifteen to twenty revealed that those who perceived their favourite NHL performers (almost everybody had favourites) as rough and tough exhibited higher levels of aggression (self-reported aggressive penalties) in their own games over a season's play than players whose favourite NHL performers were perceived as nonaggressive. In the second study (Russell, 1979), 205 amateur players, whose average age was eighteen, members of the twelve provincial and territorial teams competing in the 1975 Canada Winter Games in Lethbridge, Alberta, completed questionnaires in which they ranked their favourite players and teams from among those active in the NHL. NHL individual and team penalty records for the portion of the season elapsed were obtained from *The Hockey News,* a weekly digest of hockey information. The Canada Games penalty records were obtained from the official Games statistics. The results of this study indicate that Canada Games players displaying high levels of "physical aggression" (penalties for fighting, high-sticking, spearing, etc.) and/or "challenge to authority" (penalties for persistent fighting, profanity, obscene gestures etc.) were no more likely than nonaggressive Games performers to select as heroes NHL individuals and teams having high penalty totals.

More than one plausible explanation can be advanced for the discrepant results of these two investigations. To begin with, selecting a cultural hero does not necessarily entail imitating that person's behaviour. As McEvoy and Erickson (1981) point out, the degrees of influence that a cultural hero, or what they call a "reference idol," may exert range from simple admiration through identification and emulation to "worship." (The latter may even entail personal sacrifice on the hero's behalf; recall the Reverend Jim Jones and the Guyana suicides.) Neither study attempted to ascertain the *degree* of the amateur players' attachment to their NHL favourites, but perhaps inadvertently what was tapped in Russell's study was simple admiration and in Smith's some deeper level of attraction, a result possibly of the different ways the questions were phrased or the different techniques used (Russell used a written questionnaire, whereas Smith used the face-to-face interview).

Another point: it may be that a youngster's favourite NHL star is not necessarily one and the same as the individual whose behaviour the youngster imitates. The respondents in Smith's later hockey survey, when asked to name their favourite NHL player, almost invariably chose players noted, if not exactly for their prosocial comportment, for superior skills of a nonviolent nature (see Figure 5.1); yet, as pointed out below, many of the same respondents claimed to have learned certain "dirty tricks" from NHL players unlikely to be included in any ten-most popular-NHL-stars list. In short, the validity of hero selection as a measure of modelling is open to question, though this leaves Smith's positive findings unaccounted for.

Perhaps the explanation lies in the measurement of the independent variable. As Russell points out, the objective measure of NHL player aggression used in his study (penalties) is imperfectly correlated with the perceptual measure used in Smith's (interviewees' perceptions of their favourite NHL players' aggressiveness); the former, after all, is a function of the vagaries of refereeing, and the latter is vulnerable to media distortion. The positive results obtained in Smith's study suggest that the perceptual measure is the more valid.

Figure 5.1   Hockey Player Bobby Orr as a Prosocial Media Model

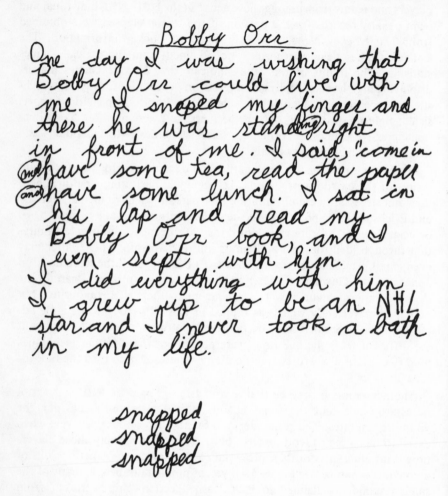

SOURCE: Stephen Smith, age eight.

Smith's (1978a,b) survey approached the modelling hypothesis more directly. The interviewees were asked: "Have you ever learned how to hit another player illegally in any way from watching professional hockey?" Fifty-six per cent of the 604 interviewees replied affirmatively, with only slight variations by age and level of competition. These players were then asked to describe *what* they had learned. A random selection of their responses is shown in summary form in Figure 5.2.

Figure 5.2   Descriptions of Illegal Hitting Learned from Watching Professional Hockey

I learned spearing and butt-ending.
You sort of go on your side like turning a corner and trip him with a skate.
Charging. You skate towards another guy who doesn't have the puck and knock him down. Or coming up from behind and knocking him down.
Sneaky elbows, little choppy slashes Bobby Clarke style.
Hitting at weak points with the stick, say at the back of the legs.
Getting a guy from behind. Getting a guy in the corner and giving him an elbow.
Coming up from behind and using your stick to hit the back of his skates and trip him.
Butt-end, spearing, slashing, high sticking, elbow in the head.
Put the elbow just a bit up and get him in the gut with your stick.
Wrap your arms over his shoulder from the back and tear his arms and stick.
Step forward and stick your foot in front of his foot.
Along the boards, if a player is coming along you angle him off by starting with your shoulder then bring up your elbow.
The way you "bug" in front of the net.
Clipping. Taking the guy's feet out by sliding underneath.
Sticking the stick between their legs. Tripping as they go into the boards.
I've seen it and use it: when you check a guy, elbow him. If you get in a corner you can hook or spear him without getting caught.
Giving him a shot in the face as he is coming up to you. The ref can't see the butt-ends.
Dirty tricks — butt-ending, spearing.
How to trip properly.
Like Gordie Howe, butt-ends when the ref isn't looking.

SOURCE: Smith (1978a:276).

Learning, however, is not necessarily doing. The above players were then asked: "How many times during this season have you actually hit another player in this way?" Two hundred and twenty-two said "at least once or twice," and ninety of these, mostly junior preprofessionals, said "five times or more." Official game records verified these verbal responses; players who said they performed such acts received significantly more major and minor penalties than those who indicated they did not. Viewing aggressive media models in hockey, and perhaps sports in general, does appear to have a systematic long-term impact on the behaviour of amateur players of different ages.

Legitimating violence

The research of George Gerbner and co-workers (1980) at the Annenberg School of Communications of the University of Pennsylvania, who have been monitoring television violence for more than a decade, is representative of a perspective that focuses not so much on violence as such, but on the messages that accompany violence, messages often serving to approve or legitimate the behaviour of violence-doers. Their research has found, tellingly, that young viewers who watch a lot of television are much more likely than those who do not to agree that it is "almost always all right" to hit someone "if you are mad at them for a good reason." As Gerbner et al. put it: the ultimate lesson of television portrayals of violence has been "to demonstrate who wins in the game of life and the rules by which the game is played." Gerbner's research has concentrated on television, but in fact this message is communicated through a broad range of media.

Nowhere does this message seem to be more blatant and pervasive than in media presentations of sports. The proportion of sports violence given a positive slant is not known, but unquestionably the media frequently convey the idea that violence is acceptable, even desirable, behaviour and that violence-doers are to be admired. This is done in a myriad of ways, some crude, some artful, some probably a simple reflection of the unwitting acceptance of proviolence values and norms by media personnel, others cynical, out-and-out attempts to merchandise a product. From a thick file of such material, and employing a broad definition of "mass media," here are some illustrations, mostly from North American hockey and football:

- A hockey writer's scouting report: "Sutter, 22, is a lean (5-foot-11, 173 pounds) lad from Viking, Alta., who played junior hockey with Lethbridge Broncos. He scored 13 goals in 103 NHL games in his first two seasons but earned 205 penalty minutes. He's an accomplished fist fighter and Plager [his coach] claims he's 11-0 in scraps this season" (*Toronto Star,* November 18, 1978:B1).
- The sweat-beaded, unshaven visage of Toronto Maple Leaf hockey brawler Dave "Tiger" Williams, complete with lumpy forehead and bent nose, a smear of dried blood on his upper lip, scowls menacingly from the front cover of a Toronto weekly magazine. The caption: "Don't hold this TIGER" (*City Magazine,* December 10, 1978).
- "Know Your Sports" is a television quiz show featuring sports celebrities as guest "experts": host Dick Irvin introduces former NHL tough guy John Ferguson by showing a film clip of one of his fights, then puts the opening question to Ferguson in approximately these words: "When Dave Schultz broke the penalty minute record last year did he get 192, 294, 348, or 472 minutes?" (Channel 11, Hamilton, Ontario, November 17, 1975)

- Topps Chewing Gum, Inc., Card No. 67: "Andre is one of the roughest players in the NHL. Opponents have learned to keep their heads up when he is on the ice. Andre won't score many goals, but he moves the puck well, and he's a handy guy to have around when the going gets tough."
- In the official programme of the 1979 Pickering, Ontario, Minor Hockey Association tournament, this article entitled, "Here's How to Watch a Hockey Game": "Hockey, we might say briefly, is a six man game; two wingmen, a center, two defensemen and a goal tender. They are all intent on two things, putting the puck in the other fellow's net, and reducing their opponents to a pulp as quickly as possible."
- Toronto's Better T-Shirt Company produces shirts for children emblazoned with caricatures of hockey players gleefully inflicting various indecencies upon one another. "Hooking," "Slashing," "Charging," the captions read.
- "Detroit's Fearsome Foursome" (subtitle: "Murderer's Row"): this hockey fan magazine article fawns over four Red Wing tough guys, one of whom is shown punching an opposing player. Under the picture, this message: "Dennis Polonich is earning quite a reputation with his fist. At 5-6 and 166 pounds, he better be tough" (*Hockey Illustrated,* February 1977:47).
- *Great Moments in Pro Hockey*, a book by one Allan Camelli (New York: Bantam, 1970), is about "some of the men who have made hockey great," including the likes of Ted Green, "1968-69 penalty record breaker." "Hockey," gushes the jacket blurb, "the game of brutality, blood, and beauty."
- Advertisement for a video game: "RIP THIS MAGAZINE IN HALF. A Tough Tryout for Ice Hockey by Activision. You can't be nice on the ice. You have to be tough. So, we've devised this little test to find out if you're tough enough for Ice Hockey, Activision-style" (*Sports Illustrated,* March, 15, 1982).
- "Rating the NHL's best fighters": a panel of experts (hockey writers, coaches, referees, etc.) rates the "best pure fighters" among active players and the "best fighters" and "best fights" of all time. The current Top 10 list, embellished with photos of their "classic confrontations," is highlighted. A footnote explains the scoring system, for the serious scholar (*Toronto Star,* February 25, 1983:B1). (This piece prompted the response shown in Figure 5.3)
- A *Sports Illustrated* article extolls the value of dirty play in professional football. In "A List of Naughty and Nice" readers are told: "In the NFL nice guys don't finish first. According to a straw poll of the players, Oakland is the most-hated team, Gene Upshaw the premier holder and George Atkinson the No. 1 Cheap-Shot Artist. So the Raiders are expected to win the Super Bowl again" (*Sports Illustrated,* September 19, 1977:30).
- "Killer with a Baby Face" is a *Sports Illustrated* story on NFL defensive

tackle Joe Klecko, who "may look angelic, but he has mayhem on his mind" (*Sports Illustrated*, September 24, 1979:32).

- "Conrad Dobler - Pro Football's Mr. Violence," proclaims another writer. "When He Tried to be a Nice Guy, He was Cut from the Squad. But He Came Back as the Game's No. 1 Street Fighter, and Made It (*Petersen's Pro Football Annual*, 1979:20).

- "When the Going Gets Rough" is a magazine piece on the National Basketball Association's six "premier enforcers." An accompanying portfolio of photographs depicts the six in a variety of menacing poses, including Portland Trailblazer Maurice Lucas gazing balefully at the camera from an alley. Lucas, the reader is informed, "plays even meaner than he looks" (*Sports Illustrated*, October 31, 1977:38).

Figure 5.3   A Protest to the Ontario Press Council

Mr. Fraser MacDougall   21 March 1983.
Executive Director
Ontario Press Council
151 Slater St., Suite 708
Ottawa, Ont. K1P 5H3

Dear Mr. MacDougall,

Re: Wayne Parrish, "Rating of the NHL's
    best fighters," *Toronto Star*, Feb. 25,
    1983, pp. B1 and B3.

The undersigned are writing to protest the publication of the above article by the *Toronto Star*, and to request that remedial action be taken.

The article is perhaps the most irresponsible example of sports journalism we have ever seen, for it celebrates, without a single word of critical distance, an activity which is prohibited by the rules of hockey and which has been shown over and over again to be injurious to the best interests of participants and the sport as a whole.

The article begins, "Who is the best pure fighter in the National Hockey League?" and then proceeds, after identifying a panel of "experts" and the criteria employed, to list the "top ten" and then the "best fighters." Every aspect reinforces the idea that fighting in hockey is an important and desirable skill:

— phrases such as "pure fighters," "solid support," "honourable mention" and "best fights" suggest a commendable activity, worthy of approval and emulation, as does the criterion, developed by the panel, that a player has to fight frequently to earn a top ranking;

— the use of NHL referees, the assistant director of NHL refereeing, three general managers, and the distinguished *Star* hockey writer, Frank Orr,

as panelists also gives fighting an air of credibility;
— meaning is not only conveyed by what is said but by what is left out. Completely absent from this story was any mention that fighting constitutes a *major* violation of hockey's rules and frequently is punished by the most severe penalty ever meted out in sport — the loss of competitive privileges. Also absent is mention of the fact that the three NHL officials on the panel and the three NHL general managers, all of whom lent their names to the ranking, have a professional responsibility to not only enforce the rules of the game but to discourage their violation. Parrish's failure to mention these points serves to reinforce the approval given fighting.

We all know that the NHL has practised an unsportsmanlike double standard about fighting for years. But we strenuously object when Canada's largest-circulation newspaper so uncritically joins in the celebration of rule-breaking and hypocrisy. In the last decade fighting in hockey has become an issue of public concern and has been studied at length by both government commissions and sport scholars. Not one of the persons who has studied it has concluded that it is a desirable skill to develop in hockey players, or that the rules regarding fighting in hockey should be liberalized. In fact, reports such as *The Final Report of the Saskatchewan Hockey Task Force* (1973), the (Ontario) *Investigation into Violence in Amateur Hockey* (1974), and the *Final Report of the Canadian Hockey Review* (1979) all recommended that the penalties for fighting and other violent infractions be stiffened. Recently the majority of young players interviewed in a large representative sample indicated that they would prefer not to have to fight in hockey. Unfortunately, there is a great deal of evidence to show that fighting in the professional ranks leads to modelling by the young players and legitimates rule-breaking and violence. Uncritical articles like Parrish's only reinforce this unfortunate pattern. (Michael Smith, "From Professional to Youth Hockey Violence: The Role of the Mass Media," in M.A. Beyer Gammon (ed.), *Violence in Canada* [Toronto: Methuen, 1978], 269-281).

At the time the article was published, several other readers wrote protesting letters which were published in the *Star,* but we do not think this step sufficient. The remedial action we are seeking is as follows:

1. The *Star* should acknowledge, on the front page of the sport section above the fold (the layout of the Parrish article) that the article in question was irresponsible in that it did not indicate that fighting is contrary to the rules of hockey and is unsportsmanlike; and that in publishing the article, the *Star* did not intend to suggest it condones fighting in hockey and other acts of rule-breaking in sport.

2. The *Star* should agree to publish an article by the undersigned, or by someone mutually agreeable, which would outline and discuss the biases present in the sports pages of the three Toronto dailies. This article should also be published on the front page of the sports section above the fold.

If there is any more information you require, please let us know. We shall look forward to hearing your decision.

Sincerely,

Rob Beamish, Bruce Kidd,
Physical and Health
Education,
University of Toronto.

Michael Smith,
Physical Education and
Sociology,
York University.

The net result of such communications, it would seem, is at least to condone the behaviour of violence-doers, at most to glorify it. (See also the section on spectators in Chapter 4.) There seems to be no research on the relationship between exposure to this kind of media content and subsequent violence in the sports context; in fact, as the Royal Commission on Violence in the Communications Industry concludes, there is not much consensus on the effects of exposure to such media content in general, television and films excepted. The effects are probably gradual, cumulative, long-term, and almost impossible to separate from a host of other influences. Moreover the different media probably exert their influence in different ways and with different results. One suspects, however, that these media messages amount to one more way in which consumers, including young athletes, learn that violence is legitimate sports behaviour.

Drive Theories of Aggression and Its Reduction

More than forty years ago a group of Yale University psychologists published an influential book entitled *Frustration and Aggression* (Dollard et al., 1939). The Yale group claimed that frustration (the thwarting of any ongoing goal-directed behaviour) produces a *drive* (an internal state of arousal) to injure the source of the frustration. Dollard et al. flatly declared that frustration always leads to aggression and that aggression is always caused by frustration. Furthermore, they argued, when a frustrated person performs an act of aggression, any act, that person's aggressive drive is reduced; that is, a *catharsis* of aggression occurs. Subsequent research has proven all these claims to be far too sweeping. But Dollard et al.'s formulations gave impetus to the development of two contemporary theories highly relevant to the study of media violence: arousal-aggressive cues theory, which predicts that exposure to media violence *increases* the probability of violent behaviour, and the catharsis hypothesis, which predicts that exposure to media violence *decreases* the probability of violent behaviour. Both theories are concerned chiefly with so-called impulsive or hostile aggression.

Arousal-aggressive cues theory

University of Wisconsin psychologist Leonard Berkowitz's (1969) arousal-aggressive cues perspective was not designed specifically to study the effects of media violence, but has been used for this purpose because of its reliance on film violence as an experimental stimulus. Berkowitz's experiments are of particular interest to the student of sports violence because the film violence he generally used was a scene from the 1949 boxing movie *Champion,* in which the hero, played by Kirk Douglas, is savagely beaten by his opponent in the ring.

Consider this simplified version of a typical Berkowitz experiment (Geen and Berkowitz, 1969). A male subject in a laboratory setting is given an insoluble jigsaw puzzle (frustrated) and insulted (angered) by another male subject, who is really a confederate of the investigator. Both then view the film clip from *Champion* on the pretext that it contains information to be used in a learning experiment, ostensibly the purpose of the study. The confederate then introduces himself formally to the subject as "Kirk" Anderson. (Prior to this he was simply "Mr." Anderson.) At this point the two are given a learning task involving rearranging random combinations of letters. The subject (the "teacher") is told to punish mistakes made by the confederate (the "learner") by giving him what appear to be electric shocks, using ten "shock buttons" representing different levels of intensity. The confederate, who is now out of sight in an adjoining room (teacher and learner are to communicate by means of control panel) has been trained to make prearranged mistakes. The learning task begins, the experimenter recording the intensity and duration of the shocks administered by the subject. At the end of the experiment the researcher explains the real purpose of the study to the subject and asks him if he saw through the deception. Over fifty subjects are processed in this way. In a control condition, other subjects are treated neutrally by a confederate, watch a film of an exciting but nonviolent track race, are informed that the confederate's name is Bob Anderson, then participate in the learning task. As hypothesized, the intensity and duration of shocks delivered in the experimental condition are significantly greater than in the control condition. (There are actually eight conditions in the experiment.)

According to Berkowitz, frustration and/or anger create a readiness or "drive" to aggress, but aggressive behaviour occurs only if aggressive "cues" – a person, a name, an object associated in some way with the present or previous anger or with aggression in general – are present. In the example above, the name "Kirk" linked the confederate to the boxing film and had aggressive "cue value." In another study the confederate was introduced as a "college boxer." In still another, two guns were placed conspicuously near the subject. All these aggressive cues elicited aggressive behaviour. In effect, through a process resembling classical conditioning, a neutral stimulus, e.g. the name "Kirk," by being paired a number of times with a stimulus associated with frustration, anger, or aggression, e.g. the brutal fight scene, becomes a conditioned stimulus having the capacity to elicit aggressive behaviour from frustrated, angry persons. The probability of aggressive behaviour varies additionally, other experiments have shown, with the magnitude of the frustration, the strength of the aggressive cues, the degree to which the witnessed aggression is perceived as justified, and the degree to which it is interpreted as truly aggressive, i.e., a deliberate attempt to hurt.

Berkowitz's theory is a theory of media effects because television and film violence appear to give persons, names, objects, and the like the capacity to "pull" aggressive responses from viewers whose aggressive drive has been "energized" by frustration and anger. The latter of course everyone experiences. Media violence in effect creates a supply of targets for potential aggressors; theoretically, televised professional hockey violence in the mid-1970s increased the likelihood of aggressive attacks on all players named Dave because of their association with Dave Schultz, at that time professional hockey's number-one brawler. It follows that the higher the level of televised sports violence, the higher the level of sports violence elsewhere.

This revised frustration-aggression hypothesis has its problems. One concerns the validity of administering electric shocks as a measure of aggression. Because this is a behaviour foreign to most people, we can wonder if the aggressors in Berkowitz's experiments really believed they were hurting their victims. Another problem concerns the difficulty, if not impossibility, of identifying the unconditioned stimulus in the experiments – the stimulus initially capable of eliciting aggression. In the movie *Champion* is it Kirk Douglas, Douglas's adversary, Douglas's expression of pain, or some other aspect of the situation? Suspicions have been raised that subjects in these experiments guessed that they were taking part in an aggression study, despite Berkowitz's efforts to control for this factor. If angered subjects guessed after viewing the brutal fight scene and being introduced to "Kirk" Anderson that the experimenter was expecting them to behave aggressively, may not they have behaved accordingly? That Berkowitz has reliably demonstrated an association between witnessed aggression and aggressive behaviour there is no doubt; that the mechanisms supposedly producing the association are as he claims is another matter (Baron, 1977; Zillman, 1978). 1978).

Despite these problems Berkowitz's theory has had considerable impact on the study of aggression. Not only has it stimulated a great deal of research on the linkages between frustration and aggression, it has been instrumental, as Baron points out, in directing researchers' attention toward environmental stimuli that "pull" aggression from individuals, and away from the now-outdated views of Freud, Lorenz, and others that aggression is "pushed" from human beings by instinctive forces.

The catharsis hypothesis

Dollard et al. claimed that performing an aggressive act of any sort, in fantasy, even against a target unrelated to the source of the frustration, reduces aggressive drive. The ethologist Konrad Lorenz (1963) later argued, on the basis of animal observations, that watching others aggress, as when attending a violent sports contest, is cathartic. More recently Feshbach and Singer (1971) demonstrated experimentally that observing others aggress on television lowers observers' aggressiveness. From these and other sources has come the stubbornly held popular belief that *vicariously* experiencing the aggression of others "drains off" one's feelings of aggressiveness, thus reducing the probability of aggressive behaviour. The catharsis hypothesis (technically, the vicarious aggression catharsis hypothesis) has been staunchly defended historically by spokespersons for the television industry, who for obvious reasons have used it to defend the industry's predilection for violent programme content. The research evidence, however, is overwhelmingly negative.

Let us examine the hypothesis, as it applies to televised sports violence, by considering this hypothetical situation (Goranson, 1980: 131-32):

A young man is angry because he is out of work and his application for a new job has just been rejected. He is also upset because he suspects that his wife is seeing another man. On his way home to dinner he stops for a few drinks, and the boys at the bar tease him about his wife and about losing his job. He arrives home to find a note from his wife giving a flimsy excuse as to why she went out instead of making dinner. He is angry and confused and he imagines scenes of beating his wife when she returns. As he sits down to wait for her, he turns on the TV. (Reprinted with permission.)

Now consider, says Goranson, two alternative versions of this unfolding scenario:

In the first version, the TV programme shows an exciting hockey game in which hard checking quickly escalates to an incident of high-sticking and a spectacular fight that empties both benches. The fighting continues for several minutes while the crowd roars with excitement. Finally the ice is cleared, and at this point the wife returns.
In the second version, the TV programme shows an equally exciting mile race in which the lead shifts back and forth between the lead runners, and then in the last lap a third runner makes a strong bid to overtake them. The race ends in a close finish while the crowd roars with excitement, and at this point the wife returns. (Reprinted with permission.)

Which scenario, Goranson asks, is most likely to have a violent climax? According to the catharsis hypothesis, the final act in the hockey game drama should be a tranquil one, for in this scenario, watching the violence on the ice should have "drained off" the young man's anger, thereby lowering the probability that he would attack his wife upon her return. In the track race scenario, although the race was very exciting, there was no overt violence, so presumably the young man's anger would have remained "bottled up," then vented upon his wife as she came in the door.

Does this prediction make inuitive sense, to start with? Goranson thinks it does not. Claiming that watching hockey players fight drains off feelings of aggressiveness in the watcher is as illogical as arguing that watching someone eat a sumptuous meal drains off feelings of hunger, or that looking at erotic pictures drains off feelings of sexual arousal. The idea of vicarious aggression catharsis simply does not square with common sense.

Nor does it square with the research evidence, 90 per cent of which indicates that the observation of violence on television, film, or in real life results, if anything, in *increased* feelings of hostility, anger, and aggressiveness and in aggressive, sometimes violent, behaviour. Much of this present chapter has been devoted to an analysis of this research. Goranson's (1980:137) final comment reflects the opinion of most scholars: "The idea of vicarious aggression catharsis seems to be false. I think this is one of the rare occasions in behavioural research where an unqualified conclusion is warranted."

Media Effects on Collective Violence

The mass media have been implicated in the escalation of collective violence in a variety of ways, from television camera crews and their equipment hampering crowd control to rioters performing for the cameras (LaMarsh et al., 1977, Vol. 5), but two theories of media effects seem particularly relevant to the study of sports fan violence. Both attribute continuities and discontinuities in collective violence in time and space to the way the media portray violent events.

The modelling perspective

Modelling theory is fundamentally an explanation of individual aggression. It holds that one learns aggressive acts by observing an aggressive model, live or through some form of communications medium. Whether or not the observer actually performs these acts then varies to a great extent on the observer's perceptions of the rewards and punishments given to the model and likely to be given the observer's own matching behaviour. The work of Pitcher et al. (1978) indicates that these propositions, the latter one especially, have explanatory power at the group as well as the individual level. Employing extensive sets of data on ten different types of group violence, including revolution, civil disorder, vandalism, and air hijacking, they conclude that what happens to violent small groups, organizations, and crowds instigates or inhibits violence on the part of other potentially aggressive groups and collectivities. The Pitcher et al. perspective is a theory of media effects because the potentially aggressive groups and collectivities typically learn the techniques and outcomes of their predecessors' aggression through the media. In fact Pitcher and his colleagues develop a mathematical model that predicts the diffusion over time of collective violence initially reported in the media. (It tends to take on a flattened S shape.)

Perhaps it was not just by chance that soccer field invasions in Britain seemed to increase following the first *televised* invasion in 1961. The prospect of merely appearing in the media is probably inviting to would-be hooligans. Also the media do not just report information but reward and punish by the tone of their reportage; the *way* a violent event is covered may affect the probability of subsequent violence. If early hooligan escapades were made to appear, say, dangerous and exciting, then such escapades were undoubtedly attractive to prospective hooligans. There appears to be no research from a modelling perspective specifically concerned with sports crowd violence, but the theory is supported by enough empirical research at the individual level that such work ought to have high priority.

The deviance amplification perspective

This perspective, a variation on the notion of "deviance amplification," itself a version of labelling theory, has generated considerable speculation with regard to football hooliganism. According to the media-based theory of deviance amplification, the media select and sensationalize an initial deviant behaviour, like violence, thereby creating a public sensitivity to the "problem" and stimulating a reaction whereby the "deviants" are increasingly denigrated and isolated by conventional society. Retreating into the company of their own, the deviants then engage in more deviance, which results in more public vilification and punitive sanctions at the hands of the authorities. An "amplification spiral" is thus set in motion – a kind of stimulus-response sequence – which results in those labelled deviant increasingly living up to the label, the media playing a central role throughout.

According to British sociologist Stanley Cohen (1973), "folk devils" and "moral panics" are continually being created in this fashion. It so happens that youths, in their sometimes outrageous efforts to distance themselves from the adult world, are likely candidates for the role of folk devil; Britain, for example, has seen the rise and fall of the Teddy Boys, the Mods and Rockers, and the Skinheads and Hippies, among other bizarre social types identified by society, in Cohen's words, as "visible reminders of what we should not be." Currently the Football Hooligan is cast in this part.

The treatment of football hooliganism in the British media provides what appears to be a clear illustration of deviance amplification. Early in the 1960s, possibly motivated by the fear of being embarrassed internationally by rowdy fans during the 1966 World Cup scheduled for England, the media began to build up football hooliganism as a major new social problem, the latest in a seemingly endless list since the last war. Television cameras and commentary began to focus on the crowd as well as the match. Reporters went to games specifically to cover the terrace shenanigans. The hooligan story became a weekly fixture in the popular press, Monday's "impact-edited" headlines decrying the atrocities perpetrated at Saturday's matches (Taylor, 1982; Dunning et al., 1982).

The central element of the standard newspaper hooligan story, according to Whannel (1979), is the "quote": an interview with a club official, magistrate, or "outraged bystander," who gives not so much a description of a hooligan incident but a personal reaction to it, often accompanied by an opinion on how the miscreants should be handled. (A return to public flogging and use of the stocks has been suggested.) The language of the hooligan story smacks of what in Chapter 7 is referred to as "riffraff theory," the essence of which is captured in this list of typical newspaper catchwords (Whannel, 1979:331):

Foul-mouthed chants, fans on the rampage, the thugs, the rowdies, rowdy mob, mindless moronic maniacs, brainless wonders, bird-brained maniacs, a ridiculous so-called supporter, English Yobboes sowed panic, soccer louts, the hysterical fans, soccer savages, battling fans worse than animals, latest outbreak of soccer lunacy....

Generally neglecting in-depth analysis (stereotyping hooligans as "moronic maniacs" tends to foreclose further investigation), the press has instead concentrated, according to Whannel and others, on establishing "proof" of a trend toward greater violence ("MORE VIOLENCE AT...") and demanding severer controls ("CAGE THE ANIMALS"). The self-fulfilling prophecy of deviance amplification unfolds: media dramatization leads to public hysteria, which leads to tougher policing, which generates more arrests, which are reported in the press as evidence of an alarming rise in hooligan violence (and coincidentally that extraordinary steps are required to combat it). Hooligans themselves, no doubt revelling in the notoriety, are increasingly drawn to the terraces, already defined for them as dangerous places ideally suited for diversion, excitement, and acting out norms of violent masculinity.

What concrete evidence is there in support of the deviance amplification approach to fan violence? Most social scientists would probably concede that the media have had something to do with the apparent escalation of football hooliganism, but none, one guesses, would claim that the media are the main source of the problem. In fact there has been very little *systematic* analysis of media coverage of hooliganism. The most systematic is Whannel's, and even it is more impressionistic than scientific. Theorists in this tradition, it seems, are guilty of selectively presenting media content to make their points in much the same way that the media are guilty of selectively presenting material for a story.

In any event, there is not much *evidence* that the public either accepts the media's view of social problems, or is affected by it. An English study of the impact of crime news on public perceptions of crime found that though a variety of newspapers did give a consistently distorted impression of crime and criminals over time, the perceptions of the problem held by a sample of the public bore little relationship to the media view (Roshier, 1973). Also, whatever impact the media may have on the public perception of social problems probably depends on a given problem's stage of development.

Hubbard et al.'s (1975) research in the United States, for example, indicates that the media play a significant role in shaping public opinion when a social problem is emerging, but not when it is established as a "problem." Much more careful research is needed before accepting or rejecting the role imputed to the media in the creation of folk devils and moral panics associated with sports fans in Britain or anywhere else.

Conclusion   *intro??*

The relationship between violence in the mass media and violence in society has been a subject of intense interest to the public, to government, and to the academic community for decades. A large volume of research now points unequivocally to a positive correlation between the two, though nagging questions of cause and effect remain, and a considerable amount of controversy still attends the subject.

Beyond dispute is the ubiquity of violence in the popular media. Although levels of sports violence have not been precisely determined, anecdotal evidence and casual observation indicate that sports violence in one form or another is certainly not unusual media fare. Survey research indicates that young athletes consume large amounts of professional sports, through television and newspapers especially, and therefore consume whatever violence is presented. Research indicates as well that a sizeable proportion of fans *want* violence in sports presentations; 39 per cent of a sample of television-viewing amateur hockey players said they would like to see about the same amount of or more fighting in professional hockey.

Attempts to ascertain the effects of media portrayals of sports violence fall into several different theoretical camps. From a learning point of view, modelling studies indicate that young athletes learn how to perform assaultive acts by watching big-league models on television and subsequently enact what they have learned, especially in sports leagues where such conduct is rewarded. This effect seems to be cumulative and long term. Legitimation studies, focusing more on the media messages that accompany violence than on violent acts themselves, suggest that the media approve of sports violence and violence-doers in a myriad of subtle and not-so-subtle ways, including hawking products on the basis of their violence appeal. Such messages add up to one more way in which people learn that violence is legitimate sports behaviour. Drive theories of aggression are less convincing. The arousal-aggressive cues approach, which suggests that the media imbue persons and objects in sports contexts with the capacity to "pull" aggressive reactions from frustrated or angry players (or fans), has been criticized on methodological grounds; the catharsis hypothesis has been proven just plain wrong. Two theories of collective violence – the modelling and deviance amplification approaches – suggest in different ways that the media play a major role in the spread of fan violence. Both theories are intriguing but need empirical support from research directly related to sport.

All told, the evidence is that media presentations of sports violence, particularly at the professional level, contribute to a social climate in amateur and professional sports conducive to violent behaviour. It is a fact that most people are exposed to sports violence not directly but indirectly through the media. For this reason alone the mass media are of considerable importance in any comprehensive attempt to understand violence in sports.

6 Sports Crowd Violence: Descriptive Patterns

Montreal: Horse race-goers smash windows, set fires, and destroy electronic pari-mutuel machines. New York: Boxing enthusiasts brandish revolvers and pelt the ring with bottles following an unpopular referee's decision. Kingston, Jamaica: Rival factions brawl at a cricket match. Veracruz, Mexico: 200 baseball fans spend the night in jail after a ball-park riot. London: Police lay siege to a "supporters' special" football train filled with drunken youths. Milan: A dozen spectators are stabbed and several others killed and beaten before and after a soccer game. Auckland: Police battle a 6,000-strong mob hurling gasoline bombs at the end of a New Zealand-South Africa rugby match. And so it goes. This chapter and the following are an attempt to make sense of such seemingly senseless eruptions.

Several shifts in viewpoint differentiate these chapters from the preceeding ones. In the first place, although spectator violence was dealt with to a limited degree in earlier chapters, especially Chapter 5, this one and the next focus almost entirely on the crowd. Accordingly the emphasis here is on collective, as opposed to interpersonal, violence. Both entail the use of physical force against others with intent to injure, but collective violence also entails at least several and usually a much larger number of people acting to some degree in concert. Additionally, while sports fans attack players, referees, police, and other fans, they also attack property. We thus go from an almost exclusive emphasis on persons as objects of attack to an interest in property as well, even to an interest in disorder involving disruptive, but not necessarily violent, behaviour. Finally, most fan violence takes place in or around the sports ground, but some of it occurs on public transit and elsewhere; we look therefore beyond the sports ground to a greater extent than in earlier chapters.

The Violent Sports Crowd in History

Historical research on sports crowd disorder is in short supply, but a handful of studies - most of them concerned with British football - reveal that the phenomenon is as ancient as it is currently ubiquitous.

Among the first documented cases of sports riots are those involving spectators at the games in ancient Rome. In the fourth, fifth, and sixth centuries A.D. fights between rival spectator factions - particularly those known as the blues and the greens - were a regular feature of the chariot races throughout the Roman and Byzantine Empires. Spectators set Constantinople's Hippodrome on fire four times between 491 and 532. The imperial guard was frequently called upon to suppress the circus factions, slaughtering 30,000 in the famous Nika riots of 532 A.D. Forerunners of the twentieth-century football hooligan, these groups wore their team's colours, chanted and cheered during races, brawled with opposing fans, and vandalized property in and around stadiums (Cameron, 1976; Guttman, 1981).

Isolated accounts can be found of disorders associated with sports in medieval and post-medieval Europe. The disorders never approached the magnitude of those occurring in Rome and Constantinople, probably, Guttman observes, because medieval sports were much smaller in scale and the gap between the roles of participant and spectator much narrower than in imperial Rome; even so, several people were killed in a riot during a tournament in Châlons in 1274, and contemporary documents reveal a general concern with crowd control at tournaments, especially in the fifteenth and sixteenth centuries when the tournaments became grandiose and attracted sizeable crowds. Sixteenth-century Italian duels were plagued by disorderly onlookers who yelled at and spat on the duellists, and occasionally entered the fray, despite warnings by duel officials of severe penalties for doing so (Bryson, 1938). Cockfight crowds in seventeenth-century London, according to Samuel Pepys and other contemporary observers, usually angered by betting irregularities and other suspected dupery, not infrequently stormed the pits, forcing pit owners to hire armed guards to protect valued patrons (Atyeo, 1979). In 1667 a public sword fight in a London beargarden, featuring a butcher versus a waterman, turned into a battle royal between their supporters, triggered purportedly by a foul blow on the part of the butcher (Atyeo, 1979).

Wray Vamplew (1979, 1980), a historian at Flinders University in Australia, has shown that spectators in Britain often got out of hand in the late nineteenth and early twentieth centuries, with the advent of commercialized horse racing, football, and cricket. Boisterous crowds of 10-15,000 regularly showed up to watch horse races in the newly enclosed race courses. Pugilists were paid to protect horses and track property, and police were on hand to guard respectable patrons from the "rough element." In 1879 the British Parliament felt it necessary to pass legislation aimed at suppressing some of the rowdier race meetings. At the new pay-at-the-gate football grounds, upward of 30,000 fans might turn out for an important match. Rowdy behaviour was the order of the day. The 1892 Scottish Cup football final featured an invasion of the field despite the presence of 150 police. Seventeen years later a full-scale riot broke out following a Rangers-Celtic game (See Figure 6.1). Between 1895-97 the English Football Association closed twenty-one grounds and cautioned another twenty-three clubs because of fan misbehaviour. Cricket crowds mainly expressed themselves verbally – whistling, jeering, and booing – but spectators at a 1907

Middlesex-Lancashire match, irate because of an unexplained delay of the game, overran the pitch and tore it up.

Figure 6.1   Glasgow Rangers versus Glasgow Celtic: April 17, 1909

At full time in the replay the scores were level, and, due to a false press report, many fans expected extra time to be played. When it became apparent that this was not the case, the field was invaded by an estimated six thousand disgruntled spectators. A few policemen attempted to stem the flow but they were beaten savagely. Police reinforcements were able to prevent the mob from reaching the dressing rooms, but that was all they could accomplish. Rioters tore out the goalposts, ripped up the nets, and smashed down fencing. Bonfires were made out of the broken barricading and the uprooted goalposts were used as battering rams against the turnstile entrances which were also set on fire. The arrival of the fire brigade signalled further trouble and the firemen were attacked and their hoses slashed. Not till early evening, two and a half hours after the match ended, were the rioters forced out of the grounds and the fires brought under control. Much of the stadium was damaged: Five gates and payboxes within twenty-two turnstiles had been destroyed, a substantial proportion of fencing had been smashed and burned, and a large part of the playing area had been scarred by fire and broken glass; in all, some £1000 worth of damage. Casualties were heavy: Only by a miracle was no one killed.

SOURCE: Vamplew (1980:6). Reprinted with permission.

Nor were the British colonies immune to this kind of misbehaviour. In Montreal, on several occasions between 1875 and 1894, Irish working-class supporters of the Shamrock Lacrosse Club ran onto the field and assaulted players during games against the Protestant middle-class Montreal Lacrosse Club (Metcalfe, 1978). In Sydney an 1879 cricket test match between Australia and England was marked by sustained booing from the stands. When the umpire made an unpopular call, about 2,000 fans took possession of the grounds and scuffled with the players. Order was restored, but later the crowd again invaded the wicket and the match was finally abandoned (Dunstan, 1973). When Australian boxer Leo Darcy lost in twenty rounds to American Fritz Holland in 1914, Darcy's supporters tried to burn down Sydney Stadium and had to be dispersed with fire hoses (Dunstan, 1973).

The history of fan violence from World War I until about 1960, insofar as it has been recorded, seems principally a history of football violence. In fact Dunning et al. (1982) have documented some form of football hooliganism for every decade of this period in Britain. They point out, however, on the basis of newspaper accounts, Football Association Disciplinary Committee minutes, and other contemporary documents, that these years seem to have been marked by a gradual decline in the frequency of fan misbehaviour. Ugly incidents did occur, as when Leicester fans, returning from an away match in Birmingham in 1934, smashed windows, slashed seats, and wrought other damage to the trains, but football crowds in the main were apparently more high-spirited than violent. The increasing presence of women at matches bolsters this impression. An estimated 50 per cent of the passengers on the supporter train bound for an important match at Wembley in 1929 were female, for instance. Dunning et al. question whether women would have attended games in such large numbers if the stadiums had been the dangerous places they apparently once were.

Dunning and his colleagues attribute the relative tranquillity on the terraces in this period to changes in the composition of the British working class, changes that were reflected in the composition of the typical football crowd. A growing portion of the upper strata of the working class during the inter-war years and afterward, they try to show, was incorporated into the middle class. This segment, increasingly adopting middle-class standards of behaviour, began to leave behind, so to speak, a diminished lower or "rough" working class. By the end of the 1950s there was a distinct line between the "respectable" lower-class majority and the "rough" lower-class minority in all areas of social life, including the stadium terraces. There the growing majority increasingly refrained from disorderly conduct and looked with more and more distaste upon the diminishing minority that continued to disrupt soccer matches.

Truly destructive riots erupted from time to time elsewhere. South American fans, with their fanatic devotion to soccer, seemed especially prone to them. Following the 1930 World Cup final between Argentina and Uruguay in Buenos Aires, an Argentinian crowd stoned the Uruguayan consulate, prompting police to fire their carbines into the crowd. Eighteen years later in the same city a soccer referee was beaten to death by players and fans who disagreed with a call. More fortunate was the referee of a 1954 game in Rio de Janeiro who was beaten unconscious by spectators who then proceeded to set his dressing room afire (Smith, 1976). And so it went. Spectator disorder at sporting events is not a new phenomenon.

Frequency of Disorder

How prevalent is spectator violence today? No one seems to have addressed this question directly, but rough estimates of disorder frequency can be gleaned from a handful of studies.

> 1. Bryan and Horton (1976), employing a team of nine participant observers, studied "violent-aggressive" and "unsportsmanlike" behaviour among spectators at a university sports facility in the U.S. rural West during the fall of 1974. They were present at thirty-eight college and high-school football and basketball games, during which they observed three ar-

rests; six weapons confiscations by security officers; eighteen fights; ten outbursts of "rowdiness" (encroaching on the playing area, baiting police, "mobbing" a game official without actually harming him, jeering and harassing half-time performers); six outbreaks of missile throwing (bottles, cups, etc.) at players and officials; four instances of vandalism (destroying stadium seats, damaging automobiles in the parking lot, a locker room theft). These add up to forty-seven incidents, twenty-eight of which clearly involved violence (fighting, missile throwing, and vandalism). None of the forty-seven incidents could be described as "major," according to the authors of this report.

2. Dewar (1979) and an unspecified number of other "trained observers" recorded thirty-nine "spectator fights" during nineteen of forty major professional baseball games (the entire 1975 home season) in a U.S. city. This account says little about how the "trained observers" went about their work and nothing about what constitutes a "spectator fight."

3. Pilz et al. (1981) report that the West German police intervened in twenty-five "brawls" (involving 140 fans and producing 35 injured persons) that took place during the seventeen home games of the first division Stuttgart Football Club in 1979-80. "Brawl" was not defined.

4. Lewis (1982b) inspected the front sports page of every issue of six U.S. eastern and midwestern "regional" newspapers, plus the *New York Times,* the country's widest circulation or "national" newspaper, from 1960-1972, and collected information on 170 episodes of American fan violence. Fan violence was defined as five or more spectators who, during or after a formally organized sports event, invaded the playing area and disrupted the event, fought against other fans or players, threw missiles, and/or damaged property. Lewis's sample best represents the eastern and midwestern U.S., for reasons that will be specified shortly.

5. Smith (1978c) perused the front page and all the sports pages of every issue of the Toronto *Globe and Mail,* Canada's "national" newspaper, from April 1, 1963 to April 1, 1973 and abstracted twenty-seven accounts of "crowd violence" associated with North American sport. Crowd violence was defined as ten or more sports spectators engaged in violence against persons and /or property. Most of the episodes took place in Ontario, chiefly Toronto, with a handful occurring in the U.S.

6. Mann (1979) reports a count of sixty-two "sports riots" listed in the *New York Times Index* between 1950 and 1974. He

estimates that these riots represent less than 10 per cent of "major outbursts" worldwide, but provides no rationale for this estimate, no criteria regarding what constitutes a "sports riot," and no speculation about the sample's geographical representativeness.

The results of these six studies are summarized in Table 6.1. The data are all underestimates, of course, for not all disorders are officially observed, nor are all of those officially observed, reported. Probably the incidents witnessed by Bryan and Horton, Dewar, and the West German police come closest to exhausting the population of events that they represent. But to what extent do the Lewis, Smith, and Mann data, which were derived from newspapers, underestimate disorder frequency?

A study by Snyder and Kelly (1977) is helpful in addressing this question. They found that only about *one in five* of 120 "collective protests" reported in the newspapers of forty-three U.S. cities during a six-month period in 1968 were *also* written up in the *New York Times*. Most of these "protests" were small in scale and only seven actually involved violence, but most sports riots are small-scale. A computation of newspaper-derived data on "collective conflict" in Canada in the early 1960s reported by Jackson et al. (1977) yields roughly the same ratio of conflicts receiving national attention to total number of conflicts. Extrapolating from these findings, perhaps about one out of every five sports crowd riots reported in local newspapers is reported as well in "national" ones like the *New York Times* and the Toronto *Globe and Mail*. The proportion of disorders unnoticed even by local newspapers is not known, but Snyder and Kelly demonstrate statistically that *high magnitude* affairs and those *geographically close* to the reporting sources have the highest probability of finding their way into print.

Using the data shown in Table 6.1 and Snyder and Kelly's findings, estimates of disorder frequency may be computed by dividing the number of disorders by the unit of time (number of games or number of years) to obtain average figures of frequency, and for the Smith and Mann data, which came solely from "national" newspapers, multiplying by five, as Snyder and Kelly's research suggests. The Lewis data need not be expanded in this way; they were taken mainly from regional newspapers and presumably are a closer approximation of the actual total number of disorders. The categories "minor," "serious," and "major" below are those used in the report of the National Advisory Commission on Civil Disorders (1968).

Based on Bryan and Horton's very broad criteria of disorder (arrests, presence of weapons, fighting, rowdiness, missile throwing, vandalism), an average of 1.2 *minor disorders* per game took place (47 disorders ÷ 38 games), 0.7 of which unmistakably involved violence (28 violent disorders ÷ 38 games). Dewar's data work out to 0.98 "spectator fights" per game (39 fights ÷ 40 games).

Table 6.1   Frequency of Sports Crowd Disorder

Study	Data Source	Time Period	Total Number of Disorders	Average Number of Disorders per Time Period	Sports	Geographical Representativeness	Definition of Disorder
1. Bryan and Horton (1976)	participant observation	38 games, 1974	47	1.2 per game	football and basketball	U.S. rural West	arrests, weapons confiscations, fighting, rowdiness, missile throwing, vandalism
2. Dewar (1979)	participant observation	40 games, 1975	39	0.98 per game	baseball	a U.S. city	"spectator fights"
3. Pilz et al. (1981)	police report	17 games, 1979-80	25	1.5 per game	soccer	Federal Republic of Germany	"spectator brawls"
4. Lewis (1982b)	7 U.S. newspapers including *New York Times*	12 years, 1960-72	170	14.2 per year	86 per cent football, basketball, baseball, boxing, and hockey	mainly U.S. East and Midwest	5 or more participants invading playing area and/or engaging in violence against persons and/or property
5. Smith (1978)	Toronto *Globe and Mail*	10 years, 1963-73	27	13.5 per year*	80 per cent soccer and hockey	mainly Ontario	10 or more participants engaging in violence against persons and/or property
6. Mann (1979)	*N.Y. Times Index*	24 years, 1950-74	62	12.9 per year*	77 per cent soccer	mainly U.S., also world	none given

*average number of disorders x 5 (see text)

Employing Lewis's more restrictive criteria (five or more participants, disruption of play, violence against persons and/or property), an average of 14.2 *serious disorders* per year took place (170 disorders ÷ 12 years), some unknown proportion of which could be called "major." Note that some unspecified number of these episodes entailed "disruption of play" but not necessarily "violence." Let us include the Pilz data in this category; they average out to 5.6 participants per "brawl" (140 participants ÷ 25 brawls) and 1.5 brawls per game (25 brawls ÷ 17 games).

Using Smith's even more restrictive criteria (ten or more participants, violence against persons and/or property) an average of 13.5 *major disorders* per year took place (27 disorders ÷ 10 years x Snyder and Kelly's multiplier of five). Mann's average works out to 12.9 disorders per year (62 disorders ÷ 24 years x five).

It must be emphasized, first, that these estimates of frequency are very crude. Second, they are almost certainly underestimates even though they include, in the cases of Bryan and Horton and Lewis, some behaviour that we would not define as violence. Third, as Snyder and Kelly's work suggests, the estimates of the higher magnitude incidents are almost certainly more accurate than the estimates of the lower. Fourth, arithmetic averaging hides fluctuations over time; conceivably the majority of the disorders occurred in one or two brief periods. Fifth, the estimates apply to rather specific places and times; extrapolation to other places and times should be made only with great caution, if at all.

To put the above figures into greater perspective, crowd violence is not limited to sports. Jackson et al. (1977), using a definition of disorder similar to but more restrictive than Smith's (fifty or more people engaged in violence against persons and/or property, compared to Smith's ten) and using the Toronto *Globe and Mail* as a data source, report a count of 129 episodes of "collective violence" between 1965 and 1975 in the province of Ontario, a per year average of 11.7. Most of the incidents were industrial or political disputes. This number would obviously be much higher had Smith's less restrictive definition of collective violence been applied. A more dramatic comparison is provided by Feagin and Hahn (1973), who, using roughly the same definition of disorder as Lewis (four or more participants, damage to persons or property, defiance of civil authority, disruption of civil law), report a count of over 1,000 racial disturbances in the U.S. between 1964 and 1971, an average of 135 per year.

Although not to be dismissed as inconsequential, sports crowd violence, in North America at least, seems relatively infrequent. This is especially true in light of the countless opportunities for such disturbances.

Is Disorder Increasing?

Perhaps of greater interest is whether or not spectator violence has *increased* in frequency since about 1960, as the popular media are wont to declare (e.g., Kram, 1982). In terms of absolute numbers of disorders, this is probably so. But absolute numbers of sporting events have also risen in general – certainly in most major North American professional sports – and increases in disorder *incidence* have not been demonstrated. Nevertheless there is considerable indirect evidence that such a trend has been taking place, beginning around 1960.

Some isolated facts pertaining to soccer in Great Britain and the Federal Republic of Germany, to begin with: between 1946 and 1960 an average of thirteen cases of "disorderly behaviour by spectators" came to the attention of the British Football Association; in the next six years this figure almost doubled (Joint Councils, 1978). Observers of the British soccer scene generally agree that pitch invasions were rare before 1961, when the first *televised* invasion occurred during a game between Sunderland and Tottenham Hotspur, but snowballed after that (Taylor, 1982). In 1977, 7,391 soccer fans were arrested in the greater London area, whereas only 3,500 were arrested "a few years back" (*Toronto Star,* February 27, 1978). On the other hand, arrests at Manchester United's home ground went down between 1972 and 1976, from 280 to 122, while attendance rose (Joint Councils, 1978). A report on fan violence in West Germany sponsored by the Council of Europe states that virtually every first division soccer match now produces police and press reports of injuries, property damage, confiscated weapons, and arrests (Pilz et al., 1981). Police statistics supplied by Pilz reveal an average of 4.5 arrests per game during the 1977-78 Bundesliga (highest league) season and a property damage bill equivalent to $5 million.

There is little doubt that those who have to cope with fan misbehaviour *believe* it is on the rise. In Britain the Harrington Report (1968) on soccer hooliganism noted that over 80 per cent of thirty-three team managers polled, 72 per cent of sixty-eight team Boards of Directors, and fifty per cent of fifty-one police authorities felt that hooliganism was increasing, as did 90 per cent of 1,753 newspaper readers who responded to the same poll. Eighty-four per cent of 944 football supporters surveyed in 1976 by the same newspaper thought that hooliganism was a "serious problem" and an important contributing factor to a 13 per cent drop in soccer attendance in Britain over the preceding five years (Joint Councils, 1978). In the United States a 1978 national opinion poll found that 58 per cent of 839 self-described sports fans thought there was more "unruliness in the stands" than in past years (Kennedy and Williamson, 1978). In 1979, twelve of seventeen U.S. professional sports team executives polled by Burns Security said that "disorderly patrons" were their number one security problem, fourteen agreeing that the problem had increased in the past decade (Whelton, 1978). In West Germany the Münster Hiltrup Police Training School has recently instituted courses in sports crowd control for police officers, and the German Football Federation now sponsors conferences on the subject for club and stadium officials (Pilz et al., 1981).

Control measures are increasingly extraordinary, even in North America where "kid glove" crowd handing is the norm (Whelton, 1978).

- Kiev: a solid wall of green-uniformed troops, three deep, isolates the players from the crowd during a soccer game against Tbilisi Dynamo: soldiers man every entrance and are scattered throughout the stands. A lone fan produces a banner, which is immediately confiscated and torn up by one of the soldiers (*Toronto Star,* September 12, 1973:C6).
- Cardiff: specially trained police greet the "supporters' special" soccer train from Manchester. All incoming fans are lined up, spread-eagled against the station wall, frisked for weapons. Outside the station, police with dogs form a corridor to the stadium over a mile away – one policeman every twenty-five yards (Murray, 1974).
- Madrid: 5,000 police with water cannons are on duty in Vicente Calderon Stadium (known as the "Boiling Cauldron of Hate") for a European Cup soccer match between Atletico Madrid and Glasgow Celtic (*Sports Illustrated,* May 6, 1974).
- Newark: water hoses mounted on trucks are used to douse six to eight thousand overly exuberant baseball fans, an airport welcoming committe for the World Series champion New York Yankees (*Toronto Star,* October 19, 1978:B1)
- Leeds: in a windowless room in the Leeds United soccer ground, police officers sit scanning a bank of television monitors and operating remote control cameras that zoom in on stadium trouble spots (Marsh et al., 1978).
- Lake Placid: plans for crowd control at the 1980 Olympic Winter Games include 1,000 state troopers, 800 security guards, local police forces, National Guardsmen, assorted FBI types, including bomb disposal experts, and a $3.8 million "troop headquarters" and "command post"(Kmet, 1979).
- Berlin: Hertha, a second division soccer team, bans the notorious Hertha Frogs fan club members from its home games and asks other teams to do the same for away games. Members of more orderly fan clubs are issued identity cards with mug shots that gain them access to grounds. Among the Frogs' exploits is setting a soccer supporters' train afire, to the tune of several million dollars damage (*Toronto Star,* February 9, 1980).
- Rome: in a noon address, Pope John Paul II begs Italian soccer fans to watch their favourite teams in peace (*Toronto Star,* March 3, 1980).
- London: the European Football Union fines West Ham United approximately $18,000 for failure to control its fans and orders its game against Castilla of Spain to be played *in camera:* no spectators (*The Times,* October 3, 1980).
- Philadelphia: anticipating an invasion of the field after the sixth game of the World Series, NBC-TV hires attack dogs to protect its equipment. By the seventh inning the outfield is lined with policemen and dogs (*Toronto Star,* October 21, 1980:B1).
- London: British Rail imposes a six-day ban on alcohol on trains between

Scotland and London at the time of the annual England-Scotland soccer match. Any alcohol-carrying fans are to be taken off the trains (*Toronto Star,* December 30, 1980:B3)

- Detroit: in 1980 the Detroit Tigers baseball club temporarily closes a section of Tiger Stadium to "retake it" from "chronically violent" fans (Gilbert and Twyman, 1983).
- Madrid: plans for crowd control at the 1982 World Cup soccer finals to be held in several Spanish cities include 30,000 police and helicopters to fly out severely wounded fans or to ferry in riot equipment (*Toronto Star,* January 5, 1982).
- Pontiac: on duty in Michigan's Silverdome for the National Football League's 1982 Super Bowl Game are, in unspecified numbers, private security guards, local police, state troopers, sheriff's deputies, the League's own security force, the FBI, the Secret Service, and, looking for counterfeit and stolen tickets, a complement of postal inspectors (*Toronto Star,* January 23, 1982:D2).

It could be claimed that the media, by focusing on and exaggerating the problem of fan unruliness, has set in motion a social process that produces spurious evidence of the problem's growing presence – a "moral panic," as it were, in which evidence is generated that the problem is increasing, apart from any *actual* increase. The validity of this claim is discussed in Chapter 5 under "deviance amplification."

Magnitude of Disorder

As for the magnitude, or severity, of sports crowd violence, as already suggested most episodes are relatively minor compared to some forms of violent turmoil, the occasional dramatic exception notwithstanding, though this statement may be truer for North America than elsewhere. In Lewis' 170 "serious" and "major" disorders there were only three deaths. In Smith's 27 "major" disorders there were no deaths and very few reported injuries; no control forces besides local police were ever summoned; the vast majority of the incidents were over quickly and confined to the sports ground. Compare with 238 reported deaths, 9,006 injuries, and 54,494 arrests in U.S. "ghetto riots and interracial clashes" between 1963 and 1970, some of which went on for days (Gurr, 1979b).

The report of the Joint Sports Council/Social Science Research Council (1978) presents no systematic data on violence magnitude in British soccer but does describe a "typical match" as containing more sound than fury. Likewise Marsh et al.'s (1978) videotape recordings of Oxford United hooligans in action show they stop short of real violence most of the time. Marsh reports that during the 1974 season 83 arrests were made at the Oxford ground, an average of only 4 per game, and only 5 of these arrests were for violent offences. During the 1974 and 1975 seasons 311 injuries were treated by St. John's Ambulance, an average of about 7 per game, but over half the injuries resulted from accidents, like falling down stairs. Those injuries that did involve violence were mostly minor cuts and bruises. Marsh's observations are corroborated by Trivizaz (1980), who obtained data on 652 criminal offences committed by football spectators in the London Metropolitan Police Area, 1974-76 (see Table 6.2). Sixty-seven per cent of the offences come under the heading of "threatening or insulting words or behaviour." Only 8 per cent involved bodily assault of any kind, and only 3.7 per cent vandalism. Either the dominant stereotype of the hooligan as a dangerous vandal is erroneous, Trivizaz concludes, or the police tend not to arrest violence-doers. The latter, he argues, is unlikely.

Dunning et al. (1981) demur. Citing reports of court proceedings, they point out that police often charge fans involved in physical "assault" with the lesser charge, "threatening or insulting words or behaviour," because it is more easily sustained. To sustain a charge of assault a constable must identify both assailant and victim, a near impossibility in a melee on a crowded terrace or street. Furthermore the victim, if the victim can be distinguished from the assailant, must be willing to press charges. This he is not usually inclined to do because it means co-operating with the police and taking a "fellow hooligan" to court, actions not held in high regard in the hooligan world.

Additionally, notes Lewis (1982a), based on his experience as an observer with the Birmingham police during the 1980 soccer season at the Aston-Villa grounds, Birmingham police strategy was to "contain" gang fights involving more than a few people and not to worry about arresting the fighters. With respect to Marsh's comments about a lack of "real" violence, Lewis points out that Oxford United is a third division team that neither draws large numbers of visiting supporters nor generates the excite-

Table 6.2   Football Crowd Arrests: London, 1974-76

Offence Category	Number of Offences	Per Cent of Total Offences
Assault on police	50	7.7
Obstructing police	19	2.9
Threatening or insulting words or behaviour	438	67.1
Obstructing highway	46	7.1
Possessing offensive weapon	33	5.1
Criminal damage (vandalism)	24	3.7
Other assault	2	0.3
Drunkenness	24	3.7
Theft	11	1.7
Other	5	0.8
Total	652	100.0

Adapted from Trivizas (1980:278). Reprinted with permission.

ment of, say, a first division Manchester United. The violence of the latter fans may be more virulent, as is suggested below. It seems that on several counts both Marsh et al. and Trivizaz underestimate the amount of genuine violence in hooligan confrontations.

In any case, claims that hooligan violence is of generally low magnitude may be less applicable to the late 1970s and early 1980s than to preceding years. The first soccer hooliganism death in decades seems to have occurred in 1974. It was followed by several more deaths in 1975 and 1976. Six soccer fans were murdered at matches between 1979 and 1982, two others were killed accidently, a dozen or so others were slashed or stabbed with knives, and scores were maimed by other weapons, according to a report in the *Toronto Star* (December 21, 1982). The same report notes that there were also aerial bombardments at games of coins, darts, bricks, bottles, billiard balls, wrenches, screwdrivers, metal washers, ball bearings, and even Molotov cocktails. By the late 1970s, supporters of Chelsea, Millwall, Manchester, and several other English and Scottish League clubs had acquired truly fearsome reputations. The activities of some supporter groups now extended to allegedly National-Front-inspired attacks on blacks, destroying the interior of pubs and shops near football grounds, and extensive vandalism in and around railway stations and city centres (Taylor, 1982). In West Germany, in recent years, more violence has occurred among fans on their way to and from the match than during it, a result of tough control measures within the stadium, according to Pilz et al., (1981). Because some of these goings-on are marginal to the actual football match they may not be reported as football hooliganism. Trivizaz' data, for instance, include only arrests in football crowds. Observations of this sort strongly suggest that there is more genuine violence associated with soccer fans than earlier studies indicate and that violence is increasing.

There seem to be no systematic data on sports crowd riots outside of Europe and North America. One gets the impression from the occasional case study that they are awesomely destructive in, for example, South America, and, indeed, occasionally they are. But in the absence of any systematic evidence to the contrary, it must be assumed that such high magnitude affairs are the exception, not the rule.

Numerous indexes for ordering collective violence in terms of magnitude can be found in the social science literature. But most have only limited applicability to sport because they employ criteria (number of deaths, number of riot days, etc.) that poorly differentiate sports riots, almost all of which would fall at the low end of the scales. In his book *Why Men Rebel* Ted Gurr (1970) shows that the magnitude of collective violence has three underlying dimensions: scope, intensity, and duration. A provisional attempt at constructing an index for coding sports crowd violence based on these dimensions is presented in Table 6.3.

Because newspaper accounts, the major source of data on sports and other kinds of riots, are sometimes ambiguous and incomplete, rather arbitrary coding decisions must be made, like the one regarding the extent of property damage in the example below. Coding decision rules can be constructed to produce coding consistency – Tilly's (1978) research on collective violence in France provides a good illustration – but the present scheme is offered as is for now. The index ranges from zero to fourteen. This soccer riot, an unusually high magnitude affair, would receive a final designation of ten.

A riot erupted during the final of the UEFA Cup Soccer match between Feyenoord of Holland and England's Tottenham Hotspur last night when more than 200 English supporters attacked Feyenoord fans. Tottenham lost the game, 2-0, and the two-leg series, 4-2.

A spokesman for the Red Cross said 130 persons were injured, some of them seriously. Police said about 50 arrests were made.

The fighting erupted at the end of the first half when Feyenoord took a 1-0 lead. Tottenham fans attacked Dutch spectators sitting next to them on the top tier of the 67,000 capacity stadium with bottles and sticks.

The fighting lasted for 10 minutes before police baton-charged the entire section of Tottenham supporters and forced them out of the stadium.

About 4,000 Tottenham supporters came over from London. Police in Rotterdam earlier made 17 arrests when small bands of Tottenham supporters rampaged through the town, breaking shop windows and ripping up traffic signs (Toronto Star, May 30, 1974:C1.) (Reprinted by permission of UPI.)

Table 6.3   An Index for Determining the Magnitude of Sports Crowd Violence

Magnitude	Code			Soccer Riot Example
	0	1	2	
Scope				
Participants	5-19	20-99	100 +	2
Sites	1	2	3 +	1
Intensity				
Dead	0	1-4	5 +	0
Injured	0	1-19	20 +	2
Property damage	none	minor	major	2
Arrests	0	1-19	20 +	2
Duration (days)	1/2 or less	1	2 +	1
Total (number of items x code number)	0	7	14	10

A Typology of Sports Crowd Riots

A typology, as was pointed out in Chapter 1, is a classification scheme whose units of analysis are divided into two or more categories or types on each of one or more dimensions. Most typologies in the social sciences are heuristic: they provide *direction* in the solution of a problem by clarifying concepts, identifying gaps in knowledge, and suggesting hypotheses (Schmitt, 1972). The typology of sports crowd riots developed here is no exception. The thinness of the materials from which it is built - newspaper accounts and a handful of empirical studies - renders it greatly subject to revision as more and better data accumulate. Mann (1979) has constructed a somewhat similar scheme based in part on rioters' emotional states. The following draws slightly from his work, but my preference is to focus on characteristics of riots and rioters that are more amenable to direct observation. Let us begin by making a distinction between an issue-oriented and an issueless riot.

A thumbnail sketch of the changing image of the crowd in history is helpful in making this distinction. During the late 1800s and the first few decades of the twentieth century, European and American crowd theorists, most of whom were socially and politically of a markedly conservative bent, almost invariably depicted riotous crowds in negative and psychological terms: the crowd was irrational, fickle, impulsive, irresponsible, and destructive; the sources of its behaviour lay not in social issues but in mysterious psychological processes, like "mental contagion" (Bramson, 1961). This "mob psychology" imagery still suffuses much popular writing on sports crowds (e.g., Kram, 1982).

Then during the 1950s and increasingly during the 1960s, in the wake of the first waves of black, student, and Third World turmoil of that decade, North American social scientists, on the basis of their usually liberal-to-left ideological predispositions, with, for the first time, a considerable amount of empirical data, began to portray riots and rioters in sympathetic and sociological terms: riot participants were motivated by deeply felt grievances, political ideologies, and legitimating beliefs; they were oriented to issues whose sources lay in conflicts, deprivations, and other problems in the social environment (Marx, 1972; Smith, 1975a).

More recently a handful of scholars have pointed out that while the latter position is definitely a "healthy corrective" to the former, neither position completely reflects reality. Although a spate of research conducted in the 1960s and 1970s ties riots to grievance, protest, and social issues, there is also evidence, historical and current, that some kinds of riot are only tenuously, or not at all, associated with these elements, offensive as this suggestion may be to liberal ideologues. Riots erupting when the police go on strike and in victory and celebration (Marx, 1972), riots "for the fun of it" (Tilly, 1979) and for "recreation" (Beisser, 1979) appear to be several such types. These perturbations Gary Marx (1972:50) terms "issueless," in the sense "that a critique of the social order and the belief that violence will bring about needed social change are relatively unimportant as motivating factors."

I shall designate a riot issue-oriented or issueless depending on the answer to this key question, posed among others by Marx: to what degree was there present a "legitimating belief"? By "legitimating belief" I mean any belief, attitude, grievance, ideology, or definition of the situation held by riot participants that directly ties the riot to some problem in the social structure and justifies or explains participants' behaviour, at least to themselves. Where a legitimating belief is significantly present an episode is issue-oriented; where a legitimating belief is not significantly present an episode is issueless. This is not to imply that issueless riots materialize out of thin air. One can assume that they are rooted, however tenuously, in the conditions of people's lives. It is only to suggest that participants in these eruptions do not develop legitimating beliefs "explaining" their actions in terms of such conditions, that there is no "issue" at stake as far as rioters are concerned. Protest and demands for social change are not significant elements in the genesis of the issueless riot, nor does the issueless riot tend to result in changes in people's life conditions.

A few additional complications and clarifications must be dealt with before proceeding further. With respect to the legitimating belief, a number of questions arise: should the beliefs of leaders be taken as representing the beliefs of crowd members in general? How is one to deal with cases in which people have multiple, perhaps conflicting, legitimating beliefs, or are unsure of their beliefs? What proportion of riot participants must profess a legitimating belief in order to conclude that such a belief was significantly present (Brown and Goldin, 1973)? These questions are apt, but they seem mainly methodological questions and not unsolvable. I shall not attempt to deal with them except to cite Marx who warns that if one searches assiduously into the "nooks and crannies" of any complex body of riot data one can probably find *some* evidence of a legitimating belief, of an issue. To label an episode "issue-oriented" thus requires that such evidence be *substantial*.

Second, the social structural underpinnings of an issue need not be extant for the issue itself to be kept alive. Some issues seem to last in a group memory almost indefinitely. The structural bases of Protestant-Catholic conflict in Scotland may lie more in the past than the present, but the ancient prejudices live on, and Rangers and Celtic soccer fans still fight (see Hay, 1979).

Third, sport itself may have varying degrees of importance in the production of a sports crowd riot. In issue-oriented riots, sport may (1) simply supply the physical setting for the disturbance, (2) fuel an already existing non-sport conflict, (3) provide the catalyst or precipitating factor for the riot, (4) generate both the issue and the riot. In issueless riots sport mainly provides the occasion – the excuse – for the disorder.

Fourth, as Smelser (1962) has noted, some riots have "real" and "derived" phases. In the "real" or initial phase participants act on the basis of the original riot determinants. In the "derived" or "drawing in" phase, participants are motivated by factors partly or wholly divorced from the original determinants; a victory riot, say, turns into a clash between citizens and police as some crowd members use the occasion to vent their hostility toward the latter. The sports riots whose descriptions follow are categorized on the basis of their "real" phases, to the extent these can be determined.

Issue-oriented and issueless riots are "ideal," or purely analytical, types, needless to say. Most actual riots would fall somewhere on an issue-oriented-issueless continuum, as depicted in Table 6.4. The sub-types in the middle of the continuum (the entry riot and defeat riot) are conceived as characterized by an issue emanating solely or principally from some immediate situational problem, like being denied access to a sports ground, rather than a social structural problem, like racial discrimination. The legitimating beliefs of participants in these episodes are superficial and short-lived in the sense that they stem only from the problem at hand.

Table 6.4 A Typology of Sports Crowd Riots

Issue-Oriented Riots		
Structural Sources	Demonstration: relatively organized attempt to disrupt an event and draw attention to a cause	
	Confrontation: relatively spontaneous clash between traditional enemies	
Situational Sources	Entry: relatively spontaneous reaction to being denied a performance	
	Defeat: relatively spontaneous reaction to being denied a victory	
Issueless Riots	Victory: semi-institutionalized revelry following a victory; minimal social control	
	Time Out: institutionalized revelry; minimal social control	

The demonstration riot

> *SYDNEY, AUSTRALIA - The South African rugby team seem to be sleeping well tonight after earlier noisier demonstrations outside their hotel in Bondi were stopped by the police. A young man was arrested and the crowd sang "We Shall Overcome."*
>
> *Yesterday's match in Melbourne, when 650 policemen with truncheons and horses took on about twice as many demonstrators inside the ground and prevented several thousand more from getting inside, has further divided Australia. (The Times, July 5, 1971:1). (Reprinted by permission of The Times.)*

This riot type is the product of a planned attempt to make what is essentially a political statement. Groups of protesters express grievances, make demands, shout slogans, challenge the authorities, march, erect barriers, sit in, destroy property, or otherwise attempt to use a sports event as a forum for drawing attention to a social or political cause; goals may range from merely demonstrating a position to disrupting or terminating the event. The demonstration riot is a form of "modern violence," a term Tilly (1979) uses for the highly rationalized, organized, politicized, instrumental collective violence increasingly characteristic of our time. On the fringe of this category are certain forms of terrorism.

A demonstration per se is not necessarily violent, of course but it often becomes so when the authorities, counter-demonstrators, or others antagonistic to the demonstrators, react with hostility or force. This has been the case on several occasions during the sports anti-apartheid movements of the past two decades. Most of the organizations opposing apartheid profess nonviolence, though they are not above minor vandalism, like spreading automobile oil on tennis courts and tearing up golf greens and cricket pitches. When violence against persons does occur it is mostly counter-violence, as when white South African "rugby vigilantes" living in London assaulted "hippie demonstrators" protesting the South African rugby tours of England in the early 1970s (Thompson, 1975). This division of labour seems to hold for collective violence in general, at least in the modern European experience: the police and other agents of the state do the lion's share of the wounding and killing; the groups they are trying to suppress do most of the damage to property (Tilly, 1978).

The confrontation riot

> LONDON - A bottle flies through the air into the ring at Wembley arena on Saturday evening as Marvin Hagler of the United States, the new world middleweight champion, is shielded by his cornermen at the end of his bout with Britain's Alan Minter.... Bottles, mostly plastic containers filled with beer, and abuse were hurled at the ring.
>
> The trouble was caused by about twenty hooligans in the capacity 10,000 crowd, some of whom booed the American National Anthem. Hagler and his cornermen had to be bundled out by police when the barrage started and a man jumped into the ring to attack the new champion. (**The Times,** September 29, 1980:7) (Reprinted by permission of The Times.)

Participants in a confrontation riot seek more to vent their hostility on a disliked group, its representatives, or symbols than to advance a cause or ideology. In sport, communal spectator groups may clash before, during, or after a contest, attack opposing players, officials, police, and security personnel, vandalize property in and around sports grounds. This type of riot is akin to Tilly's "primitive violence": a relatively spontaneous, expressive, inchoate, small-scale feud, brawl, or mutual attack by antagonistic groups.

At the root of the confrontation riot is social conflict: a struggle between groups over any tangible or symbolic scarce resource in which each side seeks to neutralize, injure, or eliminate the other (see Coser, 1967). Typically such conflict is rooted in racial, ethnic, religious, economic, cultural, political, territorial, national, or other institutionalized differences. Boxing fans' reaction to black American Marvin Hagler's victory over white Briton Alan Minter, described above, seems a blend of national chauvinism and racism. Weeks prior to the fight, Minter had announced publicly, "I am not letting any black man take the title from me," a reaction to an earlier, much publicized refusal by Hagler to shake Minter's hand, along with the words: "I don't touch white flesh." After the fight, outside the arena, crowd members chanted racist slogans (Gammon, 1980: 26-28).

Some manifestations of events that tend to get lumped under the heading of hooliganism are probably best described as confrontation riots. Once a phenomenon associated amost exclusively with soccer in the United Kingdom, so-called hooligan violence has diffused in recent years to other sports, such as rugby league (Murray, 1977), and other countries, such as West Germany, (Pilz et al., 1981; Stemme, 1978), the latter possibly via what Lewis (1982) refers to as "international travelling supporters," hardcore hooligans who follow their teams around Europe. Its most extensive, sustained, and dramatic manifestations, however, are still associated with British soccer. Hooliganism in fact spans several riot types, but when it is based on social conflict, as in a classic Celtic-Rangers clash, it seems best viewed as a confrontation riot.

The entry riot

> *NAPLES, ITALY (UPI) - Gatecrashers battled police at San Paolo Stadium yesterday in its second bloody incident in one week. Police said 13 policemen and at least two civilians, who described themselves as passers-by, were injured in the fight.*
>
> *They said about 4,000 persons trying to crash the Napoli-Catanzaro Italian Cup game, pelted police with stones and bottles. Police fought back with tear gas and baton charges. (Toronto Star, September 16, 1974:C5)* (Reprinted by permission of UPI.)

"Entry riot" is a label for any fracas resulting from fans being denied an event they expected or hoped to see. Its chief variant occurs when would-be spectators are refused entrance to the sports ground. They may have tickets, hope to acquire them, or simply try to force their way in ticketless, as seems to have happened in the case above. Entry rioters may ravage property outside the stadium, fight with police and even with each other.

Knowing the lengths to which fans will go to obtain tickets to important sports events helps in trying to comprehend the depth of their feelings when ultimately thwarted. In the mid-1960s in Melbourne up to 10,000 fans queued on several occasions for eight days to obtain tickets to the Victorian League rugby finals (Dunstan, 1973). Marathon queues are generally orderly (Mann, 1979), but not always. Forty thousand people lined up for as long as thirty-six hours for tickets to a 1967 Liverpool-Everton soccer match, then fought each other for access to the ticket windows when they opened (*Globe and Mail,* January 3, 1967).

Related disturbances are those taking place inside or outside sports grounds (1) when performers fail to appear as scheduled, (2) when there is a long, usually unexplained delay of the event, and (3) following a markedly shoddy performance by a team or individual.

The defeat riot

> VERACRUZ, Mexico (AP) - An estimated 200 baseball fans spent the night in jail yesterday after a riot in a stadium here when the local team lost.
>
> Scores of persons were injured when fans threw empty beer bottles, balloons filled with water and cushions after the umpire suspended the game when hundreds of spectators invaded the playing area.
>
> The Veracruz Eagles were losing, 2-1, to Mexico City Red Devils in one of the final games of the Mexican baseball season. If the local team had won, it would have gained the finals, but when the fans invaded the field, the umpire gave the victory to Red Devils. (**Toronto Star**, August 9, 1973:C6) (Reprinted by permission of the Canadian Press.)

The riot in defeat is produced by a defeat, an event that seems to guarantee a defeat, or some other bitterly felt "loss" associated with a game, team, or sport. An "unjust" or unpopular decision by an official is usually implicated: the referee disallows a goal, allows a disputed goal, awards a penalty, fails to award a penalty, terminates a contest resulting in forfeiture of the game, as in the baseball example above, or makes some other massively unpopular call. The "loss" need not be tied to a specific game. In the Italian city of Caserta, soccer league authorities vacillated for several days in 1969 over whether or not to demote the local team to the second division because of an alleged bribery attempt. When they decided on demotion a general strike ensued, which featured two days of clashes between police and protestors, thirty injured persons, seventy-five arrests, and widespread property destruction, including the gutting of the railway station (Smith, 1975a).

An unpopular official decision, however, does not invariably play a part in defeat riots. Twenty-five people were injured and one person killed in 1973 in Obera, Argentina when fans of the local soccer team rioted after the visiting team, Rio Cuarto of Cordoba, scored two goals within twenty minutes. The account of this episode makes no mention of any disputed ruling on the part of an official. Sore loser fans, it seems, simply reacted badly to what appeared would be a certain defeat (*Toronto Star,* November 20, 1973). In San Diego, California, several years ago, 300 resentful National Football League fans similarly tried to attack the San Diego Chargers' coach after a humiliating loss (Beisser, 1979).

The victory riot

> PITTSBURGH - An estimated 20,000 Pittsburgh Steelers fans braved a snowfall and flooded the city's downtown area yesterday to celebrate their

team's first Super Bowl victory. Pitched battles flamed and more than 200
fans were arrested.

The revellers staged several fights with the estimated 620 city and county
police officers who had been stationed downtown. At least 70 persons were in-
jured and 224 arrested, mostly for drunk and disorderly conduct, before police
finally dispersed the crowd.

Several department stores suffered broken windows as the crowd began
their slow move uptown – and eventually home. (Toronto Star, January 13,
1975:C1) (Reprinted by permission of *Toronto Star.*)

The victory riot is characterized by high spirits, drunkenness, and general
revelry, also vandalism, looting, and brawling. Policing is often minimal. In
1968 when Ohio State defeated the University of Michigan in football,
6,000 revellers turned out in Columbus, Ohio, for a nine-hour binge of vandalism while police looked on benignly (Hoch, 1972). In the Pittsburgh
Super Bowl shenanigans the police stepped in only after the celebration was
perceived as getting out of hand (Lewis, 1982). A victory riot apparently is
seen more as "boys-will-be-boys" high spirits than a threat to public order.

Looting, principally for the purpose of acquiring souvenirs, is sometimes
the chief, and occasionally the only, activity in a victory riot. Raiding rugby
supporters took corner posts, goal posts, line flags, water buckets, and
anything else moveable when Australia triumphed over England in the
Third Rugby Test of 1950 (Dunstan, 1973). In 1969 when the New York
Mets won baseball's World Series in Shea Stadium, ecstatic fans ran onto
the field and ripped up pieces of "magic sod," pulled out dugout
telephones, tore seats from chairs and boards from the backfield fence.
They tried to wheel away the batting cage. Police and security personnel
watched and in some cases even assisted (Klapp, 1972).

The time-out riot

VANCOUVER – Some 5,000 Grey Cup fans, most of them youths, rioted for
five hours here during the night, smashing windows, pelting police and fellow
revellers with beer bottles, and screaming "let's kill them" as police moved in.

It took 150 policemen and 12 dogs to quell the riot. At 1:30 a.m. they moved
in a solid block down Hornby Street in the downtown hotel district, driving
the mob before them and arresting anyone who refused to go quietly.

The crowd pelted paddy wagons with beer bottles and hurled bottles and
drinking glasses against the front of hotels. Some guests replied with bottles
from hotel windows. (Toronto Telegram, November 26, 1966:1) (Reprinted by
permission of *Toronto Telegram*)

This type of riot occurs during what anthropologists refer to as a "time
out": a holiday, festival, ceremony, or any special occasion in which the
usual proscriptions against violating moral norms are relaxed or suspended.
During such interludes, drunkenness, debauchery, minor property damage,
fighting, and other illicit and semi-illicit activities are more or less winked at

by citizens and authorities. The time out is apparently a cultural universal (Nieburg, 1969).

Sometimes sports events provide the excuse for a time out, and sometimes the general boisterousness spills over into rioting. Canada's 1966 Grey Cup festival, described above (the Grey Cup is emblematic of the Canadian Football League Championship), is a notable case in point: celebrants smashed store windows, destroyed street decorations, lit fires in trash cans, and skirmished with the police. Police arrested and charged 260, mainly for unlawful assembly and drunkenness (*Vancouver Sun,* November, 1966). Unlike the victory riot, which it closely resembles, the time-out riot does not require a victory, or even a game. The Vancouver high jinks took place on the evening *prior* to the football game.

Much of what is called soccer hooliganism smacks strongly of time-out behaviour. Most of the scholarly literature on the subject suggests that hooligans are as much motivated by the desire for fun, excitement, and peer status as they are by ethnic, regional, or other animosities. The latter seem more a pretext for trouble than a cause of it. One is reminded of the election day rough-and-tumble of Victorian times. Supporters of each candidate treated the day as a holiday, "sporting their colours, drinking amply to the health of their champion, jeering his rivals, brawling with bearers of other colours" (Tilly, 1978:173).

Conclusion

Based on admittedly skimpy evidence this much seems true: spectator disorder associated with sport is almost universal. It occurred sporadically throughout history but became a more or less regular feature of the sporting scene with the rise of commercialized sport for the masses beginning around the end of the nineteenth century. Since about 1960, possibly earlier, minor disorder has been a regular feature of sport at most levels. Serious and major disorders – genuine riots – while erupting fairly regularly, are infrequent given the innumerable occasions on which they could occur. Indications are, however, that disorder in general and violent disorder in particular has been on the rise since the mid-1970s.

Sports crowd disorder is not a unitary phenomenon; it springs from different sources and assumes a variety of forms. An attempt has been made to differentiate disorders by constructing a riot typology composed of a number of types and subtypes arrayed along an issue-oriented – issueless continuum. It is important to emphasize that *all* these categories are conceived as continua, not dichotomies; each category overlaps and merges with its neighbours. Although the requirements of formal typologies sometimes include mutually exclusive categories, and although it is convenient to speak of "types" as if they were independent of one another, the social world is not so easily compartmentalized in reality. The ultimate purpose of typology building is to pave the way for the development of theory, and it is to this task that we turn next.

7 Sports Crowd Violence: Theoretical Perspectives

> *I'm beginning to see that the real source of the madness is the unconsciousness of the crowd.... Those fans today were murderous. Wildeyed. Angry. Excited. Ready to kill. It's a huge circle. No one is responsible.... It's everywhere, in all of us. (Mandell, 1976:166)*

Such melodramatic exaggeration is standard fare in popular accounts of sports crowd misbehaviour. Rooted in nineteenth-century "mob psychology," it suggests that disorder stems from mysterious pathological forces that compel people in crowds to act like "maniacs" or "animals." The problem with such "theories" is not merely that they are wrong but that they are so entrenched they divert attention from the real determinants of crowd violence. Theories addressing the latter are the subject of this chapter. Our task is to replace outdated beast-with-many-heads stereotypes with social theory grounded in empirical data.

The Roots of Riots: Issue-Oriented Theories

In his classic *Theory of Collective Behavior,* sociologist Neil Smelser (1962) sets out to answer the question, why does collective behaviour occur when it does, where it does, and in the ways it does? The key in his theory to explaining the distribution of collective episodes in time, space, and form lies in the concept of "structural strain." In the case of a riot – what Smelser calls a "hostile outburst" – "strain" seems mainly to consist of social conflicts, deprivations, and frustrations. Indeed a great deal of work in all the social sciences has concentrated on these conditions as root causes of issue-oriented collective violence of every description.

The social conflict perspective

We defined social conflict in the last chapter as a struggle between groups over some scarce resource in which each group attempts to neutralize, injure, or eliminate the other. The scarce resource may be material (wealth, territory) or symbolic (social status, values). Struggles over symbols, Oberschall (1973:50) argues, tend to create more enmity and hostility and are fought harder and more mercilessly than struggles over material resources, because symbols express "the moral worth, claim to status, and collective identity" of groups and communities. Struggles based on symbols also tend to be more difficult to resolve because symbols are indivisible:

what one side wins the other loses absolutely. Conflict based on material resources, in contrast, can often be resolved in such a way that both parties get at least a slice of the pie. In sport the scarce resource is sometimes material, but it almost always is symbolic as well, and often exclusively so. Therein lies the potency of sport as a generator of intergroup confict.

Social conflict typically is based on class, racial, religious, or other institutionalized group differences, but not necessarily. In their famous field experiments on intergroup competition and conflict, the Sherifs (1969) and their collaborators demonstrated that given a *competitive structure* conflict, negative stereotyping, hostility, and violence may occur even between groups whose members have *similar* backgrounds, provided the competition takes place repeatedly over time and focuses on goals that are highly valued by both sides but that can be attained by only one. Thus sport alone can generate conflict, less virulent perhaps than that produced by more fundamental group cleavages, but conflict nonetheless. Recall the animosity, name-calling, and occasional exchange of fisticuffs between rival minor hockey parents described in Chapter 4.

Social conflict tends to produce a sense of collective identity. The latter, according to Klapp (1972), can be considered in terms of two extremes: there is the relatively shallow and transitory "we" feeling shared by sports spectators who have little else in common but allegiance to their team or individual athlete; then there is the deeper, more permanent "we" felt by people who have a common background, especially if it has been one of deprivation and persecution. The identification, for example, of black Americans with the boxer Joe Louis in his heyday was apparently extraordinarily intense. Louis was what Klapp (1972:77) would call a "group superself": an individual who embodies "on a large scale – through acts, style, or personality traits – what the group believes and wishes itself to be." A special pride is felt when a "group superself" succeeds, a special disappointment when a superself fails, a special bitterness when a superself is wronged.

Nowhere is all this more vividly enacted than in Jamaica on the occasion of a West Indies-England cricket match. In Figure 7.1 Orlando Patterson (1969), lecturer in sociology at the University of the West Indies, describes the scene at Sabina Park, Kingston, prior to a 1968 test match that ended in a pitched battle between spectators and police. "The wonder of it," writes Patterson, "is not that there have been so many confrontations of this sort, but that there have been so few!"

Figure 7.1   The 1968 Kingston Cricket Riot

At Sabina Park, on that Monday afternoon, both the setting and the game were like a microcosm of Jamaican society.

At the western end of the ground was the pavilion, its members over 90 per cent white or very light in colour — the rich and the upper class. The few browns and blacks were typical of those outsiders who have made it in this group: the Governor-General — black, resplendently attired; his wife a little way down, amid a group of patronising white ladies — cheerful, chubby and well dressed, looking like a black version of the Queen Mother. A few government ministers, the odd uppity civil servant, the occasional black businessman.

Opposite the pavilion, at the eastern end of the ground, were the "bleachers" — i.e., the hard wooden benches beneath the hot sun, every inch of which exploded with people. Here were the masses, securely fenced off from the rest of the ground with chicken wire. Their faces were nearly all black. The very rare white or "high brown" face belonged, as often as not, to some too-earnest member of the university.

Then, at the northern end, were the covered stands with concrete seats. The spectators here were better clad; their colour, on average, a cooler shade of black. There were fences here, too. But not as high as the ones in front of the bleachers. Here it was possible to move about more freely. With the naked eye one could from here just about scan the cream on the pavilion.

Finally, there was the southern grandstand: clean, shaded, comfortable, the view excellent, the spectators orderly and well dressed. They shared with the pavilion the privilege of having no fences. And occasionally there was an exchange of greetings between a spectator from this grandstand with one from the pavilion — always polite, always cordial but with a lingering flavour of awkwardness.

And now the game. Cricket is the Englishman's game. The very name, cricket, has become a byword. Its vocabulary is a pool of stock images for Tory statesmen. No better symbol of English culture could be found. Yet this is the game which West Indians have usurped, have come to master. The former colonial has learnt, often, how to beat his ex-master at his own game.

This brings out all the ambivalence of the black lower-class West Indian towards English culture. If we West Indians love cricket it is because it is the only game we can play well, the only activity which gives us some international prestige. But it is the game, deep down, which we must hate — the game of the master. So victory — victory against the Englishmen — is a matter of great moment.

Cricket also gives the West Indian masses a weapon against their current oppressors, the carriers of the dominant English culture in local society. The present West Indian team is almost entirely dark brown or black and of lower-class origin. During the bad old days, when the West Indian team was dominated by whites, no riots ever took place. The really popular West Indian cricketers are not Sobers, the captain, or the spectacular batsman, Kanhai (who is of Indian origin), but the fast bowlers, Hall and Griffith, whose colour is very dark.

One reason perhaps is that they are pacemen. No one who has seen Hall making his long muscular run-up to the wicket can fail to be impressed by the beautiful, sweet violence of the act — the slow, menacing beginning, the gathering pace, the sudden climactic explosion of energy on delivery, the dashing follow-through, the plight of the lonely batsman. In this moment of truth, it is "Us" versus "Them."

A test match is in fact one of the few exceptional occasions when the West Indian lower classes feel solidarity. The atomism created by poverty, conflicting values and charismatic politics loses its divisiveness in the presence of the game. Here at last, via the medium of genuine heroes — the only heroes in a land barren of other heroes or a heroic tradition — the masses respond as one, share a common experience, bite their nails in a common war of nerves against a common enemy — against "Them."

SOURCE: Patterson (1969:988-89). Reprinted with permission.

Where there is a "we" there is a "they." Collective identity is sharpened by, and sometimes contributes to, conflict with other groups. The outgroup is negatively stereotyped; in-group members draw closer together in common cause. This had been empirically demonstrated time and again, probably most dramatically by the Sherifs. Promoters of commercial sport are only too aware of these dynamics, "hyping" the gate by staging contests that capitalize on intergroup conflict and identity. Such contests are euphemistically termed "natural rivalries." The role of the media in this process is illustrated in Figure 7.2, in this case an attempt to create fan interest by playing on Canadian Anglophone-Francophone friction. One is immediately reminded of Canada's most famous sports riot, the 1955 "Rocket" Richard hockey row. In an analysis of "l'Affaire Richard," Duperreault (1981) fixes the lion's share of the blame for the riot on the Montreal press, whose frenzied, inflammatory reporting turned the suspension of French-Canadian scoring star Maurice "Rocket" Richard by Anglo-Saxon National Hockey League President Clarence Campbell into a case of English racism. It is not hard to see in such instances how the struggle on the sports field takes on the dimension of the wider conflict.

Figure 7.2   Sports Journalism as Gate "Hyping": Playing on Collective Identity and Conflict

A HOCKEY WAR IS BREWING

Unless everybody is dead wrong, there's a very untidy little war brewing at the moment which evokes, though on a much smaller scale, memories of the Wolfe-Montcalm scrap of earlier years on nearby Plains of Abraham.

Toronto Toros venture into Quebec City Saturday night for their World Hockey Association season opener against the Nordiques.

The trumpets have been sounding a couple of days now. Forget the English Canada versus French Canada thing. That's secondary to the sports issues.

Here are two clubs attempting to shake off reputations as patsies and assert themselves more physically. Both have made this an important part of their sales pitch....

While neither side will admit it is coming out Saturday night with guns blazing, neither denies a readiness to meet force with more force.

"We're going in there to win and take two points out and if it requires rugged play, we're going to get the points," says Toros' manager Gilles Leger. "In case of trouble, we've got a lot of rough players."...

"Everybody tried to kill us, figuring you run at the Nordiques, you beat them," said Filion. "Well, that's all changed. We have guys who can hit pretty good, too."

SOURCE: *Toronto Star*, October 8, 1975: C2. Reprinted with permission.

The social deprivation perspective

This perspective centres on groups that are absolutely or relatively deprived in terms of life quality and chances. It has several variants, each of which enjoys some support from empirical research.

The "absolute deprivation" hypothesis suggests that riots occur when a group's living conditions are very bad in objective terms. The "powder-keg" view of prison riots is in this tradition: violence supposedly erupts when overcrowding, inadequate food, guard brutality, and other oppressive conditions create a mood of tension that eventually explodes in violence (Perry and Pugh, 1979).

The "relative deprivation" hypothesis suggests that riots break out when a group perceives a discrepancy between the conditions of life to which it feels it is rightfully entitled and those that it has actually achieved. Even though people may not appear wanting in objective terms, they may *feel* deprived when they compare themselves with what they once had or with what some other group has. The "rising expectations" version of this thesis predicts that violence is most likely to occur when a prolonged period of improvement in the objective living conditions of a deprived group is followed by a short, sharp setback. The period of improvement, it seems, produces an expectation that life will continue to get better, even in the face of objective evidence that it will not; violence erupts when an "intolerable gap" develops between what people expect and what they get (Gurr, 1970).

Then there is the "deprivation-frustration-aggression" hypothesis. Most research on social deprivation and collective violence either explicitly or implicitly assumes that deprivation leads to frustration, which produces aggression in the form of rioting. Likewise, frustration-aggression approaches to collective violence usually assume some condition of social deprivation.

Rarely, however, are all three variables measured and their relationships examined empirically (McPhail, 1971). Note that frustration may be used as an aggregate-level variable and as an individual-level, or psychological, variable. The rather complex relationships between *social* deprivation and *individual* frustration and aggression are detailed in Chapter 2 of Gurr's (1970) book, *Why Men Rebel.*

Social deprivation perspectives predict that absolutely or relatively deprived or frustrated groups have a greater propensity than more advantaged ones to riot in sports contexts in the same way as they have a greater propensity to riot in other settings. This may be so, but perhaps deprivation also affects the probability of rioting indirectly via collective identification.

It has already been suggested that deprived groups are particularly prone to intense identification with "their" teams and athletes. Consider the legendary commitment to their soccer teams of the "masses" in some Latin American countries, where the bulk of the population lives in poverty, where most top-level players also come from poor backgrounds (Lever, 1972;1983), and where soccer riots have been a fact of life since the 1930s. As Hecht (1968:743) writes in *Handbook of Latin America and the Caribbean,* "Sport as a matter of patriotic pride is not uniquely a Latin American institution, but nowhere else perhaps is it so intensely identified by the people with their personal and national honour." A defeat in an important soccer match may precipitate a riot by a deprived group in part because of members' strong emotional attachment to their team.

Issue-oriented sports riots are relatively comprehensible, at least theoretically, in the sense that they can be traced more or less directly to their source, whether this be conflict, deprivation, frustration, or some other "strain." Issueless riots are less easy to explain.

The Roots of Riots: Issueless Theories

Most "theories" applicable to issueless riots are not well developed, hence we use the term loosely. Furthermore most of these theories deal with collective violence only tangentially. Nevertheless several "theoretical perspectives" go some way toward helping understand the issueless sports riot. Like issue-oriented theories, most of these perspectives begin with some notion of structural strain - life is fundamentally repressive, unrewarding, frustrating, etc., at least for some groups - but unlike issue-oriented theories, issueless theories posit no conscious association in the minds of rioters of their behaviour with the conditions under which they live - no "legitimating beliefs." To the contrary, according to a number of these theories, riotous behaviour precludes the development of such consciousness by diverting attention from, draining off, or in some other way controlling societal tensions before an "issue" can develop. Let us examine several theories relevant to the issueless riot under three headings: time out, subculture, and class.

The time-out perspective

As noted in the last chapter, a "time out" is a period of "legitimate deviance," a time when, or place where, deviant behaviour on a large scale is tolerated, even encouraged. Social controls are minimal, and almost anything goes, including, to a point, aggressive behaviour (Listiak, 1974). Some time-out theories examine the function of these interludes from the standpoint of the participants, some from the standpoint of the forces of social control.

In the first category is Elias and Dunning's (1970) view of the time out, together with other modes of thrill seeking, as a "search for excitement in unexciting societies." Time-out behaviour is a relatively acceptable way of temporarily breaking free of the social controls on the expression of excitement and other strong emotions, controls, according to Elias's theory of civilization, that are characteristic of the present stage in the "civilizing process." Presumably such controls have not yet been fully internalized in the human personality.

The "football Saturday" view of hooliganism is of this genre. As expressed by Corrigan (1977), football hooliganism is part and parcel of the working-class Saturday, a day of liberation and excitement in what for many working-class youth is an otherwise numbingly boring week of work or school. The football match and its associated activities, including perhaps a clash with rival supporters, are the focal points of the day. Rehashing last Saturday's exploits and anticipating next Saturday's are what make the weekdays bearable. Hooliganism from this perspective is a product of the relationship between working-class youth and the social institutions that repress them, a relationship apparently largely unperceived by the boys themselves.

In approaches emphasizing the function of the time out for the controllers, time-out behaviour is thought to siphon off or otherwise manage in a relatively safe way the tensions, frustrations, and discontents of daily life that might otherwise explode in a truly destructive way – in a way, that is, that seriously threatens established society, i.e., the state.

Consider the sociobiological explanation of aggression put forward by Peter Marsh and his colleagues at Oxford University (Marsh, 1978; Marsh et al., 1978). The Oxford group has attempted to show that young males in all human societies throughout history have engaged in "ritualized aggression" (one manifestation of which is football hooliganism), which, like the instinct-governed confrontations between nonhuman animals of a given species, almost always fall short of genuine violence. Among humans cultural "rules" are what restrain combatants from doing serious injury to one another. Marsh et al. (1978:134) do not exactly say that ritualized aggression is genetically determined in humans, but they do claim it is ubiquitous and inevitable and that eradicating it could result in more "real" violence. In their own words: if we "take away the opportunities for boys and young men to engage in structured aggro, then we might very well be faced with a set of problems that are far more serious and much more difficult to control." Tolerating ritualized aggression thus becomes a way for the authorities to manage the real thing. Dunning et al. (1981) object. It is too simple, they write, to conceptualize aggression as either "ritualized" or "real." What about intervening types and grades of violence? Just because British hooligan confrontations, say, are not as serious as, say, genocide, this does not mean that the former are innocuous. Recent aerial bombardments involving darts, gasoline bombs, and other potentially lethal missiles attest to that.

In the "integration" hypothesis the function of the time out is to bind the masses to the ruling group in a kind of "false consciousness," to use Karl Marx's term for the stage in a society in which the beliefs, attitudes, and values of the subordinate classes serve the interests of the dominant class, not their own. Janet Lever (1983:61) suggests, for instance, that unofficial government policy in Brazil "seems to include the notion that soccer can be used to distract workers from their serious grievances." After Brazil won its third World Cup in Mexico, in 1970, the president of the military regime, in an address to the nation, identified the victory with the "rise of faith in our fight for national development." Photographs of President Médici holding the Cup, surrounded by the national team, appeared in newspapers throughout Brazil. Médici declared a national holiday (an incredible two-day celebration in which forty-four people died). Subsequently, the government's slogan, "No one will hold Brazil back now," popped up on billboards everywhere, juxtaposed with a picture of Pelé in midair after a goal. A marching song, "Pra Frente, Brasil" (Forward, Brazil), written to inspire the World Cup team, became the regime's theme, played by military bands on all official occasions.

Ian Taylor (1971b) makes a similar case with respect to Mexico. In 1970 the highly repressive government of that country (which two years before had authorized the machine-gunning of students protesting Mexico's holding of the Olympic Games) used the success of the Mexican soccer team (it reached the quarter finals of the World Cup for the first time) to bolster the government's own position. While the government's control agents allowed an estimated 50,000 people to revel unchecked in the streets of Mexico City for twelve hours after the victory advancing the team to the quarter-final round, the government, Taylor claims, sought to associate itself, mainly through public pronouncements, with the team's success. For Taylor this is evidence of "state-licensed relief" for the masses, the same kind of "repressive tolerance" exercised by Brazil's military junta.

Such claims may be exaggerated. In terms of numbers alone, though an impressive 50,000 revelers may have danced in the streets of Mexico City, the city's population after all is over 17 million. It seems unlikely that an interlude of this nature could serve to blind the populace to the true nature of a system that exploits it when less than one per cent of the populace is involved. Hay (1979:14) makes the same point with respect to the allegedly mesmerizing effect of football on the Scottish working class. On a typical Saturday in Glasgow, he estimates, less than 8 per cent of the population, at best, attends the five Scottish League games available, including Celtic and Rangers matches. "Anyone who tries to make a case for social control in terms of the numbers of people directly involved or influenced by the game, even in a football-besotted area like Scotland," Hay concludes, "has an uphill struggle on his hands." On the other hand, 92 per cent of the population of Rio de Janeiro bets at least once a month in the national soccer lottery. Seventy million blank lottery flyers are distributed each week throughout Brazil (Lever, 1983)!

The subculture perspective

Several attempts to account for soccer hooliganism in Britain may be put very loosely under the heading of subculture theory. Some of these approaches take as their starting point the post-World-War-II disintegration of the English working-class community and the subsequent alienation of some of its fragments, brought about by the "redevelopment" of old neighbourhoods, the breaking of family ties, and the creation of a large army of unemployed youth, among other factors. Hooliganism supposedly has been a reaction to these changes. The hooligan subculture espouses a set of values that are at once derived from and at odds with traditional working-class culture.

Taylor's (1971a) "theory of the game" has to do with the decline of the professional soccer club as a local working-class institution and the largely unconscious response of the "soccer subculture" to this decline. Prior to World War II, Taylor attempts to show, fans, players, and management were bound together in mutual support of the local professional club. Fans and players shared the same background and values, players being local products for the most part. Fans felt they had some influence on club decisions and style of play. The soccer club was a "participatory democracy," or so supporters felt. After the war, professionalism, commercialism, and internationalism began to alter these relationships. Contractual relationships replaced subcultural ones. Local styles of play and strategy with which supporters could identify disappeared. As the game became increasingly removed from their real or imagined influence, remnants of the soccer subculture attempted to reassert themselves, to regain control of a sort, through disruptive acts of hooliganism. From this perspective the hooligan riot seems an example of what historian George Rudé (1964) calls the "backward looking riot" – an attempt to restore a prior state of affairs – but in this case apparently without conscious motivation on the part of rioters. Taylor's thesis is intriguing, but there is little hard evidence that "participatory democracy" actually existed in the old days. Even if it did it was probably gone by the turn of the century, for of the sixty-six current Football Association clubs founded in the nineteenth century, forty had become limited companies by 1900 and nineteen more by 1914 (Whannel,

1979). Nor is there any compelling evidence that modern hooligans are aware that such control may have existed in the past, let alone evidence that they want to regain it. In any case, Taylor (1982) subsequently repudiated much of his own position on similar grounds.

Clarke's (1978) theory of "subcultural style" views hooliganism in the same light as other postwar youth subcultures, from Teddy Boys to New Wave. All have been attempts by working-class youth to establish a sense of identity and community by separating themselves from adults and the middle class. Increased freedom and wealth for the young have helped enable this separation. In the soccer stadium this has taken the form of the physical and social disjoining of adults and young supporters. Adult restraints on youth behaviour are now gone. Previous generations of young working-class fans also engaged in pushing, swearing, and fighting, but less actively, owing to the presence of adults. The modern hooligan, freed from adult control, engages in a more "active" style of supporting, offensive to adults, especially the middle-class soccer consumer, but a style nevertheless perpetuating the old traditions and values, such as loyalty to the team. Hooliganism, according to Clarke, is merely a "different" way of supporting. The problem with this formulation is that it is silent on the great majority of working-class youth who are not hooligans. Why, asks Taylor (1982), do some become hooligans while others do not?

The class perspective

The most recent attempts to make theoretical sense of hooligan violence have been made by Taylor (1982) and Dunning (Dunning, 1981; Dunning et al., 1982). Both ground the phenomenon explicitly and historically in the structure of class relations in Britain, at which point they diverge, Taylor taking a Marxist viewpoint, Dunning taking Elias's configurational perspective.

Taylor's (1982) "state theory," in some ways an extension of his earlier "theory of the game," is based heavily on a book by Stuart Hall et al. (1978), *Policing the Crisis*. Taylor begins with the "fundamental inequalities and significance" of class relations in modern capitalist liberal-democratic states. The recent development of capitalism in the West, he contends, has been one of forcing a growing proportion of the working class into underemployment and unemployment. The result: frustration, resentment, disillusionment, nihilism, racism, violence. In an effort to contain these problems, the dominant class, working through the state (by way of the central government and other state institutions, like the schools, courts, and media) works to promote a consensus regarding the sources of the unrest, namely, that it is a result in Britain at least of insidious social permissiveness in every area of society. The trick is to make the interests of the dominant class seem like the interests of all. This is what neo-Marxist theorists call "hegemony": ruling-class power legitimated in popular consent. Put slightly differently, by carefully examining the activities of the institutions that comprise the state, one can begin to understand how the capitalist class, or a fragment of it, tries to present the appearance of "being on the side of the people," thus promoting popular consent to its rule. Of course the ruling class distances itself from the direct operations of the state, for if the latter is to function effectively it must be perceived by the people as "neutral" (see Gruneau, 1982).

Contemporary Britain, according to Taylor, is presently in a "crisis of hegemony." The masses have been increasingly questioning the authority of the state since the late 1960s, when capital and labour became entrenched in the struggle over the share of profits in a context of continuing poor wages and low industrial productivity. The British State, currently embodied in the British Conservative party, has attempted to deal with the "crisis" by mustering popular support for tough, authoritarian government (and tough, authoritarian schools, courts, and the rest), which will restore law and order, stamp out social permissiveness, bring back traditional standards, clamp down on soccer hooligans and other delinquent elements. Essentially this is a labelling process, conducted largely through the media (see Chapter 5), whereby Britain's economic and social malaise is attributed, not to the failure of capitalism, but to a weakening of the nation's "moral fibre" under the demoralizing influence of the social democratic welfare state. The soccer hooligan exemplifies this malaise. In Taylor's "theory of the game," hooliganism stemmed from the alienation of the football supporter from his local club; in this latest formulation, hooliganism results from the overall alienation of parts of the working class under an economic system in rapid decline. But why does hooliganism take place in the context of a sports event? This question is left unanswered.

In their "violent masculinity" thesis, Dunning and his colleagues at the University of Leicester argue that the social structure of the lower or "rough" working-class communities, which make a major contribution to the ranks of hard-core hooligans, resembles the "segmentally bonded" structure characteristic of the preindustrial societies described in Chapters 2 and 3, with their residential and ethnic solidarity, their high level of tolerance for violence in interpersonal relations, their emphasis on a "violent masculine style." In such communities, Dunning et al. assert, male adolescents are traditionally left on their own and tend to form neighbourhood gangs within which, as in the wider local context, a premium is placed on toughness and fighting ability.

Residence is important in the formation and maintenance of these groups, but the boys' notions of territory are flexible, allowing, in the case of soccer hooligan confrontations, the formation of temporary alliances between enemies (the "Bedouin syndrome") right up to the international level of soccer; thus normally hostile supporters of rival London clubs may combine to defend a stadium "end" against visiting fans from the hated North, and club and regional animosities may be subordinated to national ones when England plays France. Dunning et al. try to show that lower-working-class males have always used football as a medium for expressing norms of aggressive masculinity, unlike most other theorists who see hooliganism primarily as a post-World-War-II phenomenon. The Leicester studies constitute the most explicit and systematic theoretical attempt to date to ground soccer hooligan violence in the larger configuration of social relationships that produces it. Based on a reality not entirely unique to Britain, the violent masculinity thesis also has implications for a more general theory of spectator disorder.

The Precipitating Factor

Crucial to the understanding of issue-oriented riots are the closely related concepts of "hostile belief" and "precipitating factor," integral elements of Smelser's theory of collective behaviour. To understand the latter concept requires a brief examination of the former. According to Smelser a "hostile belief" grows out of a need to "explain" what he calls "structural strain." A hostile belief is conveyed by rumour. It usually contains "magical" elements in which "extraordinary forces" involving threats, conspiracies and the like are thought to be at work. Smelser's critics claim that the breadth and vagueness of this notion render it impossible to disprove, that its "magical" and "extraordinary" character places it in the outdated "irrationalist" camp of collective behaviour theorizing, that it is more an after-the-fact justification than a cause of collective behaviour, and so forth (see Smith, 1978c). Still, few seem to take issue with the claim that "hostile outbursts" are preceded by some sort of grievance, belief, attitude, or ideology – elements summarized in the last chapter under the heading of "legitimating belief" – which serves to legitimate the hostile actions of at least some participants. We can adhere to the general logic of Smelser's concept without accepting all its details (and without accepting the functionalist assumption of his theory that the *normal* state of social systems is one of order).

It is in the context of a legitimating belief that a "precipitating factor" takes place: some event, or series of events, that confirms or sharpens the belief and touches off the riot proper. Given a legitimating belief, what appears to be a minor incident may be defined as outrageous provocation. In their examination of the 1943 Detroit race riot, Lee and Humphrey (1943) emphasized that the incident triggering the riot – a fist-fight between a black and a white man – was itself unimportant, but in the extreme tension of that time and place acquired a major significance. Klapp (1972) maintains that if the tension is high enough, the crowd will even "search" for a "trigger." The National Advisory Commission on Civil Disorders (1968:70-71) is explicit in its conclusion that a precipitating factor can be apprehended only when viewed in context:

In virtually every case a single "triggering" or "precipitating" incident can be identified as having immediately preceded – within a few hours and in general-

ly the same location – the outburst of disorder. But this incident was usually a relatively minor, even trivial one.... As we see it, the prior incidents and the reservoir of underlying grievances contributed to a cumulative process of mounting tension that spilled over into violence when the final incident occurred.

Emphasis on the context of precipitants, however, while correct, has diverted attention from their empirical contents. Is the empirical nature of the precipitating factor as insignificant as the lack of attention paid it implicitly suggests? Or is a particular *type* of precipitant, because it conveys a particular message, most likely to be perceived as a "last straw" by riot participants?

The violence-precipitates-violence hypothesis

It can be said initially that the more intimately connected an event with the issue that underlies it, the more likely the event will come into play as a precipitating factor. Certainly the precipitants of racial disturbances typically have had a direct relationship with the grievances of the rioters. Not surprisingly, race riots are usually touched off by some sort of interracial confrontation. The National Advisory Commission notes the "typical" case of the Newark riot in which a black cab driver was hurt during an altercation with white police following a traffic accident. Feagin and Hahn's (1973:144) review of research on the U.S. ghetto revolts of the 1960s concludes that one category of precipitant was of overriding importance in the genesis of the disorders, namely "the killing of, arrest of, or interference with black men and women by policemen, commonly by white policemen." Lieberson and Silverman (1965) similarly report that most of the "immediate precipitants" of seventy-six race riots from 1913-1963 were interracial violations of strongly held norms.

Closer inspection of the Lieberson and Silverman data reveals that 75 per cent of the "immediate precipitants" involved bodily assault, from murders and rapes to fights without lethal weapons. Violent crimes against persons generate an intensity of feeling unmatched by other offences, the authors argue, an assertion buttressed by the typically harsher punishments meted out for crimes of personal injury, threat, and intimidation, than for crimes against property. An act of assault that is perceived as illegitimate – too extreme, unwarranted in the circumstances, perpetrated by a member of a disliked group, or in some other way norm-violating – seems to communicate such a contempt for the victim's "self," and by extension *those whom the victim represents,* that a powerful sense of outrage is felt by the latter, the more motivated of whom may act violently in retaliation. "Violence redresses wrongs," as Lang and Lang (1970:100) put it, "or at least gives the appearance of doing so." Such observations suggest that violence – perhaps even the rumour or threat of violence – is the stuff of which the precipitants of issue-oriented riots are made.

Some support can be mustered for the hypothesis that interpersonal or relatively small-scale collective violence touches off larger outbreaks in sports crowds. Recall the data in Table 6.1, showing that the great majority of spectator outbursts occur in contact sports where player violence is common. In an examination of seventeen major soccer riots reported in the *New York Times,* Smith (1976) found that about half the episodes were preceded by assault, or the threat of it, by players, spectators, or police – but usually players. Occasionally a major incident precipitated the disorder, but more frequently there was evidence merely that the contests were rougher than usual, as when Napoli met Rapid of Vienna, June 1959 in New York City, in a riot-capped game in which "players' tempers flared all afternoon." In other instances an escalating series of incidents took place. The crowd protested a last-minute penalty against a Naples player in a 1955 Milan-Naples encounter by throwing objects at the referee, whereupon the police, presumably on edge because a game between the two teams a year before had erupted in a melee that had hospitalized 120 fans and police, turned water cannons on the stands. Crowd members then attacked the police.

Unpopular decisions by referees appear to constitute a second class of precipitant. (In defeat riots they may be *the* issue.) Disallowing a goal, calling a penalty, ejecting a player from the game, and the like tend to be selectively defined by partisan crowd members as discrimination against "their" team. Hastorf and Cantril (1954) showed in an experiment over thirty years ago that sports fans tend to see fouls committed by the opposing team but somehow miss those committed by their own. In a field study of Australian football crowds, Mann (1974) found that immediately after an important game, fans of the losing team, compared to winning-team and nonpartisan fans, tended to "explain" the defeat by reference to bad luck and poor officiating and to see more "dirty play" by the other team than actually occurred. Such rationalizations apparently assuage the bitterness of losing. A visit to almost any North American hockey arena or baseball field will confirm that these distortions of perception and judgement cut across national boundaries.

It does seem that it is often the referee's decision – or lack of one – that ignites a riot. Yet examples that bolster this observation often reveal that player violence was the cause of the official's decision (Smith, 1976). An act of assault on the field, if not always the last straw, seems frequently a link in a chain of precipitating factors.

It is perhaps best to think in terms of a series of precipitants rather than attempting to isolate one final act that mobilizes the crowd. Final acts tend to be preceded by similar acts that intensify legitimating beliefs and create an expectation that events confirming these beliefs will occur. Furthermore, as suggested by the Milan-Naples incident described above, one collective outburst may precipitate another.

One other line of research bears on the violence-precipitates-violence hypothesis, a series of field studies of the effects of viewing violent sports on spectators' hostility levels. In an initial study, Goldstein and Arms (1971) had student interviewers administer a shortened version of the Buss-Durkee hostility scale, plus other background questions, to a random sample of male spectators before and after an Army-Navy football game and before and after a "competitive, though nonaggressive" Army-Temple University gymnastics meet, both held in Philadelphia. Hostility scores were significantly higher after the football game than before it (no matter whether the subject's favoured team won or lost) but were not higher after the gymnastics meet than prior to it.

In a Canadian replication of this investigation, Arms, Russell, and Sandilands (1979) randomly assigned male and female students at the University of Lethbridge to view either a professional wrestling match ("stylized aggression"), a hockey game ("realistic aggression"), or a swim meet (the control event). The subjects were further assigned to either a pre-event or postevent session with the investigators during which they completed three measures of hostility: the shortened Buss-Durkee hostility scale, the aggression scale of the Nowlis Mood Adjective Check List, and a number of items assessing "punitiveness." The subjects were told the study was of spectators' impressions of sports events. Although the three measures yielded somewhat different results for the three events, in general, post-event hostility levels were significantly higher than pre-event levels in the wrestling and hockey crowds, but not the swim crowd. These results bolster those of Goldstein and Arms.

In a third study Russell (1981) had student interviewers administer the short form of the Nowlis Mood Adjective Check List to 117 adult spectators at a rather violent (184 penalty minutes) game, and to 159 spectators at a relatively nonviolent (46 penalty minutes) game, both in the Western Hockey League. Both games were played in Lethbridge, and both were won by the home team. The subjects were interviewed either prior to the game, during the first or second period intermission, or following the game. Once again, viewing the aggressive contest increased hostility, while viewing the nonaggressive contest did not. Russell's procedures determined further that the effect of viewing the aggressive game was curvilinear; hostility increased during the first two periods of this game, peaked at the end of the second period (when most of the rough play occurred), then fell during the third period. If indeed hostility generally dissipates as rapidly as these findings indicate, the timing of its measurement in research is clearly important. As Russell observes, the earlier studies may have underestimated hostility levels by measuring it only after the contests.

In any event the evidence is consistent: observing sports violence live, as on television, tends to heighten spectator's hostility, not reduce it, as proponents of catharsis theory claim, on the basis of virtually no reliable evidence. These results may be interpreted as supporting elements of social learning theory (Bandura, 1973) or Berkowitz's (1969) revision of frustration-aggression theory, but they are also compatible with the hypothesis developed here, which emphasizes the *meaning* of acts of violence within the context of a legitimating belief.

Testing the violence-precipitates-violence hypothesis

Let us systematically test the violence-precipitates-violent hypothesis using data from Smith's crowd violence study outlined in the previous chapter. In addition to the twenty-seven cases of "crowd violence" already mentioned, reports were obtained on twelve spectator incidents stopping just short of culmination ("near violence") and twenty-nine cases primarily involving players ("player violence"). These latter two categories are included in the analysis because they bear on the proposition at hand and increase the sample size.

Recall that "crowd violence" was defined as ten or more spectators engaged in violence against persons and/or property. This abbreviated account of a melee during a 1971 Toronto soccer game between Yugoslavia Zagreb and the Greek All Stars conveys the character of the "crowd violence" data. On this occasion fifty extra police officers were called to restore order after spectators had invaded the pitch.

> *Zagreb goalkeeper Fahria Doutbegovic tripped Georgios Viohos of the Greek team as he was racing for the goal.*
> *Bell [the referee] awarded a penalty kick and Doutbegovic promptly protested. There was a shoving match and then fans raced to the field. The spectators started kicking at the players who returned the blows. (Globe and Mail, July 10, 1971:30)*

"Near violence" refers to spectator outbursts involving ten or more people that failed to reach a climax. In the twelve cases that come under this heading, precipitating incidents were followed by the mobilization of crowd members, but the action was nipped in the bud in every instance by the police. A ruckus that interrupted a National Soccer League game in Toronto between Portuguese and Italia in 1972 is typical. Italia was leading the "hard tackling" game 1-0 when a Portuguese player kneed an Italia player in the back. Players on both teams crowded around the injured performer who lay "writhing on the field."

> *Suddenly, Armando Costa of the Portuguese ran from his bench and started swinging at an Italian player.*
> *Many of the 4,500 spectators rushed to the barriers surrounding the playing field but were restrained from going further by about 30 policemen, some mounted, who lined the field facing the covered stand. (Globe and Mail, July 31, 1972:S3)*

The twenty-nine cases of "player violence" were brawls involving all or most performers on both teams. Some of these free-for-alls had a ritualized, institutionalized character, but so have some spectator episodes. Most theorists in any case no longer make a sharp distinction between "institutional" and "collective" behaviour. Consider this 1968 incident involving the Philadelphia Flyers and St. Louis Blues hockey teams. Two opposing players collided behind the St. Louis net, slashed each other with their sticks, then began to fight, at which point

> *other players on both teams paired off in a mixture of wrestling and*
> *fighting, which continued for about a minute. Just when officials appeared to*
> *be restoring order, players Pat Hannigan and Don Blackburn came off the*
> *Philadelphia bench and entered the fight. They were quickly followed by all*
> *their teammates and all the St. Louis players. (**Globe and Mail**, April 16,*
> *1968:30)*

Table 7.1 indicates that violence is the chief precipitant of collective violence in sport. Forty-nine of the sixty-eight episodes were preceded by some sort of assaultive behaviour, with only slight variations in frequency among the three types.

Seventy-four per cent of the crowd violence was ignited by player assaults (mainly attacks on opposing players), ranging from individual fouls to bench-emptying brawls (the latter typically escalations of lesser affairs). The majority of these encounters were described as two-person fights; a typical case was a 1972 Ontario Hockey Association Junior A game between Ottawa and London in which a cross-checking incident sparked a fight, which eventually included most players from both teams, several hundred spectators, and twenty city policemen. Other player frays apparently involved from the start a large number of combatants. Such was the case in 1968 when Buffalo and Cleveland (American Hockey League) players brawled, touching off a paroxysm of chair-throwing by fans, whereupon players, sticks flailing, went into the stands to fight with the fans. Performers attacked game officials on a few occasions. In a 1963 Niagara Falls-Streetsville Ontario Junior lacrosse match, a Falls player leaped out of the penalty box and began swinging at the referee. When a Streetsville boy tried to intercede, he was knocked down by another Falls player. The referee and several Streetsville players were then chased back to their bench and into the stands by the Falls team, where they were set upon by Falls supporters. Two crowd outbursts were preceded by unspecified rough play: one when 1,000 fans brawled at the end of a particularly hard-tackling Toronto and District Soccer League match, the other a hockey incident following a penalty-strewn game in which "hard feelings prevailed on the ice."

Three-quarters of the "near violence" was precipitated by assaults of the types noted above, save one outburst not explicitly tied to events on the field (or in this case, floor) of play. The exception was a 1967 Toronto high-school basketball game, during which a spectator took a kick at a student, instigating an altercation that was broken up by teachers in the stands. At the end of the contest, about 100 students milled about on the street, ostensibly to waylay the teachers as they left the building, but the crowd was forestalled by the arrival of city police.

Table 7.1   Precipitants of Issue-Oriented Sports Riots

Precipitants	Crowd Violence		Near Violence		Player Violence		All Precipitants	
	N	(%)	N	(%)	N	(%)	N	(%)
Violence	20	(74)	9	(75)	20	(69)	49	(73)
Officials's decision	4	(15)	3	(25)	1	(3)	8	(12)
Spectator baiting	3	(11)	0	(0)	0	(0)	3	(3)
Unknown	0	(0)	0	(0)	8	(28)	8	(12)

SOURCE: Smith (1978c:127).

Most of the "player violence" too was activated by violent or "dirty" play ("the Greyhounds preferred slugging to shooting"), which spiralled into two-man fights and then into rows encompassing all or most performers. The report of a 1968 Los Angeles Angel-Boston Red Sox baseball game provides a case in point: during the early innings of the game, three Angel batters were hit by pitched balls. In the eighth inning the Angel catcher was similarly smitten and rushed to the mound with his fists swinging. Both dugouts emptied, blows were exchanged, and players rolled on the ground locked in combat.

Unpopular decisions by officials make up the second category of precipitants in Table 7.1. The four "crowd violence" episodes were preceded by, on two occasions, a soccer referee awarding a penalty kick, and on one occasion, a hockey judge allowing a disputed goal. In the fourth case, a race-track disturbance, a mob of about 200 hurled trash cans and benches onto the track, set them ablaze, and pelted firemen with missiles after the message board had flashed a lower-than-expected payoff. The few "near violence" and "player violence" episodes in this category were similarly instigated.

Spectators baiting performers – the third type of precipitant – touched off three outbursts, players in each case invading the seats in search of their tormenters. As for the "unknown" precipitants, the newspaper accounts offered no hints as to what preceded the eight player outbursts in this category.

One final note regarding the last three categories of precipitant: that no violence was reported in these cases does not preclude the possibility that it was present. Borderline violence is so taken for granted in some sports that failure to perceive it as extraordinary by observers not particularly sensitized to it would not be surprising. Violence may have figured as part of a spiral of precipitating factors in an even greater proportion of disorders than indicated by the data. All told, the evidence points to violence as the main precipitant of collective violence in sport.

A note on the use of newspaper reports

Because research on collective violence relies so heavily on newspaper reports as sources of data, an aside on their value in social science research is in order. Newspaper reports are open to criticism on several counts, the most important of which are inaccuracies and distortions of facts, editorial slanting, and suppression of information. Danzger (1975), however, in an examination of critiques of the validity of news, has found that many of the critiques themselves are flawed.

With respect to inaccuracies and distortions of facts, it appears that most critiques are based on the view of news as a "straight line process of communication," whereas in fact most news is transmitted via self-correcting networks of communication, namely the wire services. Although in competition with one another, the wire services utilize and check each other, resulting in a progressive correction of errors. Unfortunately, it is not known which of the above sports violence reports were wire service-generated, but one may assume that a substantial proportion were, especially in light of the fact that Toronto has a United Press International office. It may be, furthermore, that the unreliability of the press has been exaggerated. The National Advisory Commission on Civil Disorders (1968:364) checked the reliability of 3,779 newspaper articles on racial disorders by interviewing media people, police, and ghetto residents, and by cross-checking facts against other newspapers and news magazines, and concluded that the articles on the whole were "... calm, factual, and restrained." Smith assumed that the *Globe and Mail* accounts were sufficiently accurate to be used as data.

Danzger found the second charge of editorial bias well substantiated. He notes, however, that researchers can skirt this difficulty by using only observable or "hard" facts and not "soft" facts or *interpretations* of facts. A report that crowd members assaulted a referee would be an example of the former; an interpretation of this action as a response to frustration, without direct evidence of frustration, would be an example of the latter. Smith employed only "hard" news in his study. To test the hypothesis that violence precedes collective violence, he sought evidence merely that a contest featured extraordinary violence prior to the collective outburst proper, whether or not the extraordinary violence was explicitly reported as a precipitating factor (as it frequently was).

Regarding the suppression of information (underreporting), Danzger determined that cities with wire service offices report more conflicts than cities without such offices, although this difference disappears once a certain number of stories of conflict in a given city has been filed (a "ceiling effect"). But Snyder and Kelly (1977), in an analysis of racial disorders in 673 cities, challenge Danzger's findings. They discovered that the probability of these disorders being reported correlates positively with both riot severity and "media sensitivity" (the latter a combination of the riot's proximity to the reporting source and "political climate"), but *not* with the presence or absence of wire service offices. Snyder and Kelly conclude that studies of conflict frequency based on newspaper reports are "generally valid," especially when it comes to "high intensity" affairs. In any case our concern here has been not with the frequency or rate of conflict, but with the precipitants of conflict.

Despite Danzger's corrective to previous images of the inaccuracy of news, it would be wrong to overstate the case for the use of newspaper reports as data in social scientific research. Newspaper stories are inherently weak as scientific data because they are not produced according to the rules of scientific method. For this reason, if for no other, Smith's results should be regarded as provisional.

Who Riots?

"Rowdies," "mindless moronic maniacs," "savages," "irresponsible louts," "whackos," "sickos," "hoodlums," "teenage thugs" – popular journalistic descriptions of sports riots often portray rioters in these unflattering terms. The image is not new. It goes back at least to the nineteenth-century writings of Gustave Le Bon (1895), most notably his compilation of "inferior forms of evolution" ("primitives," "the insane," "degenerates," "socialists," and members of the "Latin races," among others) who supposedly were especially prone to involvement in crowds. Similar notions surfaced periodically in ensuing decades. The modern view of rioters as subhumans goes under the name of "riffraff theory."

Riffraff theory

This approach holds that riotous crowds are composed principally of deviants, vagrants, petty criminals, teenage hoodlums, recent migrants, the uneducated, the chronically unemployed, and various other "losers" – people on the margins of society. It assumes that such types have no stake in maintaining societal norms and institutions and hence no compunctions about engaging in actions that undermine them (Lupsha, 1969).

Riffraff theory fares poorly in the light of concrete evidence concerning past and present riots unrelated to sport, as a number of studies based on extensive, carefully collected empirical data indicate. Rudé (1964) has shown through analysis of police, court, and other public records that most riotous crowds in eighteenth- and nineteenth-century Britain and France were composed chiefly of shopkeepers, apprentices, craftsmen, and labourers, not riffraff. The National Advisory Commission Report (1968) concludes, based on extensive sample surveys, arrest records, and eyewitness accounts, that the typical 1967 ghetto rioter was an unmarried black male between the ages of fifteen and twenty-five, economically in about the same position as his nonrioting neighbour, a lifelong resident of the city in which the riot took place, slightly better educated than the average inner-city black, and working in a low-status job, albeit with frequent periods of unemployment – but not riffraff. McPhail (1971) found in a secondary analysis of ten studies of civil disorder in the U.S., that only 23 of 287 different correlations between variables measuring individual attitudes, socioeconomic attributes, and demographic characteristics, on the one hand, and variables measuring riot participation, on the other, correlated .30 or better. McPhail concluded that the characteristics of individuals were simply poor predictors of participation in civil disorders.

What about participants in sports riots? The evidence, though not extensive, is consistent. It confirms what may already appear obvious, but self-evident truths have a way of turning out to be false, and it seems prudent to examine such data as exist. About the gender, age, occupation, and criminal record of sports crowd rioters, this much can be said:

Gender   Trivizaz (1980) compared the police records of 652 football crowd arrests in London between 1974 and 1976 with the records of a control sample of 410 arrests for the same offences committed in the same area during the same period but not associated with football. Ninety-nine per cent of the football arrestees were male, compared to only 87.3 per cent of the control arrestees. True, most British football spectators are male to begin with, but the ratio of male to female spectators is considerably lower than 99:1, according to two public opinion surveys conducted in the early 1970s (Joint Councils, 1978). Trivizaz' findings corroborate earlier, less systematic data on arrested hooligans assembled by the Harrington (1968) and Joint Councils Reports.

Limited visual evidence paints the same picture. Lewis (1982b) viewed a Birmingham police-made videotape of ten violent hooligan confrontations and observed only one female in forty-two minutes of tape. In "The Good Stiff Fist," a fifteen-minute film on Millwall (London) hooligans made in 1980 for the Canadian Television Network programme "W5," not one female is to be seen.

There are no North American data comparable to those of Trivizaz, but there are bits and pieces of relevant information. Only one female name appears on a list published in the *Vancouver Sun* (November 26, 1966:2) of the 260 people charged with offences in the 1966 Vancouver Grey Cup Riot. A five-minute Canadian Broadcasting Corporation film clip of the 1955 "Rocket" Richard hockey riot shows only male rioters in the streets following the game, and all 37 arrestees were males (Katz, 1955). According to Lewis (1982b), 95 per cent of the roughly 200 people arrested in the 1975 Pittsburgh Super Bowl Riot were males, and no female appears in photographs of the 1974 Cleveland 10¢ Beer Night Baseball Riot. Lewis also reports the results of an experiment he conducted at Kent State University in which male and female undergraduate students read vignettes of football riots of varying degrees of "severity" or magnitude, then indicated whether or not they would participate in such disturbances. The students were told the vignettes were from newspaper stories of actual occurrences. The low severity riots involved only vandalism, the high severity, vandalism, injuries, and two deaths. Not one woman reported that she would participate in a football riot of any kind, but 5 per cent of the men said they would or probably would, even in the high severity episode.

The British pattern of greater female representation in riots unrelated to sport is apparent in some American data; 11 per cent of over 11,000 people arrested in twenty-one cities during the 1967 racial upheavals were female, for instance (National Advisory Commission, 1968). Women have always taken part in politically oriented protests, Feinman (1980) asserts, for political activity has not usually been regarded as a denial of womanhood. Of course this does not mean that they necessarily take part in actual violence; of 437 women arrested in the 1968 Martin Luther King Riots in Washington, D.C., a mere handful were arrested for violent offences. Most were taken in for innocuous breaches of law, like curfew violation (Miller, 1981).

Age   The mean age of all arrestees in Trivizaz' football sample was nineteen. Table 7.2 gives the percentages of offenders twenty-five years and younger in the two violent offence categories (assaulting police and criminal damage) and three other categories marginal to violence (possessing a dangerous weapon, threatening or insulting words or behaviour, drunkenness). These percentages range from 86 for assaulting police to 100 for criminal (property) damage. The mean age for the former offence is twenty and for the latter fifteen, writes Trivizaz. In contrast, the mean age of all control arrestees was twenty-nine, and the percentages of the control sample twenty-five years and younger in each offence category are markedly lower than the football sample. The football arrestees' age profile is broadly the same as those reported previously in the Harrington and the Joint Councils reports. The mean age of sixty-five Oxford United supporters interviewed by Marsh et al. (1978) was a considerably younger sixteen.

The North American evidence, as far as it goes, yields a slightly older age distribution. The average age of persons charged in the 1966 Grey Cup Riot was about twenty-one, the average age of those arrested in the Richard and

Table 7.2   Percentage of Arrestees under 26 in Football and Nonfootball Crowds: London, 1974-76

Offence	Football		Nonfootball	
	%	(N)	%	(N)
Assaulting police	86	(50)	48	(93)
Offensive weapon	94	(32)	73	(16)
Criminal (property) damage	100	(24)	50	(12)
Threatening or insulting words or behaviour	97	(432)	54	(203)
Drunkenness	92	(24)	30	(10)

Adapted from Trivizaz (1980:285). Reprinted with permission.

Super Bowl fracases about twenty-three. (Katz mentions that hundreds of "juveniles" were picked up but not charged in the Richard affair.) The Cleveland Beer Riot photographs and the Richard Riot film support the conclusion that most fan misbehaviour is perpetrated by adolescents and young adults. Again the National Advisory Commission Report offers a nonsport comparison: of 10,000 arrestees in sixteen cities in 1967, 52.5 per cent were between the ages of fifteen to twenty-five and 28.3 per cent were twenty-five to thirty-five, older on the average than sports rioters, insofar as the ages of the latter are known.

Occupation   Sixty-eight per cent of all Trivizaz' football arrestees were manual workers, apprentices for the most part. Twelve per cent were unemployed, 10 per cent in school. Together these three groups account for nine of every ten persons arrested for a football-related offence. The remaining arrestees were distributed among six other occupational categories. The percentages of occupational groups in each offence category in Table 7.2 roughly parallel these overall percentages, except for criminal damage, about half of which (53 per cent) was perpetrated by "schoolboys." A quite different pattern emerges from the control sample data. For every offence save criminal damage, a lower proportion of manual workers and a higher proportion of unemployed can be seen.

Trivizaz' findings again confirm those of Harrington and the Joint Councils, and the observations of almost everyone else who has studied soccer hooliganism. Furthermore, according to survey results presented in the Joint Councils' Report, the occupational mix of the typical football crowd is far more heterogeneous than the occupational mix of convicted football hooligans; that is to say, working-class males are overrepresented in the ranks of arrested hooligans relative to working-class representation in football crowds. Regarding the occupational status of North American sports crowd rioters, nothing of substance is known.

Criminal record   About one-third of all the offences in Trivizaz' data were committed by persons with previous convictions, the control group outnumbering the football group in this respect. The largest percentages of prior offenders were from those arrested for assaulting police (59.5 per cent in the football sample, 75 in the control sample). The football arrest figures differ greatly from earlier ones, which in turn differ greatly from each other; 64 per cent of arrestees in the Harrington Report had criminal records compared to only 7 per cent in the Joint Councils' Report. There seems to be no significant information on the criminal records, or lack of them, of persons involved in North American sports riots.

To summarize, the typical individual arrested for a football-crowd related offence in Britain is a nineteen-year-old working-class male. The chances are roughly one in three that he has had at least one previous conviction, though not necessarily for hooliganism (Trivizaz is unclear on this point). The three reports on conviction rates differ considerably from one

Table 7.3:   Occupation of Arrestees in Football and Nonfootball Crowds: London, 1974-76 (in Per Cent)

Offence	Manual		Unemployed		Schoolboys		Other		Number of Cases	
	football	nf	football	nf	football	nf	football	nf	football	nf
Assaulting police	71	51	13	27	5	0	11	22	(38)	(94)
Offensive weapon	71	56	21	38	8	0	0	6	(24)	(16)
Criminal (property) damage	33	58	7	17	53	0	7	25	(15)	(12)
Threatening or insulting words or behaviour	68	48	11	30	11	0	10	22	(362)	(194)
Drunkenness	64	78	18	11	0	0	18	11	(22)	(9)

Adapted from Trivizaz (1980:282). Reprinted with permission.

another, however. The soccer hooligan is younger, of lower occupational status, more likely to be male, and less likely to have a criminal record than the typical arrestee in a crowd disorder not associated with football. The typical North American sports rioter, according to very sparse evidence, is male and somewhat older than his British counterpart. His occupational status is not known, nor is the probability of his having a criminal record. This individual is younger than the typical participant in the 1967 racial upheavals, and more likely to be male.

Qualifications must be made. To begin with, the small number of cases in some of Trivizaz' offence categories greatly limits the meaningfulness of those particular data. The violent offences, assaulting a police officer and criminal damage, those of greatest relevance here, fall into this category. One can be less confident that the sample of *violent* offences is representative of the population of violent offences than one can be that the sample of *all* offences is representative of the population of all offences.

How representative are arrested hooligans of hooligans in general? Perhaps police tend to apprehend hooligans with criminal records (known hooligans) more readily than hooligans with no records, males more readily than females, older youths more quickly than younger ones. Trivizaz generalizes his findings to all hooligans, but I am inclined to be more cautious, particularly since only a tiny fraction of hooligans are ever arrested; only three arrests per game were made on the average during the 1975-76 Manchester United home season, and Manchester supporters are infamous for their bad behaviour (Joint Councils, 1978). Countering this caveat is the fact that bits of evidence based on sources other than arrest records essentially support the arrest-based evidence, thus boosting one's confidence that the foregoing profile does apply to hooligans in general.

Finally, the rioter profiles may be a function of the riot types represented by the data. Let us presume that the football crowd episodes were predominantly issueless. Perhaps people who get involved in issue-oriented riots, sports-related or otherwise, are more likely to be female, older, and of higher occupational status. Tivizaz' control data, which probably represent a wider array of riot types than the sports data, suggest as much. We should be wary of generalizing about all sports riots on the basis of only some riot types.

Caveats aside, the typical sports crowd rioter can be roughly described, but ought he to be described as riffraff? Unless one wished to label manual workers as riffraff, the only pertinent evidence is the British data regarding occupation and previous arrests. Only 12 per cent of Trivizaz' arrested hooligans were unemployed. One in three did have a criminal record, but this figure is suspect because it is at odds with earlier ones; besides this datum by itself seems insufficient to justify the label "riffraff." The typical sports riot participant may indeed behave outrageously, but insofar as his social characteristics are known, he is not riffraff as earlier defined. Clearly one should not impute antisocial predispositions to him based on characteristics he does not possess.

The assembling instructions approach

An alternative way of answering the question, who riots? is the "assembling instructions" approach of McPhail and Miller (1973). This approach focuses not on the characteristics of people who form crowds but on communication processes and ecological factors that result in the formation of crowds.

The McPhail-Miller position attributes the convergence of people toward the location of a relatively unscheduled or "nonperiodic" event to the "instructions" they receive regarding, initially, the event's location in time and space and, then, the desirability of assembling. The authors identify three basic patterns of assembling instructions. "Short range" instructions are provided by sights and sounds that inform nearby people that "something is happening." These sensory notices may be followed by verbal suggestions to "go and see." A fight or a loud argument often has this effect. "Long range" instructions are provided initially by the mass media, leaflets, sound trucks, or word of mouth to people relatively distant from the event. These instructions may be accompanied or followed by additional verbal messages to converge. Rallies, demonstrations, and riots in progress often develop in this way. The third pattern of instructions develops after the first two. In this pattern the convergent movement of people and the growing size of the crowd attract passers-by who in turn move toward the assemblage.

The majority of unscheduled crowds are formed by some combination of these patterns of communication, McPhail and Miller argue. What the patterns have in common is the occurrence of nonverbal and verbal instructions establishing the time-space location of an event and specifying movement thereto. One's access or proximity to the disturbance, one's availability or freedom from competing scheduled demands, and one's past behaviour (a known "radical" hears first about a demonstration) are a few variables affecting the probability of a given person receiving and acting on assembling instructions.

A victory celebration and riot after a U.S. college basketball game gave McPhail and Miller an opportunity to test their formulations empirically. A radio broadcast reported an upset win by the state university team over a nationally ranked rival. The game had taken place in a neighbouring state. The announcer reported that the victorious team would be arriving at the airport around midnight. About two and one-half hours later approximately 4,000 people assembled at the airport to greet the victors. A riot ensued, resulting in several hundred dollars property damage, several arrests, and police use of tear gas to disperse the crowd.

Within three weeks of this episode the authors administered a questionnaire to 531 sociology and psychology students in the state university. The questionnaire sought information on whether or not the respondents (1) had received assembling instruction in some form (heard the broadcast, been invited to welcome home the team, etc.); (2) had actually gone to the airport; (3) had access to the airport (transportation); (4) had been available to go to the airport (absence of scheduled competing demands); (5) had behaved in the past in a way that would make them probable recipients of assembling instructions (attended home basketball games).

Analysis of the data yielded a strong positive statistical relationship between *receiving assembling instructions* and actually going to the airport (controlling for all other variables). Having transportation to the airport, relative absence of scheduled competing demands, and number of home games attended were moderately positively correlated with going to the airport. The data strongly support the assembling instructions approach to crowd formation.

Unfortunately McPhail and Miller did not address the question of who rioted, among the 4,000 students who assembled, i.e. the question of variation in behaviour *within* the crowd. But they suggest that this problem be tackled in the same way: by determining who within the crowd is in a position to receive and act upon instructions for behaving violently, rather than by determining who is predisposed to behave violently, as in the riffraff approach.

It seems clear that some people *are* more "riot-prone" than others. But perhaps this is true not so much because of motivations or predispositions that supposedly accompany certain social attributes, but because these attributes (e.g., young, male, working-class) determine, as McPhail (1971:171) puts it, "the presence or absence of [people's] contacts and relationships with others which decrease or increase their availability for riot participation...." The emphasis on what people "do with, and in relation to, one another," as opposed to what people "carry within them," is continued below.

Crowd Dynamics: A Gaming Approach

The development of theory in the study of crowd behaviour has been punctuated by increasing recognition that the social and psychological forces affecting people in crowds are essentially the same as those affecting people in other settings. Sociologist Richard Berk's (1974) "gaming approach" to crowd behaviour is an important theoretical effort in this vein. Berk's work is used to structure the discussion that follows because it is representative of current thinking, because it allows the incorporation of valid elements of other theories, and because it is applicable to both issue-oriented and issueless riots.

The theory

Drawing first on "decision theory," a basically mathematical approach to decision-making based on maximizing the rewards and minimizing the costs of behaving in any given way, Berk contends that one engages in the same rational, decision-making process in the crowd as in any other social context; namely, one attempts to calculate the psychological and/or material rewards and costs of an anticipated act, then behaves so as to produce the "best" outcome, i.e., the "net" of the matrix of rewards and costs. It seems that humans are capable of considering complex alternatives and making decisions in this fashion very rapidly when necessary. Of course one may behave rationally but still end up with a negative payoff, owing, say to an error in judgement. But Berk does not claim that people in a crowd, or anywhere else, always behave perfectly rationally; rationality and irrationality are relative terms. He claims only that conscious motivation and cognitive processes figure much more strongly in crowd dynamics than earlier "irrationalist" theorists recognized and that they figure as strongly in crowd situations as in others.

The difficulties inherent in the "problematic environment" in which crowds generally operate, writes Berk, account for the apparent irrationality of crowd members, not their impaired cognitive functioning, as some theorists have claimed. This problematic environment includes a number of factors that differ only in degree from those affecting people in other circumstances. First, the information available to crowd members is incomplete and unreliable because established conduits of information (television, newspapers, etc.) are usually not functioning. It is hard to know what is going on, and hence to make accurate judgements. Second, communication among crowd members, necessary for collective decision-making, is difficult in the sense that established communications structures and networks are absent. Who is the crowd member to believe, in the absence of a preestablished hierarchy of authority? Third, there is no prior agreement in most crowds on what constitutes a collective decision, no preestablished voting mechanism, so to speak. What then constitutes a consensus? Fourth, a selection process operates whereby the least highly motivated individuals screen themselves out of the goings-on for fear of a negative payoff. Those who remain tend to be the most impatient, the most frustrated, the most angry, the most committed to an extreme course of action, and it is their extreme points of view that often prevail. Fifth, crowds usually operate under great time pressure, and collective decisions must be made before alternative courses of action can be fully considered. These factors, not the loss of ability to think critically, make the actions of people in crowds sometimes appear illogical.

Berk merges decision theory with game theory by considering decision theory in the group context. Briefly, when the "best" outcome for one individual depends on what others do, that individual is in a "game" situation. As in any game, if one wants to win, one tries to anticipate what the other players will do. In a crowd, winning, obtaining the best outcome, is usually contingent upon crowd members acting collectively, for the potential costs of an act for any given individual diminish as the number of like-acting individuals increases. One looks therefore for support from others. How might this work in a stadium riot?

Gauging the support of others

On May 24, 1964, in Lima's National Stadium one of sport's worst tragedies took place – a defeat riot and panic during a soccer game between Peru and Argentina that left between 287 and 328 dead, about 400 injured, and caused extensive property damage. The riot segment of this episode, described in detail in Figure 7.3, unfolded briefly as follows: the referee disallowed a Peru goal that would have tied the game with six minutes left to play. A fan managed to gain the field to attack the referee. Another followed. They were intercepted by the police. The crowd's anger turned on the police. Dozens of crowd members began to break through the chain-link fence surrounding the field. The question for the game theorist is: how would an individual in the stands who is motivated to run onto the field gauge the probability that others would support this behaviour?

Number of supportive others   Initially the individual might try to estimate how many others were acting in ways that seemed to support his preferred behaviour. The greater the number of people acting supportively, the lower the risk for him. The first fan to invade the field, a man called Bomba, might be seen as half-crazed since he was certain to be apprehended by the police. But if in Bomba's mind the benefits of notoriety (other reports indicate he had a reputation for attacking referees) overrode the costs of arrest, the act was rational from his standpoint. The fan considering following his example, but not quite as highly motivated, would probably be buoyed by the general outpouring of rage, first directed against the referee and the scorekeeper, then against the police – the shouts, the angry, contorted faces, the flying projectiles – and then by the dozens of fans who managed to smash holes in the fence. The greater the number of fans who gained the field, the lower the probability of any given fan being manhandled or arrested by the police, and the lower the probability of that fan being censured for his action by those who know him – or punished by his own conscience; it seems that a large number of like-acting people allows the "diffusion of responsibility" for an antisocial act, though exactly why is unclear (Perry and Pugh, 1978).

Figure 7.3   The 1964 Lima Soccer Riot

In the stands the spectators were loud and boisterous. Some men were drinking a liquor called pisco and beer. They organized small cheering squads. Spectators laughed a great deal and waved to acquaintances in various parts of the stand around them. A group of some twenty boys from one neighbourhood raised a huge flag of Peru that they had laboriously sewn together. They planned to parade the victorious Peruvian team around the stadium on their shoulders.

On the field, police Comandante Jorge Azambujar Reyes broke up his force of 173 men and distributed them in small groups around the margin of land between the playing field and the stands. The steelhelmeted police, several of whom held dogs on leashes, were armed with pistols and truncheons and carried tear-gas grenades in pouches on their hips....

At 3:00 p.m. the crowd let out a booming roar. The game was on. The Argentinians, dressed in dark blue shorts, played with smooth competence. The white-uniformed Peruvians were eager and aggressive. The first half ended in a scoreless tie.

At the opening of the final half the crowd was tense and fired up. The stadium was in a continual uproar as the fans jeered at the Argentinians, shouted obscenities at Uruguayan referee Angel Eduardo Pazos, and cheered the home team with a staccato "Peru! Peru! Peru"! At the twenty-third minute of the second half Argentina scored the first goal of the game. Peru attacked fiercely and six minutes before the end of the game Peruvian Victor Lobaton kicked the ball between several defenders. It was stopped near the goal posts by Argentinian Horacio Morales who tried to kick it out of bounds. In the melee for the ball Morales booted it between his own posts, which meant a goal for Peru and a 1-1 game.

Referee Pazos disallowed it, explaining that he had blown his whistle to indicate a foul by Peru against Argentina before the goal had been made. The Peruvian players argued against the call, but the referee shook his head and held firm.

The decision triggered a tremendous outcry of anger and frustration in the stands. Spectators bellowed and threw hundreds of bottles and seat cushions on the field.

Scoreboard-keeper Dionisio Aucaruri Pinas was astonished by the ferocity of the crowd. "I've been working in this stadium for twenty-three years and I never saw people with a temper like this," he said, in describing the scene to me. "When the ball went into the Argentine goal I changed the scoreboard to read 1-1 and the spectators cheered. When the referee annulled the goal I changed it back to 1-0. The crowd was furious and they threw bottles at me. I closed the door of the booth and locked it, but people threw bottles through the window. I was scared and I stayed locked in the booth until it was all over."

At that a moment a brute of a man called Bomba (the bomb), a nickname earned by his violent temper and wild efforts to attack referees, charged onto the field and dashed for Pazos. The police intercepted him and roughly hustled him off the field. Then, to the encouraging shouts of the crowd, another man broke into the field and a police officer tripped him. He fell flat, with the wind knocked out of him. The police picked him up bodily, gave him several wallops with their truncheons and carried him off the field. Now the anger of the crowd switched from the referee to the police. In the North stands, which were closest to the Argentine goal posts and the scene of the action, men shouted "Police brutality!" and threw more bottles, cushions, and even shoes on the field. Pazos saw that the crowd's anger was only rising, so he cancelled the remainder of the match and the police quickly escorted him from the field.

With cries of angry anguish several dozen men and youths in the North stands stormed down the aisles. They threw themselves at the seven-foot-high steel-link fence that surrounded the playing field. The fence, topped by several lines of barbed wire, was supported by steel pipes imbedded in concrete. The men tried to climb over the fence by putting seat cushions over the barbed wire, but the police beat away their hands with clubs. Then the fans sat down at the foot of the fence and, by pushing in rhythm with their feet, incredibly tore three large holes in the steel links. Several dozen raced onto the field where they were met by police clubs and police dogs. Some men retreated to the stands for newspapers, lit them, and attacked the dogs with burning brands. In the stands, others started bonfires. Men tore apart a retaining wall with their hands and feet and began hurling bricks at the police....

[Afterward on the surrounding streets] Men and youths formed into roving bands. They threw stones and bricks at the police, overturned fourteen cars and burned seven of them, burned the offices of the Jockey Club and two stores, smashed shop windows, and looted and tried to break into the stadium offices.

SOURCE: Blank (1965:34-35). Reprinted with permission.

Known identities and emergent norms   Turner and Killian's (1972) "emergent norm" theory of collective behaviour would predict that the more like-acting individuals are known to one another, the greater the probability that they will conform to a norm prescribing, in our case, aggressive behaviour, for recognizable individual and group identities rather than anonymity facilitate susceptiblity to normative control. Most people probably attend sports events with one or more companions. Aveni (1977) found that three-quarters of a crowd that assembled after a Michigan-Ohio State football game were in the company of at least one friend. A survey of 2,755 roller game fans in three U.S. cities found that between 80 and 96 per cent of the fans attended games accompanied by family or friends (Hinrichs, 1979). Other acquaintances may be on the scene as well.

The potential cost of *not* invading the field, given a norm to invade and the presence of known others, becomes salient in our Lima crowd member's mental deliberations. The shared understanding as to what kind of behaviour is expected, which constitutes a norm, inhibits contrary behaviour and justifies sanctions against dissenters. Crowd norms are *emergent,* or peculiar to the situation, Turner and Killian claim, because preestablished norms are not applicable given the unstructured, uncertain nature of crowds. To the extent that conformity to emergent norms in a crowd is a *conscious* process, Turner and Killian's theory is compatible with Berk's rational approach and can be subsumed within it. To the extent that conformity to emergent norms is *unconscious,* emergent norm and game theories can perhaps coexist as explanations of crowd behaviour. The point remains in either case that known identities facilitate the imposition of crowd norms.

Visibility   Calculating the support of others is to a large degree a function of the visibility of those others. Visibility in turn depends upon crowd shape and density, among other factors. In the Lima riot the shape of the crowd was determined by the structure of the stadium, which probably afforded most spectators a reasonably good view of what a large number of others were doing. Afterward in the streets visibility would have been reduced considerably, for the advantage of elevation was gone, and people cannot see around corners, though they can get a sense of what is happening from the sounds of shouts and smashing windows, the smell of smoke, and so forth. As for density, in tightly packed crowds it may be difficult to see more than a few yards on flat terrain, whereas a tiered stadium provides a better view, density notwithstanding. The sparser the crowd, the better the visibility, all else being equal.

Density   Crowd density also seems to have a direct impact on crowd unity. In their study of Oxford United football fans Marsh et al. (1978) use the term "critical density" to refer to the number of London Road End supporters apparently required (about 100) before communal singing and other signs of collective behaviour could be observed. Prior to this point the density of the crowd was apparently insufficient to generate a sense of solidarity among members. Naturally, critical density varies with the size of the space in which people are located. In a comparison of British and North American professional soccer spectators, Roadburg (1980) speculates that the typically small, crowded British stadium, built to hold around 15,000, fosters a feeling of oneness not possible in the typically half-empty North American stadium, constructed for American football and baseball, which generally holds at least 40,000. Lima's National Stadium on the day of the riot virtually exploded with 53,000 people, while on the streets another crowd milled, unable to get in.

Ease of interpreting others' actions as supportive   Berk suggests that the ease of interpreting others' actions as supportive is a function of the symbolic content and homogeneity of the actions. Symbolic or previously explained behaviour – orchestrated gestures, slogans, songs, chants like the staccato "Peru! Peru! Peru!" of the National Stadium crowd; the waving of signs, banners, flags, scarves; the wearing of bizarre "aggro outfits" – conveys information about the probability of support for the behaviour contemplated by a given individual. The more homogenous these actions and the more homogeneous the appearance of the actors, the easier the actions are to interpret. Ironically, attempts by the authorities in some English football grounds to separate home supporters from visitors have had the unintended result of emphasizing the homogeneity and the uniqueness of each group. Opposing fans are literally "penned" in terraced sections at opposite ends of the ground, or infrequently side by side in the same end. Sometimes slices of no-man's-land patrolled by constables serve as additional barriers. From these home territories fans direct their aggression at the rival group in the form of communal gestures, chants and songs, missile barrages, and the occasional foray into enemy territory, if possible. The "Shed," the area traditionally occupied by young supporters of the Chelsea Football Club, is perhaps typical (Jacobson, 1975:702):

> *To a Shed fan, half the fun of a game is provided by the continual slanging match which occurs whenever a team with good support visits Chelsea. The football often becomes irrelevant; the effect of two large groups of fans threatening, challenging and intimidating each other from opposite ends of the ground, flying their colours and singing their war songs, is rather like two medieval armies encamped on nearby hillsides warming up before the battle. If an actual attack on the enemy is staged by the North Stand, the Shed roars with approval and excitement, encouraging its advance commando group with bloodthirsty war cries. Since most of these are chants, accompanied by rhythmic, militaristic hand-clapping, they unfortunately lose their menacing effect in print:*
>
> > *A--G*
> > *A--G--R*
> > *A--G--R--O*
> > *AGGRO!*
>
> > *Come and have a go*
> > *At the Chelsea aggro!*
> > *You're gonna get your fucking*
> > > *heads kicked in!!*   (Reprinted with permission.)

The problem of extreme behaviour

Berk's gaming approach is not without its problems. Foremost among these is the theory's failure in the eyes of some critics to account convincingly for extreme behaviour, for example that of a Bomba, behaviour, as Perry and Pugh (1978:37) put it, that "risks very high costs, yields moderate rewards, and has a low probability for success." Berk would probably concede that *individuals*, particularly unstable ones, sometimes behave irrationally in crowds – Bomba conceivably falls into this category – but Berk would also maintain that *patterns* of extreme behaviour involving many individuals cannot be accounted for in this way. Rephrasing their statement to reflect Berk's sociological orientation, Perry and Pugh ask: how can the gaming approach "explain how crowds generate sufficient support among individuals to inititate *high risk* actions?"

By way of response to their own question Perry and Pugh turn to the "risky shift" literature in small groups research. This literature indicates that group decisions made after discussion tend to be riskier than decisions made before it. Perry and Pugh then advance several plausible, if largely untested, explanations of the risky shift and apply these explanations to crowds. First, perhaps verbal (even nonverbal?) interaction serves to spread responsibility for the extreme action being considered among crowd members – the diffusion-of-responsibility argument mentioned earlier. Second, in some situations and in some groups risk-taking is highly valued for its own sake; no status-conscious hooligan wants to appear faint-hearted in the eyes of his mates, so he endorses a foolhardy action proposed by others, despite misgivings, thus contributing to the feeling of group support for the proposed action. The behaviour of leaders is a third consideration. Crowd leaders, where they exist, may tend to be intensely committed to extreme courses of action out of moral conviction or some other motivation and by their forceful speeches or actions dissolve the ambivalence of others who then shift to the leader's high-risk position. Such speculations go at least some way toward answering the question about extreme behaviour.

The gaming approach to crowd behaviour is promising, but at this stage of its development needs more support from reliable empirical data collected from crowd participants. This is not an easy task since ultimately gaming implies action based on mental states, and mental states are not directly observable. Unqualified endorsement of the gaming approach should nevertheless await the appearance of such data.

Conclusion

We set out in this chapter to organize theories relevant to the social structural roots of sports crowd violence around the idea of the issue-oriented versus the issueless riot. It was argued that all riot theories begin with the assumption of a social structural "problem" but then diverge. Issue-oriented theories posit the presence of a legitimating belief, which stems from the structural problem and justifies and explains the actions of the rioters; issueless theories posit no such belief. Issueless rioters are depicted as reacting to the social conditions in which they live, but not as consciously protesting those conditions. In most issueless riot theories, the act of rioting is thought, through one mechanism or another, to divert attention from the very conditions that generate it. Because their sources are so poorly understood, by scholars as well as others, such episodes have a strong aura of "senselessness." Issue-oriented riots seem somewhat more comprehensible because the "issue," exemplified in a legitimating belief, points more or less directly to the source of the problem.

It seems that issue-oriented riots are frequently precipitated by acts of interpersonal, or relatively small-scale, collective, violence. A study of sixty-eight sports-related riots found that approximately three-quarters of the episodes were preceded by some sort of assaultive behaviour, usually a player attack on another player. In the context of a legitimating belief even a minor act of violence seems to convey such contempt for the victim, and for those in the crowd whom the victim represents, that the more motivated of the latter sometimes seek redress by violent means.

On the question of who riots, limited data on the characteristics of sports riot participants indicate that they are more often than not working-class males in their late adolescence or early twenties. Research provides little support for "riffraff theory," the notion that crowds attract mainly transients, petty criminals, and other "lower orders" allegedly predisposed to commit antisocial acts. An alternative and more viable theory is the "assembling instructions" approach. It shifts the emphasis from the social and psychological characteristics of individuals as predictors of riot involvement to the processes of interaction among individuals and to ecological factors that determine who is likely to receive and act upon suggestions to join a crowd. From this viewpoint adolescent working-class males are overrepresented in the ranks of rioters because they, more than others, are in a position to receive and act upon "instructions" to assemble.

Regarding why people behave as they do *within* the crowd, the question of crowd processes or dynamics, the "gaming" perspective shares an emphasis on interaction processes and environmental factors with the assembling instructions approach. It suggests that individuals engage in the same more or less rational decision-making processes in crowds as elsewhere; they estimate the rewards and costs of behaving in a particular way, then act so as to produce the best outcome for themselves. But in a crowd this outcome usually turns on the degree to which others support the individual's desired behaviour. Decision-making thus becomes a process of gauging the probability of support from others for a preferred course of action, which in turn is a function of environmental factors, like crowd density. The process is collective and reciprocal, for other crowd members engage in it simultaneously; each wants to make the most of the situation, but each is constrained by the need for social support.

Theories like the assembling instructions and gaming approaches, based as they are on a recognition that the forces shaping the behaviour of people in crowds are not fundamentally different from those operating in ordinary circumstances, are a welcome alternative to the "mob psychology" stereotypes that historically have dominated thinking about sports crowd misbehaviour. What is needed now is high quality research conducted in sports contexts designed to test and advance such theories.

References

Adams, S. G.
    1978 *The Female Offender: A Statistical Perspective*. Ottawa: Ministry of the Solicitor General of Canada.
Adler, F.
    1975 *Sisters in Crime*. New York: McGraw-Hill.
Amnesty International
    1981 *Report*. London: Amnesty International Publications.
Archer, D., and R. Gartner
    1976 "Violent acts and violent times." *American Sociological Review* 41: 937-63.
Arendt, H.
    1970 *On Violence*. New York: Harcourt, Brace and World.
Arms, R. L., G. W. Russell, and M. L. Sandilands
    1979 "Effects on the hostility of spectators of viewing aggressive sports." *Social Psychology Quarterly* 42: 275-79.
Athens, L. H.
    1980 *Violent Criminal Acts and Actors*. Boston: Routledge and Kegan Paul.
Atyeo, D.
    1979 *Blood and Guts*. New York: Paddington.
Audi, R.
    1974 "Violence, legal sanctions, and the law." In S. M. Stanage, ed., *Reason and Violence*. Totowa, New Jersey: Littlefield, Adams.
Aveni, A. F.
    1977 "The not-so-lonely crowd: friendship groups in collective behavior." *Sociometry* 40:96-99.
Baker, R., and S. J. Ball
    1969 *Violence and the Media*. Washington, D.C.: United States Government Printing Office.
Bale, J.
    1980 "Women's football in England and Wales: a social-geographic perspective." *Physical Education Review* 3:137-45.
Ball-Rokeach, S. J.
    1972 "The legitimation of violence." In J. F. Short and M. E. Wolfgang, eds., *Collective Violence*. Chicago: Aldine-Atherton.
    1973 "Values and violence: a test of the subculture of violence thesis." *American Sociological Review* 38: 736-49.
Bandura, A.
    1973 *Aggression: A Social Learning Analysis*. Englewood Cliffs, New Jersey: Prentice-Hall.
Baron, R. A.
    1977 *Human Aggression*. New York: Plenum.
Beisser, A. R.
    1979 "The sports fan and recreational violence." *Psychiatric Annals* 9:78-85.
Berk. R. A.
    1974 "A gaming approach to collective behavior." *American Sociological Review* 39:355-73.
Berkowitz, L., ed.
    1969 *Roots of Aggression: A Re-examination of the Frustration-Aggression Hypothesis*. New York: Atherton.

Betts, J. R.
   1974 *America's Sporting Heritage: 1850-1950.* Reading, Massachusetts: Addison-Wesley.
Beyer Gammon, M. A., ed.
   1978 *Violence in Canada.* Toronto: Methuen.
Blank, J. P.
   1965 "Sports' worst tragedy." *The Kiwanis Magazine,* March 2:34-47.
Blishen, B. R.
   1967 "A socio-economic index for occupations in Canada." *Canadian Review of Sociology and Anthropology* 4:41-53.
Bloch, M.
   1969 "Feudal society." In C. S. Heller, ed., *Structured Social Inequality.* London: Collier-Macmillan.
Blumenthal, M. D., R. L. Kahn, F. M. Andrews, and K. B. Head
   1972 *Justifying Violence: Attitudes of American Men.* Ann Arbor: Institute for Social Research, University of Michigan.
Boulding, E.
   1978 "Women and social violence." *International Social Science Journal* 30:800-15.
Bouton, J.
   1971 *Ball Four.* New York: World.
Bowker, L.
   1978 *Women, Crime and the Criminal Justice System.* Toronto: Lexington.
Bramson, L.
   1961 *The Political Context of Sociology.* Princeton, New Jersey: Princeton University Press.
Brown, J., and N. Davies
   1978 "Attitudes towards violence among college athletes." *Journal of Sport Behavior* 1:61-70.
Brown, M., and A. Goldin
   1973 *Collective Behavior: A Review and Interpretation of the Literature.* Pacific Palisades, California: Goodyear.
Bryan C., and R. Horton
   1976 "School athletics and fan aggression." *Educational Researcher* 5:2-11.
Bryant, J., P. Comisky, and D. Zillmann
   1977 "Drama in sports commentary." *Journal of Communication* 27:140-49.
Bryson, F. R.
   1938 *The Sixteenth-Century Italian Duel.* Chicago: University of Chicago Press.
Buss, A. H.
   1961 *The Psychology of Aggression.* New York: Wiley.
Bybee, R.
   1979 "Violence toward youth: a new perspective." *Journal of Social Issues* 35:1-14.
Camelli, A.
   1970 *Great Moments in Pro Hockey.* New York: Bantam.
Cameron, A.
   1976 *Circus Factions: Blues and Greens at Rome and Byzantium.* Oxford: Clarendon Press.
Caplan, P. J.
   1975 "Sex differences in antisocial behavior: Does research methodology produce or abolish them?" *Human Development* 18: 444-60.

Carroll, R.
1980 "Football hooliganism in England." *International Review of Sport Sociology* 2: 77-92.

Chagnon, N.
1968 *Yanomamö: The Fierce People.* New York: Holt, Rinehart and Winston.

Clark, W. J., E. Vaz, V. Vetere, and T. A. Ward
1978 "Illegal aggression in minor league hockey: a causal model." In F. Landry and W. Orban, eds., *Ice Hockey: Research, Development, and New Concepts.* Miami: Symposia Specialists.

Clarke, J.
1978 "Football and working class fans: tradition and change." In R. Ingham, ed., *Football Hooliganism: The Wider Context.* London: Inter-Action Imprint.

Cohen, S.
1973 *Folk Devils and Moral Panics.* London: Paladin.

Collins, L., and D. LaPierre
1969 *Or I'll Dress You in Mourning.* Toronto: Signet.

Collins, R.
1974 "Three faces of cruelty: towards a comparative sociology of violence." *Theory and Society* 1:415-40.

Comisky, P., J. Bryant, and D. Zillmann
1977 "Commentary as a substitute for action." *Journal of Communication* 27:150-52.

Corrigan, P.
1977 *Schooling the Smash Street Kids.* London: Macmillan.

Coser, L.
1967 *Continuities in the Study of Social Conflict.* New York: Free Press.

Cullen, T., K. M. Golden, and J. B. Cullen
1979 "Sex and delinquency: a partial test of the masculinity hypothesis." *Criminology* 17:301-10.

Danzger, M. H.
1975 "Validating conflict data." *American Sociological Review* 40: 570-84.

Davis, P. H.
1971 *Football: The American Intercollegiate Game.* New York: Charles Scribner's Sons.

Dentan, R. K.
1968 *The Semai: A Nonviolent People of Malaya.* New York, Holt, Rinehart and Winston.

Dewar, C.
1979 "Spectator fights at professional baseball games." *Review of Sport and Leisure* 40:12-25.

Dietz, M. L.
1978 "The violent subculture: the genesis of violence." In M. A. Beyer Gammon, ed., *Violence in Canada.* Toronto: Methuen.

Dinitz, S., and J. P. Conrad
1980 "The dangerous two percent." In D. Shichor and D. H. Kelly, eds., *Critical Issues in Juvenile Delinquency.* Lexington, Massachusetts: Lexington Books.

Dobash R. E., and R. P. Dobash
1978 "Wives: The appropriate victims of marital violence." *Victimology* 2:426-42.

Dollard, J., L. Doob, N. Miller, O. Mowrer, and R. Sears
1939 *Frustration and Aggression.* New Haven, Connecticut: Yale University Press.

Dunning, E.
1981a "Social bonding and the socio-genesis of violence: a theoretical-empirical analysis with special reference to combat sports." In A. Tomlinson, ed., *The Sociological Study of Sport — Configurational and Interpretive Studies.* Brighton Polytechnic, Chelsea School of Human Movement.

1981b "Social bonding and violence in sport." In B. Tulloh, M. A. Herberton, and A. S. Parkes, eds., *Biosocial Aspects of Sport. Journal of Biosocial Science, Supplement No. 7,* Cambridge University.

Dunning, E., J. A. Maguire, P. J. Murphy, and J. M. Williams
1982 "The social roots of football hooligan violence." *Leisure Studies* 1:14-28.

Dunning, E., P. Murphy, and J. Williams
1981 "Ordered segmentation and the socio-genesis of football hooligan violence: a critique of Marsh's 'ritualized aggression' hypothesis and the outline of a sociological alternative." In A. Tomlinson, ed., *The Sociological Study of Sport — Configurational and Interpretive Studies.* Brighton Polytechnic, Chelsea School of Human Movement.

Dunning, E., and K. Sheard
1979 *Barbarians, Gentlemen, and Players: A Sociological Study of the Development of Rugby Football.* Oxford: Martin Robertson.

Dunstan, K.
1973 *Sports.* North Melbourne, Australia: Cassell.

Duperreault, J. R.
"L'Affaire Richard: a situational analysis of the Montreal hockey riot of 1955." *Canadian Journal of History of Sport* 12:66-83.

Durham, W. H.
1976 "Resource competition and human aggression. Part 1: a review of primitive war." *Quarterly Review of Biology* 51:385-415.

Durkheim, E. (D. F. Pocock, translator)
1974 *Sociology and Philosophy.* New York: Free Press.

Edmonds, A.
1975 "Go git a piece of her, Debbie." *Canadian Magazine,* February 8:24-26.

Eekelaar, J. M., and S. N. Katz, eds.
1978 *Family Violence: An International and Interdisciplinary Study.* Toronto: Butterworths.

Eitzen D. S., and G. H. Sage
1978 *Sociology of American Sport.* Dubuque, Iowa: Wm. C. Brown.

Elias, N.
1978a "On transformations of aggressiveness." *Theory and Society* 5:219-28.

1978b *The Civilizing Process.* (E. Jephcott, translator) London: Basil Blackwell.

1971 "The genesis of sport as a sociological problem." In E. Dunning, ed., *The Sociology of Sport.* London: Frank Cass.

Elias, N., and E. Dunning
1970 "The quest for excitement in unexciting societies." In G. Lüschen, ed., *The Cross-Cultural Analysis of Sport and Games.* Champaign, Illinois: Sipes.

1971 "Folk football in mediaeval and early modern Britain." In E. Dunning, ed., *The Sociology of Sport.* London: Frank Cass.

Ellis, D.
(forthcoming) *Prisoners, Prisons, and Prison Violence.*
Ellis, D., H. G. Grasmick, and B. Gilman
1974 "Violence in prisons: a sociological analysis." *American Journal of Sociology* 80:17-31.
Erlanger, H.S.
1979 "Estrangement, machismo and gang violence." *Social Science Quarterly* 60:235-48.
1974 "Social class and corporal punishment in childrearing: a reassessment." *American Sociological Review* 39:68-85.
Etzioni, A.
1971 "Violence." In R. K. Merton and R. Nisbet, eds., *Contemporary Social Problems.* 3rd ed. New York: Harcourt, Brace, Jovanovich.
Faulkner, R. R.
1973 "On respect and retribution: toward an ethnography of violence." *Sociological Symposium* 9:17-36.
1974 "Making violence by doing work: selves, situations, and the world of professional hockey." *Sociology of Work and Occupations* 1:288-312.
Feagin J. R., and H. Hahn
1973 *Ghetto Revolts: The Politics of Violence in American Cities.* New York: Macmillan.
Feierabend, I. K, R. L. Feierabend, and B. A. Nesvold
1969 "Social change and political violence: cross-national patterns." In H. D. Graham and T. R. Gurr, ed., *The History of Violence in America.* New York: Bantam.
Feierabend, R. L.
1978 "The role of government in violence research." *International Social Science Journal* 30:727-48.
Feinman, C.
1980 *Women in the Criminal Justice System.* New York: Praeger.
Felson, R.
1982 "Impression management and the escalation of aggression and violence." *Social Psychology Quarterly* 45:245-54.
Feshbach, N. D.
1979 "The effects of violence in childhood." In D. Gil, ed., *Child Abuse and Violence.* New York: AMS Press.
Feshbach S., and R. D. Singer
1971 *Television and Aggression.* San Francisco: Jossey Bass.
Figueira-McDonough, J., and E. Selo
1980 "A reformulation of the equal opportunity explanation of female delinquency." *Crime and Delinquency* 26:333-43.
Flakne, G. W., and A. H. Caplan
1977 "Sports violence and the prosecution." *Trial* 13: 33-35.
Flynn, E. E.
1980 "Crime and violence in American Society." *American Behavioral Scientist* 23:637-52.
Frodi, A., J. Macauley, and R. Thome
1977 "Are women more aggressive than men? A review of experimental literature." *Psychological Bulletin* 84:634-60.
Gammon, C.
1980 "It was Blood, Sweat, and Beers." *Sports Illustrated,* October 6:26-29.
Geen, R. G., and L. Berkowitz
1969 "Some conditions facilitating the occurrence of aggression after the observation of violence." In L. Berkowitz, ed., *Roots of Aggression:*

⌐ *A Re-examination of the Frustration-Aggression Hypothesis.* New York: Atherton.

Geertz, C.
1972 "Deep play: notes on the Balinese cockfight." *Daedalus* 101:1-37.

Gelles, R. J.
1974 *The Violent Home.* Beverly Hills: Sage.

Gelles, R. J., and M. A. Straus
1979 "Violence in the American family." *Journal of Social Issues* 35:15-39.

Gerbner, G., L. Gross, N. Signorielli, M. Morgan, and M. Jackson-Beeck
1979 "The demonstration of power: violence profile no. 10." *Journal of Communication* 29:177-96.

Gerbner, G., L. Gross, N. Signorielli, and M. Morgan
1980 "Television violence, victimization, and power." *American Behavioral Scientist* 23:705-16.

Gil, D.
1970 *Violence against Children.* Cambridge: Harvard University Press.

Gilbert, B., and L. Twyman
1983 "Violence: out of hand in the stands." *Sports Illustrated,* January 31:62-74.

Gilbert, B., and N. Williamson
1973 "Are you being two-faced? Women in sport." *Sports Illustrated,* June 4:45-73.

Girvetz, H.
1974 "An anatomy of violence." In S. M. Stanage, ed., *Reason and Violence.* Totowa, New Jersey: Littlefield, Adams.

Glanville, B.
1968 *Soccer.* New York: Crown.

Gluckman, M.
1973 "Sport and conflict." In O. Grupe, D. Kurz, and J. M. Teipel, eds., *Sport in the Modern World — Chances and Problems.* Berlin: Springer-Verlag.

Goffman, E.
1963 *Behavior in Public Places: Notes on the Social Organization of Gatherings.* Glencoe, Illinois: Free Press.
1967 *Interaction Ritual.* Garden City, New York: Doubleday.

Gold, R. L.
1958 "Roles in sociological field observations." *Social Forces* 36: 217-23.

Goldstein, J. H., and R. L. Arms
1971 "Effects of observing athletic contests on hostility." *Sociometry* 34:83-90.

Goode, W. J.
1972 "The place of force in human society." *American Sociological Review* 37: 507-19.

Goranson, R. E.
1977 "Television violence: issues and evidence." In J. La Marsh, L. A. Beaulieu, and S. A. Young (Commissioners), *Report of the Royal Commission on Violence in the Communications Industry, Volume 5.* Toronto: Ontario Government Bookstore.

⌐ 1980 "Sports violence and the catharsis hypothesis." In P. Klavora and K. A. Wipper, eds., *Psychological and Sociological Factors in Sport.* University of Toronto: School of Physical and Health Education.

1982 "The impact of televised hockey violence." *LaMarsh Research Programme Reports on Violence and Conflict Resolution, No. 1.* Toronto: York University.

Gordon, D. R., and L. Ibson
1977 "Content analysis of the news media: radio." In J. LaMarsh, L. A. Beaulieu, and S. A. Young (Commissioners), *Report of the Royal Commission on Violence in the Communications Industry, Volume 3.* Toronto: Ontario Government Bookstore.

Gotesky, R.
1974 "Social force, social power, and social violence." In S. M. Stanage, ed., *Reason and Violence.* Totowa, New Jersey: Littlefield, Adams.

Greenberg, D. F.
1977 "Delinquency and the age structure of society." *Contemporary Crises* 1:189-223.

Grescoe, A.
1980 "Come die with me." *Homemaker's Magazine,* September/October: 8-12.

Grescoe, P.
1972 "We asked you six questions." *Canadian Magazine,* January 29:2-4.

1973 "Volleyball is hell." *Canadian Magazine,* April 28:12-14.

Gruneau, R. S.
1976 "Class or mass: notes on the democratization of Canadian amateur sport." In R. S. Gruneau and J. G. Albinson, eds., *Canadian Sport: Sociological Perspectives.* Don Mills, Ontario: Addison-Wesley.

1982 "Sport and the debate on the state." In H. Cantelon and R. S. Gruneau, eds., *Sport, Culture, and the Modern State.* Toronto: University of Toronto Press.

Gulotta, S. J.
1980 "Torts in sports — deterring violence in professional athletics." *Fordham Law Review* 48:764-93.

Gurr, T. R.
1970 *Why Men Rebel.* Princeton, New Jersey: Princeton University Press.

1979a "On the history of violent crime in Europe and America." In H. D. Graham and T. R. Gurr, eds., *Violence in America: Historical and Comparative Perspectives.* Beverly Hills: Sage.

1979b "Political protest and rebellion in the 1960's: the United States in world perspective." In H. D. Graham and T. R. Gurr, eds., *Violence in America: Historical and Comparative Perspectives.* Beverly Hills: Sage.

Guttmann, A.
1981 "Sports spectators from antiquity to the renaissance." *Journal of Sport History* 8:5-27.

Haas, J.
1978 "Learning real feelings: a study of high steel ironworkers' reactions to fear and danger." In J. Haas and W. Shaffir, eds., *Shaping Identity in Canadian Society.* Scarborough, Ontario: Prentice-Hall.

Hagan, J. R.
1977 *The Disreputable Pleasures.* Toronto: McGraw-Hill Ryerson.

Hall, S., C. Chrichter, T. Jefferson, J. Clarke, and B. Roberts
1978 *Policing the Crisis: Mugging, the State and Law and Order.* London: Macmillan.

Hallowell, L.
1978 "Violent work and the criminal law: an historical study of professional ice hockey." In J. A. Inciardi and A. E. Pottieger, eds., *Violent Crime: Historical and Contemporary Issues.* Beverly Hills: Sage.

Hallowell, L., and R. I. Meshbesher
1977 "Sports violence and the criminal law." *Trial* 13:27-32.

Hammerstrom, I.
1976 "Hammerstrom on Hammerstrom." *Maple Leaf Magazine* 8:4-8.
Harrington, J. A.
1968 *Soccer Hooliganism: A Preliminary Report to Mr. Denis Howell, Minister of Sport.* Bristol: John Wright and Sons.
Harrison, P.
1974 "Soccer's tribal wars." *New Society* 29:622-24.
Hartnagel, T.
1979 "The perception and fear of crime: implications for neighborhood cohesion, social activity, and community affect." *Social Forces* 58:19-26.
Hastorf, A. H., and H. Cantril
1954 "They saw a game: a case study." *Journal of Abnormal and Social Psychology* 49:129-34.
Hay, R.
1979 "Soccer: social control in Scotland, 1878-1978." Paper presented at The Making of Sporting Traditions Conference. Kensington, New South Wales, Australia.
Hecht, E.
1968 "Football." In C. Véliz ed., *Latin America and the Caribbean: A Handbook.* New York: Praeger.
Hechter, W.
1977 "The criminal law and violence in sports." *The Criminal Law Quarterly* 19:425-53.
Heinilä, K.
1974 "Junior football players as cross-national interpreters of the moral concepts of sport." *Department of Sociology and Planning for Physical Culture, Research Report No. 4.* Finland: University of Jyväskylä.
Hemingway, E.
1932 *Death in the Afternoon.* New York: Scribner's.
Himelfarb, A., and C. J. Richardson
1979 *People, Power and Process: Sociology for Canadians.* Toronto: McGraw-Hill Ryerson.
Hinrichs, D. W.
1979 "Profile of audiences at roller games." Paper presented at the Southern Sociological Association Annual Meetings. Atlanta.
Hirsch, S., and J. Leff
1975 *Abnormalities in Parents of Schizophrenics.* London: Oxford University Press.
Hoch, P.
1972 *Rip Off the Big Game.* Garden City, New York: Doubleday.
Horowitz, R., and G. Schwartz
1974 "Honor, normative ambiguity and gang violence." *American Sociological Review* 39:238-51.
Horrow, R. B.
1980 *Sports Violence: The Interaction between Private Law-Making and the Criminal Law.* Arlington, Virgina: Carrollton Press.
1981 "The legal perspective: interaction between private lawmaking and the civil and criminal law." *Journal of Sport and Social Issues* 5:9-18.
1982 "Violence in professional sports: is it part of the game?" *Journal of Legislation* 9:1-15.
Hubbard, J. C., M. L. DeFleur, and L. B. DeFleur
1975 "Mass media influences on public conceptions of social problems." *Social Problems* 23:22-34.

Hughes, R. H., and J. J. Coakley
1978 "Player violence and the social organization of contact sports."
Journal of Sport Behavior 1:155-68.
Jackson, R., M. Kelly, and T. Mitchell
1977 "Collective conflict, violence and the media." In J. LaMarsh,
L. A. Beaulieu, and S. A. Young (Commissioners). *Report of the Royal
Commission on Violence in the Communications Industry, Volume 5.*
Toronto: Ontario Government Bookstore.
Jacobson, S.
1975 "Chelsea Rule-Okay." *New Society* 31:780-83.
Joint Sports Council/Social Science Research Council
1978 *Public Disorder and Sport Events.* London: The Sports Council.
Katz, S.
1955 "Strange forces behind the Richard hockey riot." *Maclean's,*
September 17:98-109.
Keiser, R. L.
1972 "The teen-age gang: an introduction." In P. K. Manning and M.
Truzzi, eds., *Youth and Society.* Englewood Cliffs, New Jersey: Prentice-
Hall.
Kennedy, R., and N. Williamson
1978 "Money in sports: the fans: are they up in arms?" *Sports Illustrated,*
July 31:34-50.
Kiefer, T. M.
1972 *The Tausug: Violence and Law in a Philippine Moslem Society.* New
York: Holt, Rinehart and Winston.
Kirkpatrick, C.
1979 "The Game is Her Dominion." *Sports Illustrated,* December 3:106-20.
Kirshenbaum, J.
1981 "Scorecard." *Sports Illustrated,* May 4:9.
Klapp, O. E.
1972 *Currents of Unrest.* New York: Holt, Rinehart and Winston.
Kmet, M. A.
1979 "Pre-game planning — 13th Olympic Winter Games — Lake Placid
(NY) 1980." *Security Management* 23:17-23.
Kram, M.
1975 "Their lives are on the line." *Sports Illustrated,* August 18:30-38.
1982 "Wild in the seats." *Playboy,* February: 83-201.
Kuhlman, W.
1975 "Violence in professional sports." *Wisconsin Law Review* 3:771-90.
LaMarsh, J., L. A. Beaulieu, and S. A. Young (Commissioners)
1977 *Report of The Royal Commission on Violence in the Communications
Industry, Volume 1.* Toronto: Ontario Government Bookstore.
Lambert, D. J.
1978 "Tort law and participant sports: the line between vigor and violence."
Journal of Contemporary Law 4:211-17.
Lambert, W. W.
1971 "Comparative studies of personality." In W. W. Lambert and P.
Weisbrod, eds., *Comparative Perspectives on Social Psychology.* Boston:
Little, Brown.
Lang, K., and G. Lang
1970 "Collective behavior theory and the escalated riots of the sixties." In
T. Shibutani, ed., *Human Nature and Collective Behavior.* Englewood Cliffs,
New Jersey: Prentice-Hall.

Lanken, D.
1972 "The Dodgers are ladies." *Canadian Magazine,* July 22:16.

Lasch, C.
1977 "The corruption of sports." *New York Review of Books* 24:30.

Le Bon, G.
1960 *The Crowd.* New York: Viking Press (first published 1895).

Lee A., and N. Humphrey
1943 *Race Riot.* New York: E. P. Dutton.

Lever, J.
1972 "Soccer as a Brazilian way of life." In G. Stone, ed., *Games, Sport, and Power.* New Brunswick, New Jersey: Transaction.

1983 *Soccer Madness.* Chicago: University of Chicago Press.

Levin, D.
1980 "Taken down a few pegs." *Sports Illustrated,* December 15:65-66.

Lewis, J. M.
1981 "British travelling football supporters: some policy implications." Paper presented at the North Central Sociological Association Annual Meeting. Cleveland, April.

1982a "Crowd control at English football matches." *Sociological Focus* 15:417-23.

1982b "Fan violence: an American social problem." *Research in Social Problems and Public Policy* 2:175-206.

Lewis, O.
1961 *Children of Sanchez.* New York: Random House.

Lieberson, S., and A. R. Silverman
1965 "The precipitants and underlying conditions of race riots. *American Sociological Review* 30:887-98.

Listiak, A.
1974 "Legitimate deviance and social class: bar behaviour during Grey Cup week." *Sociological Focus* 7:13-44.

Lorenz, K.
1963 *On Aggression.* New York: Harcourt, Brace and World.

Loy, J. W.
1969 "The study of sport and social mobility." In G. S. Kenyon, ed., *Aspects of Contemporary Sport Sociology.* Chicago: The Athletic Institute.

Luckenbill, D. F.
1977 "Criminal homicide as a situated transaction." *Social Problems* 25:176-86.

Luckenbill, D. F., and W. B. Sanders
1977 "Criminal violence." In E. Sagarin and F. Montanino, eds., *Deviants: Voluntary Actors in a Hostile World.* New York: General Learning.

Lupsha, P. A.
1969 "On theories of urban violence." *Urban Affairs Quarterly* 4: 273-96.

Lüschen, G.
1969 "Social stratification and social mobility among young sportsmen." In J. W. Loy and G. S. Kenyon, eds., *Sport, Culture, and Society.* London: Macmillan.

Lyman, S. M., and M. B. Scott
1970 *A Sociology of the Absurd.* New York: Meredith.

Lystad, M. M.
1979 "Violence at home: a review of the literature." In D. Gil, ed., *Child Abuse and Violence.* New York: AMS Press.

Mackie, M.
1979 "Gender socialization in childhood and adolescence." In K. Ishwaran, ed., *Childhood and Adolescence in Canada.* Toronto: McGraw-Hill.
Mandell, A.
1976 *The Nightmare Season.* New York: Random House.
Mann, L.
1974 "On being a sore loser: how fans react to their team's failure." *Australian Journal of Psychology* 26:37-47.
1979 "Sports crowds viewed from the perspective of collective behavior." In J. H. Goldstein, ed., *Sports, Games and Play: Social and Psychological Viewpoints.* Hillsdale, New Jersey: Lawrence Erlbaum Associates.
Marsh, P.
1978 *Aggro: The Illusion of Violence.* London: Dent.
Marsh, P., E. Rosser, and R. Harré
1978 *The Rules of Disorder.* London: Routledge and Kegan Paul.
Marshall, D.
1970 "We're more violent than we think." *Maclean's,* August: 14-17.
Martin, T. W., and K. J. Berry
1974 "Competitive sport in post-industrial society: the case of the motocross racer." *Journal of Popular Culture* 8:107-20.
Marx, G. T.
1972 "Issueless riots." In J. F. Short and M. E. Wolfgang, eds., *Collective Violence.* Chicago: Aldine-Atherton.
Matza, D.
1964 *Delinquency and Drift.* New York: Wiley.
McCormack, T.
1982 "A square called a ring: a study of Hollywood fight films." *LaMarsh Research Programme Reports on Violence and Conflict Resolution, No. 2.* Toronto: York University.
McEvoy, A., and E. L. Erickson
1981 "Heroes and villains: a conceptual strategy for assessing their influence." *Sociological Focus* 14:111-22.
McMurtry, J.
1971a "Philosophy of a corner linebacker." *The Nation,* January 18: 83-84.
1971b "Some tentative reflections on football." Paper presented at the Third International Symposium on the Sociology of Sport. University of Waterloo, Ontario, August.
McMurtry, W. R.
1974 *Investigation and Inquiry into Violence in Amateur Hockey.* Report to the Honourable René Brunelle, Ontario Minister of Community and Social Services. Toronto: Ontario Government Bookstore.
McPhail, C.
1971 "Civil disorder participation: a critical examination of recent research." *American Sociological Review* 36:1058-73.
McPhail C., and D. Miller
1973 "The assembling process." *American Sociological Review* 38: 721-35.
McPherson, B. D., and L. Davidson
1980 *Minor Hockey in Ontario: Toward a Positive Learning Environment for Children in the 1980s.* Toronto: Ontario Government Bookstore.
McRae, E.
1977 "King Kong in Minneapolis." In E. McRae, *Requiem for Reggie and Other Great Sports Stories.* Toronto: Chimo.
1977b "Requiem for Reggie." In E. McRae, *Requiem for Reggie and Other Great Sports Stories.* Toronto: Chimo.

Mead, M.
  1935 *Sex and Temperament.* New York: Mentor.
Merton, R. K.
  1957 *Social Theory and Social Structure.* New York: Free Press.
Metcalfe, A.
  1978 "Working class physical recreation in Montreal, 1860-1895." In H.
  Cantelon and R. Gruneau, eds., *Working Papers in the Sociological Study
  of Sports and Leisure, Volume 1.* Kingston, Ontario: Queen's University.
Michener, J.
  1976 *Sports in America.* New York: Random House.
Miller, E. E.
  1981 "The woman participant in Washington's riots." In L. Bowker, ed.,
  Women and Crime in America. New York: Macmillan.
Miller, R. B.
  1971 "Violence, force and coercion." In J. A. Shaffer, ed., *Violence.* New
  York: David McKay.
Miller, W. B.
  1975 *Violence by Youth Gangs and Youth Groups as a Crime Problem in
  Major American Cities.* Washington, D.C.: U.S. Government Printing
  Office.
Money, J.
  1980 "Interfaculty violence sparks concern." *The Varsity,* March 17:12.
Moriarty R., and A. McCabe
  1977 "Studies of television and youth sports." In J. LaMarsh, L. A.
  Beaulieu, and S. A. Young (Commissioners), *Report of the Royal
  Commission on Violence in the Communications Industry, Volume 5.*
  Toronto: Ontario Government Bookstore.
Mulvoy, M.
  1974 "It's sockey, the way they play it here." *Sports Illustrated,*
  May 6:28-32.
Murdock, G. P.
  1967 *Ethnographic Atlas.* Pittsburgh: University of Pittsburgh Press.
Murray, C.
  1977 "The soccer hooligans' honour system." *New Society,* October 6:9-11.
National Advisory Commission on Civil Disorders
  1968 "Patterns of disorder." In O. Kerner (Chairman), *Report of the
  National Advisory Commission on Civil Disorders.* Washington, D.C.: U.S.
  Government Printing Office.
Néron, G. E. (Président)
  1977 Rapport Final du Comité d'Étude sur la Violence au Hockey Amateur
  au Québec. Haut-Commissariat à la Jeunesse, aux Loisirs et aux Sports.
  Québec: Gouvernement du Québec.
Nieburg, H. L.
  1969 *Political Violence: The Behavioral Process.* New York: St. Martin's.
Nisbet, R.
  1973 *The Social Philosophers.* New York: Thomas Y. Crowell.
Nixon, H. L., P. J. Maresca, and M. A. Silverman
  1979 "Sex differences in college students' acceptance of females in sport."
  Adolescence. 14:755-64.
Nowak, W.
  1969 "Social aspects of Polish boxers and their environment in the light of
  questionnaires and surveys." *International Review of Sport Sociology*
  4:137-50.

Oberschall, A.
1973 *Social Conflict and Social Movements.* Englewood Cliffs, New Jersey: Prentice-Hall.
Ogilvie, B.
1979 "The child athlete: psychological implications of participation in sport." *Annals of the American Academy of Political and Social Science* 445:47-58.
Ontario Hockey Council
1975 *You and Your Child in Hockey.* Toronto: Ontario Government Bookstore.
Otero, M.
1982 "El pequeño mundo de la selección." *Hoy* 14:40-41.
Otterbein, K. F.
1979 "A cross-cultural study of rape." *Aggressive Behavior* 5:425-35.
Palmer, S.
1960 *The Psychology of Murder.* New York: Thomas Y. Crowell.
Papenek, J.
1980 "A chess game with sod." *Sports Illustrated,* October 20:37-54.
Parkhouse, B. L., and J. Lapin
1980 *Women Who Win: Exercising Your Rights in Sport.* Englewood Cliffs, New Jersey: Prentice-Hall.
Parrish, B.
1971 *They Call It a Game.* New York: Dial Press.
Patrick, J.
1973 *A Glasgow Gang Observed.* London: Eyre Methuen.
Patterson, O.
1969 "The cricket ritual in the West Indies." *New Society* June 26: 988-89.
Perry, J. B., and M. D. Pugh
1978 *Collective Behavior: Response to Social Stress.* St. Paul, Minnesota: West.
Philo, H. M., and G. Stine
1977 "The liability path to safer helmets." *Trial* 12: 38-42.
Pilz, G. A.
1979 "Attitudes toward different forms of aggressive and violent behavior in competitive sports: two empirical studies." *Journal of Sport Behavior* 2:3-26.
1982a,ed. *Sport und Körperliche Gewalt.* Hamburg: Rowohlt.
1982b "Violence in West German sport: some theoretical and empirical remarks." Paper presented at the Annual Conference of the North American Society for the Sociology of Sport. Toronto, November.
1982c *Wandlungen der Gewalt im Sport.* Hamburg: Czwalina.

Pilz, G. A. (Chairman), D. Albrecht, H. Gabler, E. Hahn, D. Peper, J. Sprenger, H. F. Voight, M. Volkamer, and K. Weis
1981 *Sport and Violence.* Report to the Council of Europe by the Sport and Violence Project Group, Federal Institute for Sport Science. Cologne, Federal Republic of Germany.
Pitcher, B. L., R. L. Hamblin, and J. L. L. Miller
1978 "The diffusion of collective violence." *American Sociological Review* 43:23-35.
Plimpton, G.
1973 *Mad Ducks and Bears.* New York: Bantam.
Rains, J.
1980 "Sports violence: a matter of societal concern." *Notre Dame Lawyer* 55:796-813.

Reed, P., T. Bleszynski, and R. Gaucher
1978 "Homicide in Canada: A statistical synopsis." In M. A. Beyer Gammon, ed., *Violence in Canada.* Toronto: Methuen.

Rennert, A.
1979 "Some came scrumming." *Women's Sports* 1:28-32.

Renson, R.
1978 "Social status symbolism of sport stratification." In F. Landry and W. A. R. Orban, eds., *Sociology of Sport.* Miami: Symposia Specialists.

Riga, P. D.
1969 "Violence: a Christian perspective." *Philosophy East and West* 19:143-53.

Roadburg, A.
1980 "Factors precipitating fan violence: a comparison of professional soccer in Britain and North America." *British Journal of Sociology* 31:265-76.

Roshier, B.
1973 "The selection of crime news by the press." In S. Cohen and J. Young, eds., *The Manufacture of News.* Beverly Hills: Sage.

Rovere, G. D., G. Gristina, and J. Nicastro
1978 "Medical problems of a professional hockey team: a three-season experience." *The Physician and Sports Medicine* 6:59-63.

Rudé, G.
1964 *The Crowd in History.* New York: Wiley.

Runfola, R. T.
1974 "He is a hockey player, seventeen, black and convicted of manslaughter." *New York Times,* October 17:2-3.

Russell, G. W.
1983 *Bibliography of Human Aggression and Violence.* University of Lethbridge, Alberta, Department of Psychology.

1979 "Hero selection by Canadian ice hockey players: skill or aggression?" *Canadian Journal of Applied Sport Science* 4:309-13.

1981 "Spectator moods at an aggressive sports event." *Journal of Social Psychology* 3:217-77.

Schmitt, R. L.
1972 *The Reference Other Orientation.* Carbondale, Illinois: Southern Illinois University Press.

Schultz, D., with S. Fischler
1981 *The Hammer: Confessions of a Hockey Enforcer.* Toronto: Collins.

Sears, R. R., E. Maccoby, and M. Levin
1957 *Patterns of Child Rearing.* Evanston, Illinois: Row Peterson.

Seefeldt, V. D., T. Gilliam, D. Blievernicht, and R. Bruce
1978 "Scope of Youth Sports Programs in the State of Michigan." In F. L. Smoll and R. E. Smith, eds., *Psychological Perspectives in Youth Sports.* Washington: Hemisphere.

Sexton, P. C.
1969 *The Feminized Male.* New York: Vintage Books.

Shaw, G.
1972 *Meat on the Hoof: The Hidden World of Texas Football.* New York: St. Martin's Press.

Sheard, K. G., and E. Dunning
1973 "The rugby football club as a type of 'male preserve': some sociological notes." *International Review of Sport Sociology* 3-4:5-24.

Sherif, M., and C. W. Sherif
1969 *Social Psychology.* New York: Harper and Row.

Sherry, J. F.
1980 "Verbal aggression in rugby ritual." In H. B. Schwartzman, ed., *Play and Culture: Proceedings of the Fourth Annual Meeting of the Association for the Anthropological Study of Play.* West Point, New York: Leisure Press.

Shoham, S. G., S. Ben-David, and G. Rahav
1974 "Interaction in violence." *Human Relations* 27:417-30.

Shover, N., S. Norland, J. James, and W. E. Thornton
1979 "Gender roles in delinquency." *Social Forces* 58:163-79.

Simmel, G.
1955 *Conflict.* (H. Wolff, Translator.) Glencoe, Illinois: Free Press.

Simon, R. J., and H. Sharma
1979 "Women and crime: does the American experience generalize?" In F. Adler and R. J. Simon, eds., *The Criminology of Deviant Women.* Boston: Houghton Mifflin.

Singer, B., and D. R. Gordon
1977 "Content analysis of the news media: newspapers and television." In J. LaMarsh, L. A. Beaulieu, and S. A. Young (Commissioners), *Report of the Royal Commission on Violence in the Communications Industry,* Volume 5. Toronto: Ontario Government Bookstore.

Sipes, R. G.
1973 "War, sports and aggression: an empirical test of two rival theories." *American Anthropologist* 75:64-86.

Skogan, W.
1979 "Crime in contemporary America." In H. D. Graham and T. R. Gurr, eds., *Violence in America: Historical and Comparative Perspectives.* Beverly Hills: Sage.

Small, M., and D. Singer
1972 "Patterns in international warfare, 1816-1965." In J. F. Short Jr. and M. E. Wolfgang, eds., *Collective Violence.* Chicago: Aldine-Atherton.

Smart, C.
1979 "The new female criminal: reality or myth." *British Journal of Criminology* 19:50-59.

Smelser, N. J.
1962 *Theory of Collective Behavior.* New York: Free Press.

Smith, D. A.
1979 "Sex and deviance: an assessment of major sociological variables." *Sociological Quarterly* 20:183-95.

Smith, D. A., and C. A. Visher
1980 "Sex and involvement in deviance/crime: a quantitative review of the empirical literature." *American Sociological Review* 45:691-701.

Smith, M. D.
1972 "Aggression and the female athlete." In D. V. Harris, ed., *Women and Sport: A National Research Conference.* Series No. 2. College Park: Penn State College of Health, Physical Education and Recreation.

1974 "Significant others' influence on the assaultive behavior of young hockey players." *International Review of Sport Sociology* 3-4:45-56.

1975a "Sport and collective violence." In D. Ball and J. Loy, eds., *Sport and Social Order.* Reading, Massachusetts: Addison-Wesley.

1975b "The legitimation of violence: hockey players' perceptions of their reference groups' sanctions for assault." *Canadian Review of Sociology and Anthropology* 12:72-80.

1976 "Hostile outbursts in sport." In A. Yiannakis, T. D. McIntyre, M. M. Melnick, and D. P. Hart, eds., *Sport Sociology: Contemporary Themes.* Dubuque, Iowa: Kendall Hunt.

1978a "From professional to youth hockey violence: the role of the mass media." In M. A. Beyer Gammon, ed., *Violence in Canada.* Toronto: Methuen.

1978b "Social learning of violence in minor hockey." In F. L. Smoll and R. E. Smith, eds., *Psychological Perspectives in Youth Sports.* Washington: Hemisphere.

1978c "Precipitants of crowd violence." *Sociological Inquiry* 48: 121-31.

1979a "Hockey Violence." *Canadian Dimension* 13: 42-45.

1979b "Hockey violence: a test of the violent subculture thesis." *Social Problems* 27:235-47.

1979c "Towards an explanation of hockey violence." *Canadian Journal of Sociology* 4: 105-24.

1983a "Female violence in society and sport." In A. Dunleavy, A. Miracle, and R. Rees, eds., Proceedings of the Second Annual Conference of the North American Society for the Sociology of Sport. Champaign, Illinois: Human Kinetics Publishers.

1983b "What is sports violence? a sociolegal perspective." In J. H. Goldstein, ed., *Sports Violence.* New York: Springer-Verlag.

Smith, M. D., and F. Diamond
1976 "Career mobility in professional hockey." In R. S. Gruneau and J. G. Albinson, eds., *Canadian Sport: Sociological Perspectives.* Don Mills, Ontario: Addison-Wesley.

Snyder, D., and W. R. Kelly
1977 "Conflict intensity, media sensitivity and the validity of newspaper data." *American Sociological Review* 42:105-23.

Stagg, A. A.
1927 *Touchdown!* New York: Longmans, Green and Company.

Stanage, S. M.
1974 "Violatives: modes and themes of violence." In S. M. Stanage, ed., *Reason and Violence.* Totowa, New Jersey: Littlefield, Adams.

Stark, R., and J. McEvoy
1970 "Middle-class violence." *Psychology Today* 4:52-112.

Steffensmeier, D. J., R. H. Steffensmeier, and A. S. Rosenthal
1979 "Trends in female violence, 1960-1977." *Sociological Focus* 12: 217-27.

Steinmetz, S. K., and M. A. Straus
1975 "The family as a training ground for societal violence." In S. K. Steinmetz and M. A. Straus, eds., *Violence in the Family.* New York: Dodd, Mead.

Stemme, F.
1978 "Jugendliche Zuschauer in Fussballstadien." *Schriftenreihe der Polizei-Fuhrungsakademie* 5:70-79.

Straus, M. A., R. J. Gelles, and S. K. Steinmetz
1980 *Behind Closed Doors: Violence in the American Family.* Garden City, New York: Anchor Press.

Sykes, G.
1971 *Society of Captives.* Princeton, New Jersey: Princeton University Press.

Tatum, J., with B. Kushner
1979 *They Call Me Assassin.* New York: Everest House.

Taylor, I.
1971a "Football mad: a speculative sociology of football hooliganism." In E. Dunning, ed., *The Sociology of Sport*. London: Frank Cass.
1971b "Social control through sport: football in Mexico." Paper presented at the British Sociological Association Annual Conference. London.
1982 "Class, violence and sport: the case of soccer hooliganism in Britain." In H. Cantelon and R. S. Gruneau, eds., *Sport, Culture, and the Modern State*. Toronto: University of Toronto Press.
Terkel, S.
1972 "Eric Nesterenko." In S. Terkel, *Working*. New York: Avon Books.
Thompson, H. S.
1967 *Hell's Angels*. New York: Ballantine.
Thompson, R.
1975 *Retreat From Apartheid*. London: Oxford University Press.
Tilly, C.
1978 *From Mobilization to Revolution*. Reading, Massachusetts: Addison-Wesley.
1979 "Collective violence in European perspective." In H. D. Graham and T. R. Gurr, eds., *Violence in America: Historical and Comparative Perspectives*. Beverly Hills: Sage.
Time Magazine, eds.
1978 "Comes the revolution." *Time,* June 26:42-47.
Tittel, K., P. Schaetz, and C. Hagen
1974 "Zur ätiologie, diagnostik, therapie und prophylaxe von verletzungen und fehlbelastungen bei handballspielern." *Medizin und Sport* 2:46-55.
Toby, J.
1975 "Violence and the masculine ideal: some qualitative data." In S. K. Steinmetz and M. A. Straus, eds., *Violence in the Family*. New York: Dodd, Mead.
Toch, H.
1979 *Violent Men*. Chicago: Aldine.
1980 "Evolving a 'science of violence.'" *American Behavioral Scientist* 23:653-65.
Trivizas, E.
1980 "Offences and offenders in football crowd disorders." *British Journal of Criminology* 20:276-88.
Tuchman, B. W.
1978 *A Distant Mirror: The Calamitous 14th Century*. New York: Ballantine.
Turner, R. H., and L. M. Killian
1972 *Collective Behavior*. Englewood Cliffs, New Jersey: Prentice-Hall.
Underwood, J.
1979 *The Death of an American Game: The Crisis in Football*. Boston: Little, Brown.
1981 "A game plan for America." *Sports Illustrated,* February 23:64-80.
Vamplew, W.
1979 "Ungentlemanly conduct: the control of soccer crowd behavior in England, 1888-1914." In T. C. Smout, ed., *The Search for Wealth and Stability*. London: Macmillan.
1980 "Sports crowd disorder in Britain, 1870-1914: causes and controls." *Journal of Sport History* 7:5-20.
van den Haag, E.
1976 "What to do about TV violence." *Alternative: An American Spectator* 9:7-8.

Vaz, E.
1976 "The culture of young hockey players: some initial observations."
In A. Yiannakis, T. D. McIntyre, M. J. Melnick, and D. P. Hart, eds.,
Sport Sociology: Contemporary Themes. Dubuque, Iowa: Kendall Hunt.
1982 *The Professionalization of Young Hockey Players.* Lincoln,
Nebraska: University of Nebraska Press.

Vaz, E., and D. Thomas
1974 "What price victory? an analysis of minor hockey league player
attitudes towards winning." *International Review of Sport Sociology* 2:33-53.

Voight, D. Q.
1974 *A Little League Journal.* Bowling Green, Ohio: Bowling Green
University Popular Press.

Weinberg, S. K., and H. Arond
1952 "The occupational culture of the boxer." *American Journal of
Sociology* 5:460-69.

Whannel, G.
1979 "Football, crowd behavior and the press." *Media, Culture and Society*
1:327-42.

Whelton, C.
1978 "Take me out of the ball game." *Black Sports* 7:6-12.

Wilson, E. O.
1978 *On Human Nature.* Cambridge, Massachusetts: Harvard University
Press.

Wolfgang, M. E., and F. Ferracuti
1967 *The Subculture of Violence: Toward an Integrated Theory in
Criminology.* London: Tavistock.

Wood, P. S.
1980 "Sex differences in sport." *New York Times Magazine,* May 18:31-104.

Yablonsky, L., and J. Brower
1979 *The Little League Game.* New York: Times Books.

Yeager, R. C.
1979 *Seasons of Shame: The New Violence in Sports.* New York: McGraw-
Hill.

Yiannakis, A.
1975 "Sport stratification." *Sport Sociology Bulletin* 4:23-32.

Zillmann, D.
1978 *Hostility and Aggression.* Hillsdale, New Jersey: Lawrence Erlbaum
Associates.

Zillmann, D., J. Bryant, and B. S. Sapolsky
1979 "The enjoyment of watching sport contests." In J. H. Goldstein, ed.,
Sports, Games, and Play: Social and Psychological Viewpoints. Hillsdale,
New Jersey: Lawrence Erlbaum Associates.

Zurcher, L. A., and A. Meadow
1967 "On bullfights and baseball: an example of interaction of social
institutions." *International Journal of Comparative Sociology* 8:99-117.

Index